Water Availability and Use Pilot: A Multiscale Assessment in the U.S. Great Lakes Basin

By Howard W. Reeves

National Water Availability and Use Pilot Program

Professional Paper 1778

U.S. Department of the Interior
U.S. Geological Survey

U.S. Department of the Interior
KEN SALAZAR, Secretary

U.S. Geological Survey
Marcia K. McNutt, Director

U.S. Geological Survey, Reston, Virginia: 2010

For more information on the USGS—the Federal source for science about the Earth, its natural and living resources, natural hazards, and the environment, visit http://www.usgs.gov or call 1–888–ASK–USGS

For an overview of USGS information products, including maps, imagery, and publications, visit http://www.usgs.gov/pubprod

To order this and other USGS information products, visit http://store.usgs.gov

Suggested citation:
Reeves, H.W., 2010, Water Availability and Use Pilot—A multiscale assessment in the U.S. Great Lakes Basin: U.S. Geological Survey Professional Paper 1778, 105 p.

Foreword

Water is one of the most important natural resources of the United States and is essential to our health and economic well-being. Increasing competition for water to meet the needs of a growing population, municipalities, agriculture, industry, ecosystems, and recreation weighs on the sustainability of this resource. The sustained use of water resources is contingent on understanding the hydrologic implications of various alternative development strategies and properly evaluating their short- and long-term implications at scales that make sense. Compounding this complexity are unforeseen factors such as climate variability and change, which can further exacerbate an already challenging situation.

The question becomes, do we have sufficient supplies of freshwater in the United States to sustain human life and property as well as critical ecosystems? To address this concern, in 2002 Congress directed the U.S. Geological Survey (USGS) to propose a national effort to assess the availability and use of freshwater resources throughout the United States. The first pilot assessment was initiated in 2005 in the U.S. portion of the Great Lakes Basin.

A major challenge in developing a sound approach for a National Assessment of Water Availability and Use has been to find effective means to deliver national-scale products while recognizing that these same water resources are commonly managed on a local scale. The USGS Great Lakes Basin pilot study focused on quantifying the source, movement, and dynamics of water resources in the Great Lakes region. New methods of hydrologic analysis and improved strategies for delivering water-related information were developed and tested in the process of assessing the region's water availability. In this report we present the results of the pilot effort and examine the challenges and limitations for implementing a National Water Availability and Use Assessment. The collaboration of multiple partners from other Federal agencies, State agencies, nongovernmental organizations, industry, and academia has been valuable to the pilot effort and will continue to be important for refining the approach and methodologies used to determine the past, present, and future conditions of our Nation's water resources. In short, our challenge is to characterize how much water is currently available, how water availability is changing, and how much water will be available in the future, and to do so at a scale that is relevant to local, State, Tribal, and Federal decision makers.

Matthew C. Larsen, Associate Director for Water
U.S. Geological Survey

Contents

Figures

Tables

Conversion Factors

Inch/Pound to SI

Multiply	By	To obtain
Length		
inch (in.)	2.54	centimeter (cm)
inch (in.)	25.4	millimeter (mm)
foot (ft)	.3048	meter (m)
mile (mi)	1.609	kilometer (km)
Area		
square mile (mi²)	259.0	hectare (ha)
square mile (mi²)	2.590	square kilometer (km²)
Volume		
gallon (gal)	3.785	liter (L)
gallon (gal)	.003785	cubic meter (m³)
million gallons (Mgal)	3,785	cubic meter (m³)
cubic foot (ft³)	.02832	cubic meter (m³)
Flow rate		
foot per day (ft/d)	0.3048	meter per day (m/d)
cubic foot per second (ft³/s)	.02832	cubic meter per second (m³/s)
cubic foot per second per square mile [(ft³/s)/mi²]	.01093	cubic meter per second per square kilometer [(m³/s)/km²]
gallon per minute (gal/min)	.06309	liter per second (L/s)
gallon per day (gal/d)	.003785	cubic meter per day (m³/d)
million gallons per day (Mgal/d)	.04381	cubic meter per second (m³/s)
inch per year (in/yr)	25.4	millimeter per year (mm/yr)
Hydraulic conductivity		
foot per day (ft/d)	0.3048	meter per day (m/d)

Temperature in degrees Fahrenheit (°F) may be converted to degrees Celsius (°C) as follows:

$$°C=(°F-32)/1.8$$

Vertical coordinate information is referenced to the International Great Lakes Datum (IGLD) of 1985.

Altitude, as used in this report, refers to distance above the IGLD.

Water Availability and Use Pilot: A Multiscale Assessment in the U.S. Great Lakes Basin

By Howard W. Reeves

Executive Summary

Beginning in 2005, water availability and use were assessed for the U.S. part of the Great Lakes Basin through the Great Lakes Basin Pilot of a U.S. Geological Survey (USGS) national assessment of water availability and use. The goals of a national assessment of water availability and use are to clarify our understanding of water-availability status and trends and improve our ability to forecast the balance between water supply and demand for future economic and environmental uses. This report outlines possible approaches for full-scale implementation of such an assessment. As such, the focus of this study was on collecting, compiling, and analyzing a wide variety of data to define the storage and dynamics of water resources and quantify the human demands on water in the Great Lakes region.

The study focused on multiple spatial and temporal scales to highlight not only the abundant regional availability of water but also the potential for local shortages or conflicts over water. Regional studies provided a framework for understanding water resources in the basin. Subregional studies directed attention to varied aspects of the water-resources system that would have been difficult to assess for the whole region because of either data limitations or time limitations for the project. The study of local issues and concerns was motivated by regional discussions that led to recent legislative action between the Great Lakes States and regional cooperation with the Canadian Great Lakes Provinces. The multiscale nature of the study findings challenges water-resource managers and the public to think about regional water resources in an integrated way and to understand how future changes to the system—driven by human uses, climate variability, or land-use change—may be accommodated by informed water-resources management.

Background and Major Issues

The Great Lakes region has abundant water resources. The Great Lakes are the largest freshwater system on Earth, and groundwater resources are widespread and typically of high quality. The average discharge from the basin to the Atlantic Ocean through the St. Lawrence River makes it the second-largest drainage basin in the United States after the Mississippi River drainage. Diversions of water into and out of the basin are notable for galvanizing discussion of regional water resources, but such diversions actually play a small role in the overall water budget for the basin. Climate variations lead to variations in water delivery (through precipitation) and removal (through evaporation and transpiration). These variations, on seasonal, annual, decadal, and longer time-frames, are crucial in determining lake levels, groundwater levels, and streamflows within the basin. Human interactions with the hydrologic system, other than hydroelectric power generation, represent a small percentage of the overall flow through the system; but drawdown of groundwater levels in the Chicago/Milwaukee area has been as much as approximately 1,000 feet, and the areal extent of the drawdown area is very large (Alley and others, 1999; Reilly and others, 2008). Mapping water withdrawals and return flows by watershed within the basin helps highlight the spatial variation in water use by various economic and water-supply sectors across the basin and illustrates the importance of subregional or local-scale analysis in quantifying the effect of water use on local water resources.

Regional Analysis

Regional water budgets were assembled from existing information. The most notable feature of the regional water budgets is the large storage volume of the surface-water system that is unique to the Great Lakes region compared to most large basins in the United States. Groundwater storage in the U.S. Great Lakes Basin was estimated, and it exceeds the storage of Lake Erie and Ontario. The annual flow through the basin is approximately 1 percent of the volume in storage. Base-flow and recharge estimates were developed from streamgage data for the region and were found to vary according to climate, landscape, and geology. Temporal trends in precipitation, lake levels, and streamflow were investigated. Water-resources development and land-use change have altered the hydrology and hydraulics of the Great Lakes Basin, and control structures on the lakes and connecting channels have dampened some of the natural variability of the system. The large size of the basin, large natural storage of water in the system, and large annual flows through the system buffer the effects of most development, so development has had relatively little overall affect on water availability at the basin scale.

Subregional Analyses

Groundwater resources, surface-water flows, and water withdrawals and returns were studied on a subregional scale in the Great Lakes Basin Pilot.

Lake Michigan Basin Groundwater-Flow Model

A subregional groundwater-flow model for the Lake Michigan Basin was developed to quantify groundwater availability and to simulate system response to changes in anthropogenic and environmental stresses. This subregional model illustrates the source of water to wells and changes in the dynamics of the groundwater system during 1865–2004 in response to development and climate-driven variations in recharge. The model also was used to show the changes in groundwater divides in response to pumping and to analyze the direct groundwater input to Lake Michigan, which is approximately 2 percent of the total groundwater discharge to surface water. The primary discharge of groundwater is to streams and other inland surface-water bodies. Pumping of groundwater produces changes in the estimates of discharge to streams but, because of the scale of the model, it does not distinguish the impact of wells on individual streams.

Water-use projections were used to develop forecast scenarios to demonstrate the use of the subregional model in predicting changes to the groundwater system in response to projected uses. Changes in pumping in the Cambrian-Ordovician aquifer system on the west side of Lake Michigan produce the most dramatic changes in groundwater levels.

Simulations indicate recovery in water levels of more than 100 feet if current conditions are held through 2040; however, additional drawdown of more than 100 feet is indicated under forecast conditions of increased groundwater withdrawal in certain areas.

Analysis of climate change was restricted to the local scale because at the subregional scale, effects of climate change cannot be adequately resolved by the groundwater-flow model. Shifts in long-term recharge rates are quickly compensated for by changes in the estimated base flow to streams such that the regional model response to climate-change scenarios is similar to its response to observed climate during 1864–2004.

Estimation of Streamflows

New methods were developed to improve estimates of surface-water delivery to the Great Lakes and streamflow in ungaged basins. Better estimates of streamflows in the basin are important because the primary discharge of groundwater in the basin is to the inland surface-water system, and surface-water delivery to the Great Lakes from direct runoff and base flow is approximately half of the water supply to the Great Lakes. The effect of water withdrawals on streamflow—especially on the flow required to maintain ecosystem health, termed "ecosystem flows" or "ecological flows"—has gained great interest in the region, and estimates of ungaged flows are an essential part of establishing and understanding ecological flow requirements in any system. A regression-based approach that is constrained to route and conserve flow in the stream network, match observed mean flows at streamgages, and account for specified water withdrawals and transfers was developed into a computer application as part of the pilot. This application also provides the analyst with a suite of tools to interrogate streamflow data, identify anomalies perhaps due to unaccounted-for water use, develop regression models with selected independent landscape and climate variables, and analyze the resulting streamflow estimates. The method was applied to a hydrologic subregion within the Lake Michigan Basin and was shown to be effective in estimating ungaged flows and providing a framework for surface-water accounting.

Water Withdrawals, Return Flows, and Consumption

Water use also was examined at the subregional scale. Seasonal and monthly variations in water withdrawal, return flow, and consumption were documented by using data from Ohio, Indiana, and Wisconsin. This analysis revealed that for all major water-use sectors, water withdrawals increase during the summer months and are lower than the respective annual average during winter months. Peak use is often coincident with or just precedes the lowest summer streamflows, implying that seasonal variation in withdrawals may be important when considering ecological flows. The implication becomes stronger if ecological flows also have seasonal components; analysis of ecological flows in the region, however, was beyond the scope of this study. Understanding the current status and recognizing trends in water withdrawals, return flow, and consumption will help water managers evaluate ecological flows, instream use, and other constraints that may influence water availability.

Local Analyses

Local analyses focused on water-availability issues that are difficult to quantify on regional and subregional scales. Notably, analyzing groundwater/surface-water interaction and the potential to affect ecological flows in streams by pumping wells are inherently local-scale issues. The local-scale analysis also included examination of the effects of climate variability and methods to estimate uncertainty using surface-water and groundwater models.

Groundwater/Surface-Water Interaction

Understanding the interaction between pumping wells and local streams is a topic of growing interest and concern; however, studies on regional and subregional scales within the pilot project were not able to directly address questions at local spatial scales or short time periods. To illustrate the relation between regional-, subregional-, and local-scale studies, a local inset groundwater-flow model was built within the Lake Michigan Basin groundwater-flow model. The inset model covered a 20-square-mile area and examined the interaction between a single, hypothetical well and the stream network that can be accurately resolved at this local scale. The inset model enables the exploration of pumping-induced effects on streamflow given a set of pumping scenarios, such as withdrawal from different aquifer layers or variations in pumping schedules. For the case studied, streamflow depletion of the closest stream by the introduced pumping well was approximately half the pumping rate of the well. Capture of water from other streams was approximately 40 percent of the pumping rate, and the remaining water delivered to the well was from aquifer storage. The presence of a layer of low hydraulic conductivity between the aquifer being pumped and the stream shifted the distribution, increasing the capture from other streams in the surrounding area and decreasing capture from the closest stream.

Assessment of Climate-Change Effects

The potential effects of climate change and variability were simulated by varying the recharge imposed on the subregional groundwater-flow model through the use of a soil-water-balance estimate. To demonstrate the technique, input to the soil-water-balance recharge estimate was from a scenario generated by an atmosphere-ocean coupled general circulation model, and base-flow changes in the system in response to a 2000–40 scenario are presented. For the scenario tested, base flow increases for part of the scenario and then decreases after approximately 2015. The simulated base flow was zero for several years in the prediction scenario showing the sensitivity of the headwater stream to relatively modest changes in estimated recharge at the local scale.

Assessment of Uncertainty of Flow, Water-Level, and Base-Flow Reduction Estimates

Much of the analysis performed in the Great Lakes Basin Pilot relied upon USGS streamgage data. In addition, the groundwater-flow model relies on groundwater-level data. For the surface-water network, the importance of streamgage stations to the uncertainty in flow estimates was studied for a watershed in southwest Michigan/northwest Indiana. At a 20-percent reduction of streamgage observations, the probability of the estimated flow being within 10 percent of measured flow at a gage was between 85 and 90 percent. This range of probability decreased dramatically to between 60 and 75 percent if half the streamgage observations were removed from the analysis.

For the local groundwater-flow model, the most effective location for future data collection to reduce uncertainty in water level and base-flow reduction estimates for hypothetical pumping within the inset model area was studied. Use of numerical techniques that estimate prediction uncertainty and sensitivity to observations were very sensitive to the conceptual model used to develop the local-scale model. A highly parameterized approach was shown to be effective in identifying locations for additional observations that would decrease prediction uncertainty. Approaches with similar structure to the underlying aquifer characterization but with fewer parameters did not clearly identify locations where additional observations would be productive. These results indicate that local inset models should have a refined spatial distribution and be highly parameterized if these types of analyses are desired.

Challenges and Lessons Learned

The Great Lakes Basin Pilot identified several challenges and lessons learned:

- Studies summarizing water use highlight inconsistencies in water-use data collection and reporting across the region. Much of the reported water use in some sectors relies heavily on estimates, and the estimation procedures may vary from state to state. Resolving these inconsistencies and developing methods to improve estimates for the broad water-use sectors and for specific categories within the broader sectors remains a challenge.

- Estimation of surface-water characteristics across the basin was hampered by the requirement that all streams in the geographic dataset used for the analysis be routed through the stream network. Existing datasets are quite well constructed in this respect, but there remains a small percentage of streams that are disconnected or improperly routed; correcting even these few problems is labor intensive and time consuming.

- The tension between developing a regional ground-water-flow model capable of representing regional hydrologic dynamics and the desire to address problems of local interest is a challenge for regional water-availability studies. Methods to allow regional models to be used to address local questions, such as the illustrative inset model discussed previously, provide insight into the potential local response in water levels and base flow to groundwater withdrawals. For site-specific questions, more refinement of the hydrogeologic characteristics would be needed to better address local issues.

One other issue that remains a challenge to both the subregional- and local-scale groundwater-flow models is that traditional models do not account for potential changes in recharge to the aquifer system in response to changes in pumping, return flow, or other specific changes to the environment. This separate treatment may be valid on the subregional scale; but as questions become more site specific, the potential for pumping to modify recharge to the local aquifer should be included in the simulation. For situations where recharge can be influenced by pumping, coupled groundwater-surface water models that generate recharge to the groundwater system as part of the simulation would be required.

Water availability is a function of water quantity and a range of other factors including water quality, physical infrastructure, water law and regulations, and economic considerations. Social decisions regarding desired instream flows for recreation, transportation, ecological support, or aesthetics may constrain water availability, and current societal decisions pertaining to water availability can be further complicated by changes in social norms with time. The legal framework for existing water use may override other considerations by granting primacy for use to senior water-rights holders or preventing any development near certain designated streams. These constraints were not studied as part of this effort.

The underlying framework controlling water availability is the interplay between storage of water in the system, flux of water through the system, and human and ecological uses of water. Understanding this underlying framework is paramount to developing estimates of water availability given the constraints that are recognized today or that may be imposed in the future. This study summarizes regional estimates of water in storage and the fluxes of water through the system. Subregional and local analyses that were part of this study quantified various aspects of the water resources, demonstrated tools and techniques capable of assessing subregional and local issues, and helped provide the requisite information to inform regional, subregional, and local water-availability decisions.

Alley, W.M., Reilly, T.E., and Franke, O.L., 1999, Sustainability of ground-water resources: U.S. Geological Survey Circular 1186, 79 p. (Also available at *http://pubs.usgs.gov/circ/circ1186/*.)

Reilly, T.E., Dennehy, K.F., Alley, W.M., and Cunningham, W.L., 2008, Ground-water availability in the United States: U.S. Geological Survey Circular 1323, 70 p. (Also available at *http://pubs.usgs.gov/circ/1323/*.)

Introduction

Water availability for the U.S. Great Lakes Basin is characterized by abundance at the regional scale but potential scarcity at local scales. Scarcity may arise from the interplay between local hydrology and hydrogeology, local demand, local water quality, and societal decisions regarding local instream use or desired ecological flows (minimum or varied flows necessary for the well-being of aquatic life). Water-availability assessment is crucial for proper resource management under complex, uncertain, and changing environmental and social conditions. Such assessments are paramount to address two issues of global concern: sustainable development and adaptation in response to climate change. Water-availability assessment also provides context for understanding how water demands interact with water resources. Population growth, increases in industrial or agricultural water use, and diversions from a basin may increase demand for water resources within a basin. Because water is a finite, open-access resource, these increased demands increase the potential for conflict over and degradation of water resources (Dietz and others, 2002). Regardless of the issue, development, climate change, or conflict, "Environmental governance[1] depends on good, trustworthy information about stocks, flows, and processes within the resource system being governed, as well as about the human-environment interactions affecting those systems" (Dietz and others, 2003).

The Great Lakes Basin Pilot of a U.S. Geological Survey (USGS) national assessment of water availability and use was prompted by the need for an increased understanding of water availability and, as Dietz and others (2003) suggest, "good, trustworthy information." Some of the water-resources issues identified in recent years by the Great Lakes Commission (2003) were addressed in this project. The project was framed by USGS Circular 1223 (U.S. Geological Survey, 2002) and the Presidential National Science and Technology Council Report on Fresh Water Availability (National Science and Technology Council, 2004). In these reports, "water-availability assessment" refers to a water-resources analysis that considers status and trends of the volume of water in storage, flow rates, and water use. These assessments also should include consideration of instream flow, water quality, data consistency, future projection analysis, and development of consistent indicators for water availability (U.S. Geological Survey, 2002).

Major tasks addressed in the Great Lakes Basin Pilot and described herein were (1) analysis of surface-water flows and storage, (2) analysis of groundwater flows and storage, and (3) analysis of water-use data in the context of assessing water availability. Constraints on use are important in the final assessment of water availability; however, this project did not inventory or research any of the various potential constraints on the system. Water quality can be an important factor in determining water availability for an area (Hirsch and others, 2008); other USGS programs focus on water quality, however, so water-quality limitations were not explicitly considered in the Great Lakes Basin Pilot.

This project built on past studies to quantify regional water availability in the U.S. Great Lakes Basin, summarized the status and trends for regional water resources, and laid the groundwork for both quantifying and monitoring stocks, flows, and processes governing regional water resources. Because local constraints are the only limitations to water availability foreseen in the near future in the Great Lakes Basin, methods to quantify subregional- and local-scale water availability were applied. Ways to build upon the regional study to address local issues were analyzed. As a pilot project, this study provided techniques and methods for both regional- and subregional-scale water-availability assessments that may be applied across the Nation.

Purpose and Scope

This report highlights and summarizes studies conducted within the Great Lakes Basin Pilot. The importance of spatial and temporal scale in the analysis of water availability is emphasized. The report is structured to provide, first, a summary of issues confronting water availability in the U.S. Great Lakes Basin and a summary of the physical conditions of the basin. Regional water budgets highlighting the regional abundance of freshwater resources in the Great Lakes Basin and the response of the system to water use and manmade controls are then presented. Next, results of more detailed studies of the processes governing water availability in the Great Lakes Basin relative to regional-, subregional-, and local-scale water availability questions are presented. These studies included (1) a subregional-scale groundwater-flow model of the Lake Michigan Basin and associated local-scale inset model focusing on headwater streams and analysis of groundwater/surface-water interaction, (2) an improved spatial regression model to estimate surface-water flows constrained by the stream geometry and streamgage data applied at the subregional scale, and (3) a subregional analysis of seasonal trends in consumptive water use illustrating the variation in water withdrawals that may influence water availability. The importance of monitoring data and key features of network analysis also are discussed through local-scale example applications.

For this project and report, the U.S. Great Lakes Basin is defined as the area where surface water drains to the Great Lakes and to the St. Lawrence River upstream from the Richelieu River drainage boundary and is designated as Hydrologic Region 04 by the USGS (Seaber and others, 1987) (fig. 1). Because of the vastness of the U.S. Great Lakes Basin, many of the detailed studies within this project focused on local areas within the basin. Other applications—groundwater and water-use studies in particular—required extension beyond

[1]Dietz and others (2003) state: "We refer to adaptive governance rather than adaptive management because the idea of governance conveys the difficulty of control, the need to proceed in the face of substantial uncertainty, and the importance of dealing with diversity and reconciling conflict among people and groups who differ in values, interests, perspectives, power and kinds of information they bring to situations."

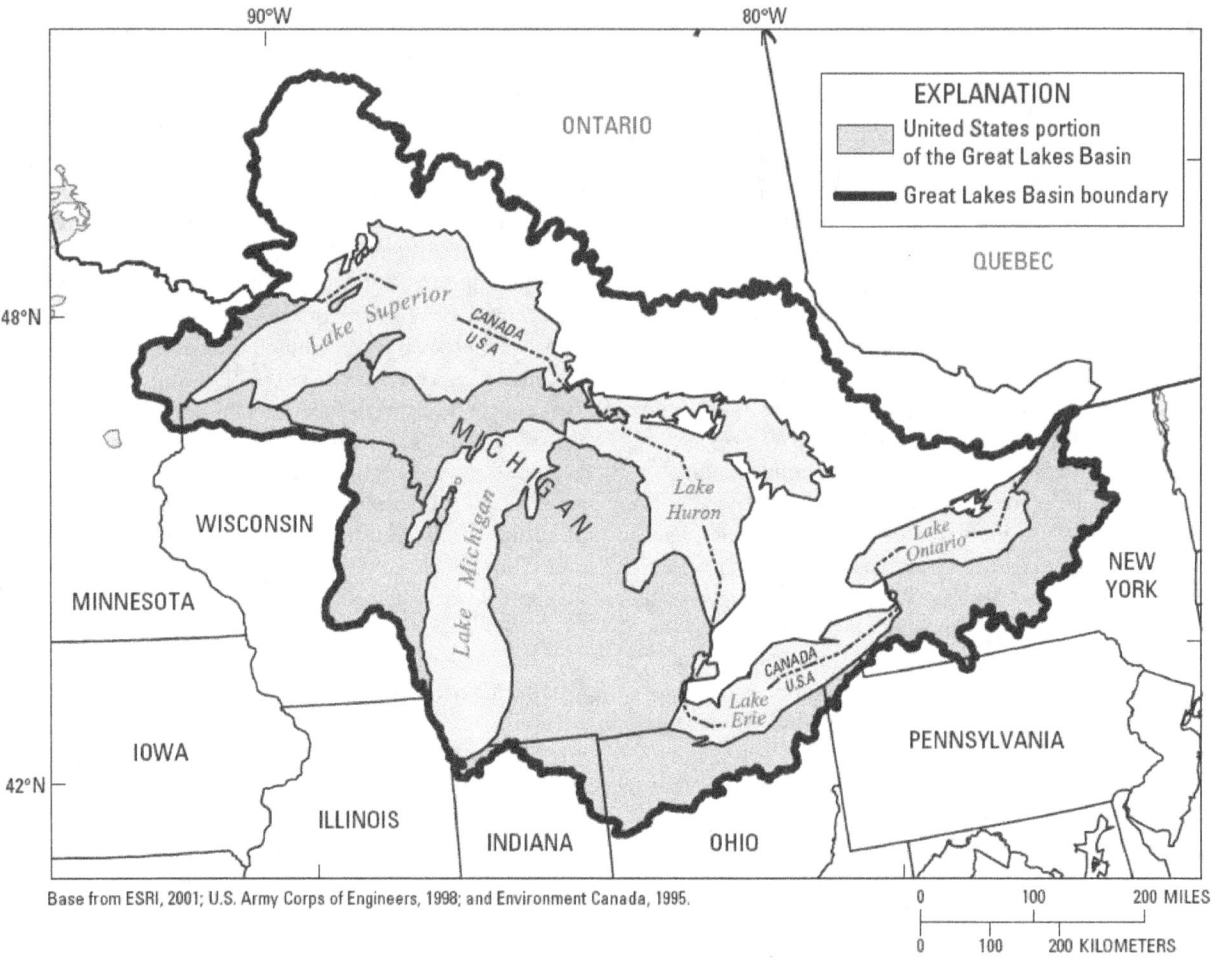

Figure 1.   Study area for Great Lakes Basin Pilot.

the surface-water drainage divide. For the groundwater studies, the extension was necessary to capture the groundwater divides of the system that lie beyond the surface-water divides. For the water-use studies, data availability and the desire to more fully analyze consumptive use and within-year variations in water withdrawals required the extension. The spatial scope for each application discussed in the report is given with each specific application.

Previous Studies

Water resources in the Great Lakes region have been studied at various scales by many researchers and entities. One comprehensive, although dated, report series by the Great Lakes Commission (1976) is an extensive overview of the natural features, economics, population, and resources of the basin, and it presents the commission's recommendations regarding multiple issues and concerns. An atlas of the Great Lakes region summarizing many features of the basin was produced by the Government of Canada and U.S. Environmental Protection Agency (1995). Previous USGS regional studies

included three Regional Aquifer-System Analysis (RASA) studies: Michigan Basin, Midwestern Basins and Arches, and Northern Midwest (Sun and others, 1997). Regional water quality has been studied by USGS through local studies and the National Water Quality Assessment (NAWQA) Program, especially NAWQA's Lake Erie-Lake Saint Clair Drainages, Upper Illinois River Basin, and Western Lake Michigan Drainages study units (see, for example, Myers and others, 2000; Groschen and others, 2004; Peters and others, 1998); the Great Lakes, Ohio, Upper Mississippi, and Souris-Red-Rainy Major River Basin Assessment (Lorenz and others, 2009); and the Glacial Principal Aquifer Regional Assessment (Arnold and others, 2008).

In addition to these regional reports, water-availability assessments and the importance of regional water budgets are discussed by U.S. Geological Survey (2002), Anderson and Woosley (2005), Healy and others (2007), and Reilly and others (2008). Hirsch and others (2008) summarize the links between water quality and water availability. Reports quantifying water availability in the Central Valley of California that include a regional groundwater-flow model were recently published (Faunt, 2009; Faunt and others, 2009).

Approach to the Pilot

The Great Lakes Basin Pilot comprised several individual studies focusing on various aspects of water availability over a range of spatial and temporal time scales. As mentioned previously, some of the studies examined the entire Great Lakes Basin, almost 300,000 mi^2, and others examined smaller parts of the basin, the smallest focusing on groundwater/surface water interaction for a 20-mi^2 area. A study summarizing research on Great Lake water levels examined lake-level variations over a timespan of approximately 4,500 years, whereas another study on water use examined monthly and seasonal variations. A team of researchers, listed in the acknowledgments section, worked on studies within the pilot to address issues of groundwater, surface water, and water use. Much of this work is detailed in a series of individual reports (table 1). This final report summarizes and highlights work from these component studies of the Great Lakes Basin Pilot. In addition to results of the individual analysis, the reports listed in table 1 discuss previous work in detail and refer to major sources of data used in the Great Lakes Basin Pilot.

Great Lakes Basin Water-Availability Issues

The U.S. Great Lakes States and Canadian Great Lakes Provinces are concerned with many water issues, including (1) water management in response to increased demand and potential conflict because of population growth, land-use change, or changes in agricultural practices; (2) diversion of water outside the basin; (3) increased societal recognition of and desire to protect environmental flows; (4) adaptation to changes and timing in supply arising from climate change; and (5) water-quality challenges from natural and human sources, both point and nonpoint. Response to these issues has led to debates and new legislation regarding water rights and governance in the region.

Among these water-availability issues, the management of Great Lakes water—in particular, control and regulation of diversions of water outside the basin—has received much attention over the past decade. Decisions regarding regional water management by representatives of the Great Lakes States and Provinces are embodied in the Great Lakes-St. Lawrence River Basin Water Resources Compact (Council of Great Lakes Governors, 2005b) and the Great Lakes-St. Lawrence River Basin Sustainable Water Resources Agreement (Council of Great Lakes Governors, 2005a). In 2008, the interstate compact between the eight Great Lakes States received consent and approval by Congress and was signed into law (U.S. Congress, 2008). The Sustainable Water Resources Agreement is a good-faith agreement among the eight Great Lakes U.S. States and two Great Lakes Canadian Provinces. This compact and agreement build upon the Great Lakes Charter Annex of 2001 (Council of Great Lakes Governors, 2001), which seeks to "protect, conserve, restore, improve and effectively manage the Waters and Water Dependent Natural Resources of the Basin." Key features that have gained significant attention in the region are regulation of diversions of water outside of the basin and development of water-management goals and policies for the states and provinces within the basin.

This legislation is important for future water-availability decisions in the region. Diversions of water outside the basin are prohibited except for limited cases. New or increased consumptive use within the basin greater than 5 Mgal/d for a 90-day period is subject to review by the Great Lakes States and Provinces and requires unanimous approval. Smaller withdrawals, those less than 5 Mgal/d for a 90-day period but greater than 100,000 gal/d for a 90-day period, also are covered in the compact and agreement. These smaller withdrawals are to be managed by the individual states and provinces to a standard that is protective of the waters of the Great Lakes and water-dependent natural features of the basin.

One type of potential diversion, water bottling, has received a great deal of scrutiny in the region (for example, Granholm, 2005; Lydersen, 2008). In the compact and agreement, water shipped in containers larger than 5.7 gal is treated as any other diversion. Water shipped in smaller containers may be regulated by individual states and provinces—but water shipped in these smaller containers is not explicitly governed. Other special cases in the compact and agreement include exemptions from diversion regulation for water used to supply vessels and aircraft or for water used for short-term noncommercial purposes such as firefighting, humanitarian need, or emergency response.

In addition to limiting diversions, the compact and agreement sets forth regional goals for water efficiency and conservation. In adopting the compact and agreement, the Great Lakes States and Provinces commit to science goals (section 1.4, Council of Great Lakes Governors, 2005a) aimed at "development of a collaborative strategy with other regional partners to strengthen the scientific basis for sound water management decision making under this Compact." The compact also seeks to prevent adverse ecological impacts by withdrawals or losses within the basin. This regional decision to prevent adverse ecological impact on all watersheds or groundwater-dependent natural resources within the Great Lakes Basin may become the limiting factor determining water availability in the region, rather than lack of water or conflict with others' water rights.

Other issues also have gained attention in the region, including priority issues outlined in a 2005 U.S. federal strategy to restore and protect the Great Lakes: aquatic invasive species, coastal health, areas of concern, toxic pollutants, habitat and species, nonpoint-source pollution, indicators and information, and sustainability (Great Lakes Regional Collaboration, 2005). In February 2008, a letter from regional representatives emphasizing these priorities was sent to each member of Congress (Council of Great Lakes Governors,

Table 1.   Great Lakes Basin Pilot reports (in U.S. Geological Survey publications series), focus topics, and predominant scale.

Report	Focus topic(s)	Scale
Great Lakes Basin Water Availability and Use: A study of the National Water Availability and Water Use Program (Grannemann and Reeves, 2005)	Overview of project	Regional.
Estimate of ground water in storage in the Great Lakes Basin, United States, 2006 (Coon and Sheets, 2006)	Groundwater	Regional.
Estimation of shallow ground-water recharge in the Great Lakes Basin (Neff and others, 2006)	Groundwater, surface water	Regional.
Historical changes in precipitation and streamflow in the U.S. Great Lakes Basin, 1915–2004 (Hodgkins and others, 2007)	Surface water	Regional.
Compilation of regional ground-water divides for principal aquifers corresponding to the Great Lakes basin, United States (Sheets and Simonson, 2006)	Groundwater, hydrogeology	Regional.
Consumptive water-use coefficients for the Great Lakes Basin and climatically similar areas (Shaffer and Runkle, 2007)	Water use	Regional.
Consumptive water use in the Great Lakes Basin (Shaffer, 2008)	Water use (fact sheet)	Regional.
Estimated withdrawals and other elements of water use in the Great Lakes Basin of the United States in 2005 (Mills and Sharpe, 2010)	Water use	Regional.
Lake-level variability and water availability in the Great Lakes (Wilcox and others, 2007)	Surface water	Subregional.
Processing, analysis, and general evaluation of well-driller logs for estimating hydrogeologic parameters of the glacial sediments in a ground-water flow model of the Lake Michigan Basin (Arihood, 2009)	Groundwater, hydrogeology	Subregional.
Application guide for AFINCH (Analysis of Flows in Networks of Channels) described by NHDPlus (Holtschlag, 2009)	Surface water	Subregional, local, methods development.
Hydrostratigraphy and salinity distribution for Lake Michigan Basin groundwater-flow model (Lampe, 2009)	Groundwater, hydrogeology	Subregional.
Variations in withdrawal, return flow, and consumptive use of water in Ohio and Indiana, with selected data from Wisconsin, 1999–2004 (Shaffer, 2009)	Water use	Subregional.
SWB—A modified Thornthwaite-Mather Soil-Water Balance code for estimating groundwater recharge (Westenbroek and others, 2009) (partially funded by Great Lakes Basin Pilot)	Groundwater recharge	Regional, subregional, local methods development.
Estimation of groundwater use for a groundwater-flow model of the Lake Michigan Basin and adjacent areas, 1864–2005 (Buchwald and others, 2010)	Water use, groundwater model	Subregional, local.
Regional groundwater-flow model of the Lake Michigan Basin in support of Great Lakes Basin water availability and use studies (Feinstein and others, 2010)	Groundwater	Subregional.
Application of AFINCH as a tool for evaluating the effects of streamflow-gaging-network size and composition on the accuracy and precision of streamflow estimates at ungaged locations in the Southeast Lake Michigan Hydrologic Subregion (Koltun and Holtschlag, 2010)	Surface water	Subregional, local, methods development.
Implementation of local grid refinement in MODFLOW for the Lake Michigan Basin regional groundwater-flow model (Hoard, 2010)	Groundwater	Local.
Using prediction uncertainty analysis to design hydrologic monitoring networks: Example applications from the Great Lakes Water Availability Pilot Project (Fienen and others, 2010)	Groundwater	Local.

2008), and a report was published describing legislative priories for fiscal year 2009 (Great Lakes Commission, 2008). The four near-term priorities highlighted in the Great Lakes Commission report are consistent with those described by the Regional Collaboration: stopping invasive species, cleanup of toxic sediments, restoration of Great Lakes wetlands, and protection of water quality. There also are treaty obligations for the United States and Canada under the Great Lakes Water Quality Agreement that was signed in 1972 and subsequently renewed and amended in 1978 and 1987. This agreement is administered by the International Joint Commission, which was formed under the 1909 Boundary Waters Treaty (International Joint Commission, 2008). In 2006, the International Joint Commission published a report reviewing and making recommendations for revisions to this agreement (International Joint Commission, 2006).

Great Lakes levels, flows in the connecting channels, and regulation of levels and flows also have been important topics in the region. Recent, (2000–2008) low levels of the Upper Great Lakes (Lakes Michigan, Huron, and Superior) have led to much interest and debate on this issue. In 2005, a report was published stating that dredging in the St. Clair River in the 1960s for a shipping channel had permanently lowered levels in Lakes Michigan and Huron (W.F. Baird Associates, 2005). Lake levels and flows are crucial factors for navigation, recreational boating, lakefront property, hydropower generation, and interaction of the St. Lawrence River with the Atlantic Ocean. The 2005 report, along with low lake levels, has motivated additional investigations in the region, among which was a study of the Upper Great Lakes coordinated by the International Joint Commission (International Upper Great Lakes Study, 2009).

Characteristics of the Great Lakes Basin

The Great Lakes Basin is approximately 575 mi from north to south and 900 mi from east to west (fig. 1). The approximate land drainage area of the basin is 201,460 mi^2; water area is 94,250 mi^2, and total area of the basin is 296,000 mi^2 (Government of Canada and U.S. Environmental Protection Agency, 1995). It is the second-largest drainage basin in the United States after the Mississippi River drainage in terms of average discharge, the third largest in terms of area, and fourth largest in terms of length from source to mouth (Kammerer, 1987). Characteristics for each of the Great Lakes are summarized in table 2. In addition to the large area of the basin, the abrupt change in altitude of the lakes between Lake Erie and Lake Ontario (Niagara Falls) is notable.

The Great Lakes Basin was formed through series of geological events and did not appear in its present form until relatively recently, after continental glaciers retreated from the region approximately 10,000 years ago. (See Hough, 1958,

and Dorr and Eshman, 1970, for discussion of the geological history of the region.) Important geological features of the Great Lakes Basin influencing water-resources stocks and flows include the Michigan Basin and the regional bedrock arches that define this structural basin, bedrock aquifers and confining units, and the veneer of glacial deposits that overlies older bedrock. Precambrian bedrock of the Canadian Shield, approximately 3.5 billion years old, crops out on the northern boundary of the Great Lakes Basin. Bedrock aquifers in the basin are formed primarily in layered Paleozoic rocks. Notable in this sequence are Middle Silurian (Niagaran) dolomite formations, which are an important structural control of the Great Lakes Basin (Hough, 1958). Glacial deposits overlie the bedrock over almost all of the Great Lakes Basin. These deposits are thickest—as thick as 1,500 ft—in the northern part of the Lower Peninsula of Michigan. The deposits include a range of materials from fine clay to gravel and can be well sorted in some areas and highly heterogeneous in others. In some parts of the basin, the glacial deposits serve as important aquifers, but in others they do not.

The Great Lakes Basin is part of the extensive Great Interior, Southern Plains, and Lowlands generalized physical climatic region that dominates the continental United States. Although, the overall climate classification for the basin is Continental (Baldwin, 1973), the large size of the basin leads to different climate characteristics across the basin. Summer mean daily air temperature ranges from 53 to 73°F, winter mean daily air temperature ranges from −4 to 28°F, and annual precipitation ranges from 25 to 50 in/yr. The Great Lakes tend to buffer changes in temperature; this buffering leads to areas, particularly to the east of each lake, that have cooler summer temperatures, warmer winter temperatures, and increased precipitation. The climate in the region is characteristically changeable because of the interaction between the buffering effects of the lakes and two competing air masses: warm, moist air from the Gulf of Mexico and cool, dry air from the Arctic (Government of Canada and U.S. Environmental Protection Agency, 1995).

Climate interacts with surficial geology, soils, and other features of the landscape to form ecoregions (fig. 2). Twelve Level-III Ecoregions have been defined for the U.S. Great Lakes Basin. These ecoregion definitions highlight differences in terms of natural productivity, land use, and human alteration of the landscape (Commission for Environmental Cooperation, 1997; U.S. Environmental Protection Agency, 2002, 2007). This diversity is important because it implies that local conditions across the region may differ greatly from the regional average condition. Dominant water use and the importance of local flows help shape the water-availability issues for a particular location.

Land use and land cover is varied across the region, from predominantly forest to agricultural and urban (fig. 3). The largest urban areas in the U.S. and Canadian parts of the basin tend to be near or on the Great Lakes. Use of the lakes for shipping and water supply helped shape this development. Forests across the basin were very important historically.

Table 2.   Physical characteristics of the Great Lakes.

[From Government of Canada and U.S. Environmental Protection Agency, 1995]

Property	Lake Superior	Lake Michigan	Lake Huron	Lake Erie	Lake Ontario
Altitude, in feet at low-water datum[1]	600	577	577	569	243
Length, in miles	350	307	206	241	193
Breadth, in miles	160	118	183	57	53
Average depth, in feet at low-water datum	483	279	195	62	283
Maximum depth, in feet at low-water datum	1,332	925	750	210	802
Water area, in square miles	31,700	22,300	23,000	9,910	7,340
Land drainage area, in square miles	49,300	45,600	51,700	30,140	24,720

[1]Low-water datum, also known as chart datum, is a reference point for water-level elevation where 95 percent of recorded/historical elevations are above the datum. It is referenced to the International Great Lakes Datum (IGLD) of 1985.

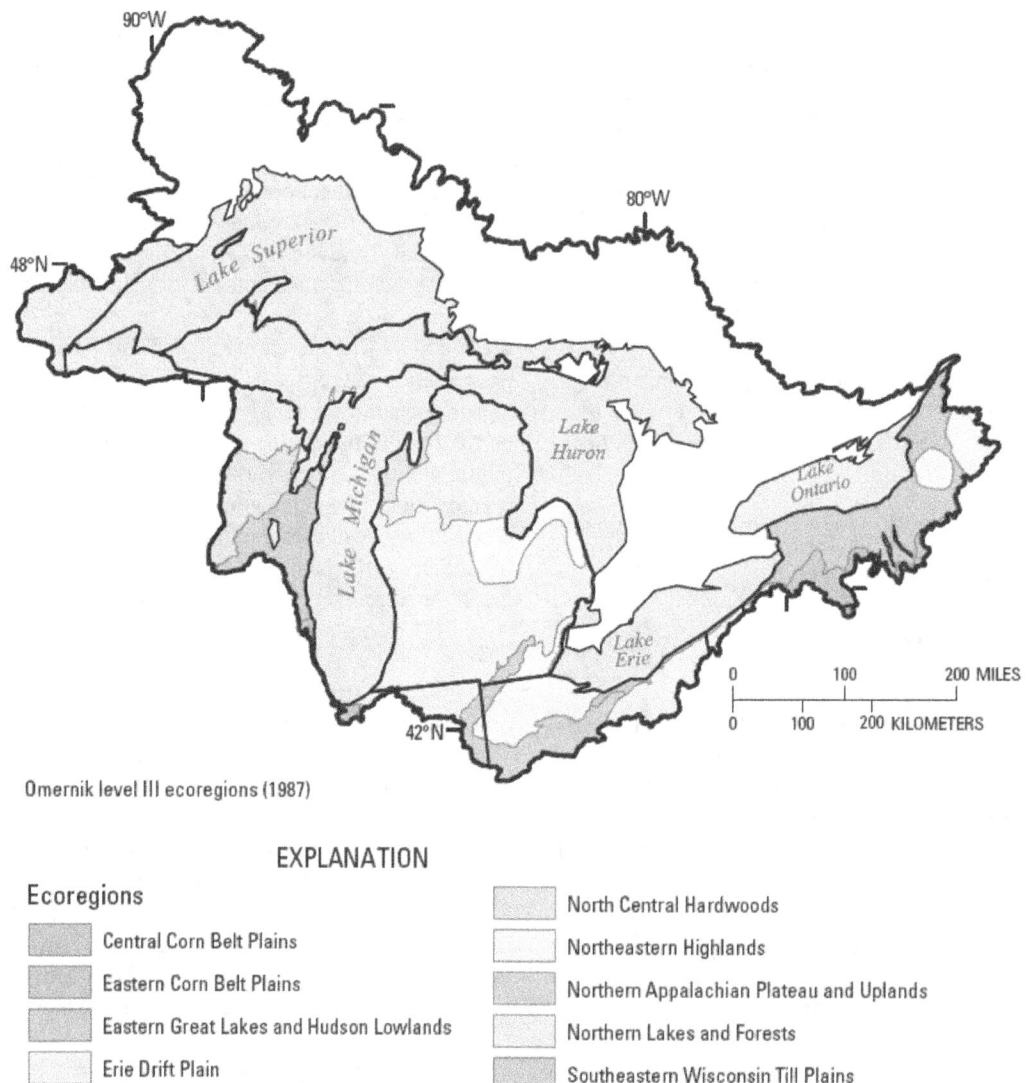

Omernik level III ecoregions (1987)

EXPLANATION

Ecoregions

- Central Corn Belt Plains
- Eastern Corn Belt Plains
- Eastern Great Lakes and Hudson Lowlands
- Erie Drift Plain
- Huron/Erie Lake Plains
- North Central Appalachians

- North Central Hardwoods
- Northeastern Highlands
- Northern Appalachian Plateau and Uplands
- Northern Lakes and Forests
- Southeastern Wisconsin Till Plains
- Southern Michigan/Northern Indiana Drift Plains
- —— Great Lakes Basin boundary

Figure 2.   Level III ecoregions for the U.S. Great Lakes Basin (U.S. Environmental Protection Agency, 2007).

Between 1870 and 1890 most of the forests in Michigan were cut, and lumber was shipped on the Great Lakes eastward to the northeast United States or through Chicago to the U.S. Plains States. Similar logging occurred in other Great Lakes States, and this logging affected water resources by changing both rainfall/runoff characteristics and sediment loads in the watersheds. These changes influenced, and continue to influence, the morphology of streams and the amount of sediment delivered to the Great Lakes (see for example, Fitzpatrick and others, 1999).

The population of the Great Lakes Basin in 2000 was greater than 34 million people, and approximately 10 percent of the U.S. population and 30 percent of the Canadian population live in the Great Lakes Basin (Government of Canada and U.S. Environmental Protection Agency, 1995; Great Lakes Commission, 2006b). Accounting for the population in the Chicago and Milwaukee metropolitan areas, however, complicates the population estimate for the basin. The surface-water

divide in this part of the basin is quite close to Lake Michigan, and many of the millions of people in the Chicago and Milwaukee metropolitan areas actually reside outside of the basin. Many of these people, however, rely on water from Lake Michigan, or water tributary to Lake Michigan, for their water supply, and the reported population estimates may either underestimate the number of people getting water from the Great Lakes Basin or overestimate the number of people living in the basin (Great Lakes Information Network, 2006).

The surface-water network of streams tributary to the Great Lakes is extensive, and the stream density across the region varies with local geological and geomorphic conditions. Typically, areas with poorly draining soils have denser stream networks than areas with more freely draining soils. USGS uses Hydrologic Unit Codes (HUCs) to classify hydrologic systems. The number of digits in the HUC code indicates drainage basins of progressively smaller areas that are embedded within larger drainage basins. Hydrologic Region 04 has

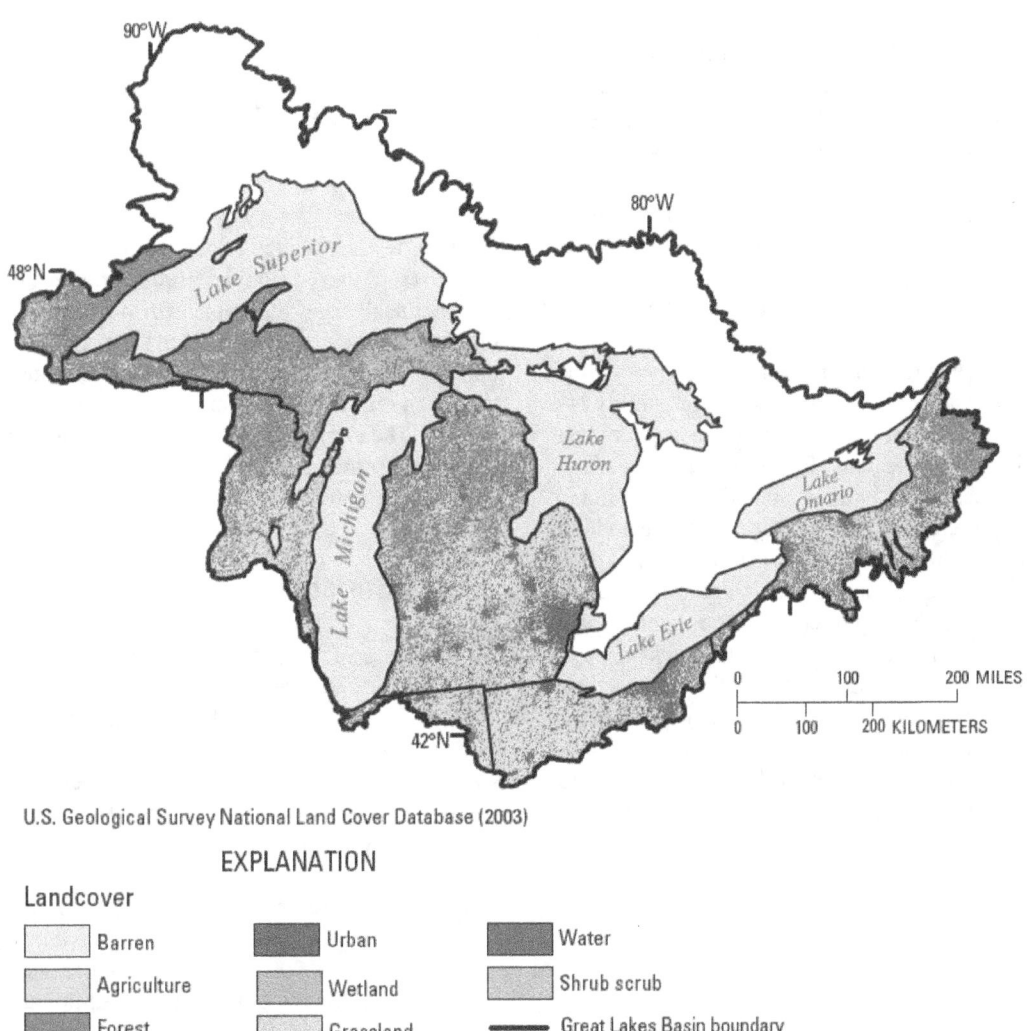

U.S. Geological Survey National Land Cover Database (2003)

EXPLANATION

Landcover

Barren   Urban   Water

Agriculture   Wetland   Shrub scrub

Forest   Grassland   ——— Great Lakes Basin boundary

Figure 3.   Land use and cover for the U.S. Great Lakes Basin from the U.S. Geological Survey National Land Cover Database.

been subdivided by USGS (Seaber and others, 1987) into 15 subregions (4-digit HUCs), 27 accounting units (6-digit HUCs), and 111 cataloging units (8-digit HUCs). Inland surface water is important as potable water supply, irrigation and industrial water supply, thermoelectric-generation cooling water, and receiving water for municipal and industrial waste disposal. Recreational use of inland surface water for fishing, boating, and swimming is important to the region economically and for the residents' quality of life.

Groundwater also is an important source of water for potable water supply, irrigation, and industrial use. Aquifers are found in parts of the highly heterogeneous glacial deposits that cover most of the region and also are formed in, primarily, Paleozoic bedrock. The USGS (Miller, 2000; U.S. Geological Survey, 2003) designates nine principal aquifers in the region: (1) localized sand and gravel aquifers in glacial deposits (Cenozoic), also called the surficial aquifer system, (2) New York sandstone aquifers, (3) Pennsylvanian aquifers, (4) Mississippian aquifer of Michigan, (5) Mississippian sandstone and carbonate-rock aquifers, (6) Silurian-Devonian aquifers, (7) New York and New England carbonate-rock aquifers, (8) Cambrian-Ordovician aquifer system, and (9) Jacobsville aquifer (Precambrian). Terminology used for the bedrock aquifer units varies across the region. The regional hydrostratigraphy used to develop a groundwater-flow model for the Lake Michigan Basin for this project (fig. 4) shows this variation and summarizes the hydrogeology in part of the overall study area. (Note that the Lake Michigan Basin model does not include three of the principal aquifers in the region: New York sandstone aquifers, Mississippian sandstone and carbonate-rock aquifers, or New York and New England carbonate-rock aquifers.)

Water quality generally does not limit water availability in the region. In some areas, however, poor water quality is an important issue. Poor water quality in the region may be a result of natural processes leading, for example, to unacceptable levels of arsenic, radon, or other potentially hazardous constituents (see for example, Thomas, 2007; Ayotte and others, 2007; Arnold and others, 2008). It also may be the result of point-source or nonpoint-source contamination. Gilbertson (2001) offers a sobering history of chemical contamination in the Great Lakes. Concerns and scientific challenges posed by these water-quality issues are raised in the priority areas listed by the Council of Great Lakes Governors, the Great Lakes Commission, and the Great Lakes Regional Collaboration, and by Lakewide Management Plans for the Great Lakes (for example, Lake Michigan Technical Committee, 2006).

Regional Water Availability Analysis for the U.S. Great Lakes Basin

The Great Lakes Basin contains a vast amount of freshwater: it is the largest system of fresh surface water on the Earth (Government of Canada and U.S. Environmental Protection Agency, 1995). In this section, predevelopment and postdevelopment regional water budget are described, and the relations between stocks, flows, and water use are discussed. In this report, "predevelopment" refers to conditions before approximately 1864; "postdevelopment" refers to conditions after 1864, but it is especially used to refer to conditions since approximately 1990. The stock and flows values presented in this section are long-term temporal averages because interannual, decadal, and long-term variations in climate are the major drivers changing stocks and flows in the system. The importance of different spatial and temporal scales is discussed in this section because short-term or local-scale water shortages or conflicts regarding water resources are quite possible even in a system that has, on average, an abundance of freshwater.

Predevelopment Conditions

Predevelopment conditions are difficult to quantify because reported direct observations of predevelopment conditions are few. Estimates of predevelopment stocks, flows, and processes, however, set the baseline and reveal the context for regional analysis of the impacts of water use and diversion on the regional water balance. Analysis of trends since predevelopment helps to illustrate changes in the system in response to human influences and variations in climate over the last century. The components of the water budget are discussed below and summarized in table 3, and their spatial distribution is shown in figure 5.

Stocks (Storage)

The largest reservoirs of freshwater in the Great Lakes Basin are the five Great Lakes. Together they contain approximately 8.0×10^{14} ft³ of freshwater. This volume, which is estimated to be approximately 84 percent of the fresh surface water in North America (U.S. Environmental Protection Agency, 2006; 2008), could cover the continents of North America, South America, and Africa to a depth of more than 1 ft (Neff and Nicholas, 2005). The volume of fresh groundwater in storage represents, in a sense, another Great Lake. For the U.S. part of the basin, it is approximately 1.4×10^{14} ft³ (Coon and Sheets, 2006), which is greater than the volume of either Lake Erie or Lake Huron. Additional water is held in the basin in (1) aquifers in the Canadian part of the basin, (2) smaller lakes and streams, (3) snowpack, and (4) soil moisture. The largest and most stable of these other reservoirs

Time-stratigraphic unit: System	Series	Wisconsin	Illinois	Indiana	Ohio	Michigan	Hydrogeologic unit (model layer)	USGS principal aquifer
Quaternary		Glacial deposits	Glacial deposits	Glacial deposits	Glacial deposits	Glacial deposits	Quaternary (1-3)	Surficial aquifer system
Jurassic	Middle	Absent	Absent	Absent	Absent	Ionia Fm	Jurassic (4)	
Pennsylvanian	Upper	Absent	Absent	Absent	Absent	Grand River Fm Saginaw Fm	Upper Pennsylvanian (5)	Pennsylvanian
Pennsylvanian	Lower	Absent	Pennsylvanian System (Undifferentiated)[1]	Absent	Absent	Saginaw Fm (Shale) Parma Sandstone	Lower Pennsylvanian (6)	
Mississippian	Upper	Absent	Absent	Absent	Absent	Bayport Ls Michigan Fm	Lower Pennsylvanian (6) Michigan (7)	
Mississippian	Lower	Absent	Mississippian System (Undifferentiated)	Coldwater Shale Sunbury Shale	Coldwater Shale Sunbury Shale	Marshall Sandstone Coldwater Shale Sunbury Shale	Marshall (8) Devonian-Mississippian (9)	Mississippian
Devonian	Upper	Antrim Shale	New Albany Shale Group	Ellsworth Shale Antrim Shale	Bedford Shale Antrim Shale	Ellsworth Shale Antrim Shale	Devonian-Mississippian (9)	
Devonian	Middle	Milwaukee Fm Thiensville Fm	Cedar Valley Limestone Wapsipinicon Limestone	Muscatatuck Group	Traverse Group Dundee Formation Detroit River Group	Traverse Group Detroit River Group	Silurian-Devonian (10)	Silurian-Devonian
Devonian	Lower	Absent	Absent	Absent	Absent	Bass Islands Group	Silurian-Devonian (11-12)	Silurian-Devonian
Silurian	Upper	Waubakee Fm	Absent	Salina Group	Salina Group	Salina Group	Silurian-Devonian (11-12)	Silurian-Devonian
Silurian	Middle	Racine Fm Manistique Fm Hendricks Fm Byron Fm	Racine Dolomite Sugar Run Dolomite Joliet Dolomite	Salamonie Dolomite	Lockport Group Rochester Shale Dayton Formation	Niagara Group Manistique Group Burnt Bluff Group	Silurian-Devonian (11-12)	Silurian-Devonian
Silurian	Lower	Mayville Fm	Kankakee Dolomite Wilhelmi Fm	Brassfield Limestone	Cataract Group	Cataract Group	Silurian-Devonian (11-12)	Silurian-Devonian
Ordovician	Upper	Neda Fm Maquoketa Fm	Maquoketa Group	Maquoketa Group	Cincinnati group	Richmond Group	Maquoketa (13)	Cambrian-Ordovician
Ordovician	Middle	Sinnipee Group Glenwood Fm St. Peter Fm	Galena Group Platteville Group Ancell Group	Trenton Limestone Black River Limestone Ancell Group	Trenton Limestone Black River Group Wells Creek Fm	Trenton Fm Black River Fm Glenwood Fm St. Peter Sandstone	Sinnipee (14) St. Peter (15)	Cambrian-Ordovician
Ordovician	Lower	Prairie du Chien Gr	Prairie du Chien Gr	Prairie du Chien Gr	Absent	Prairie du Chien Gr	Prairie du Chien-Franconia (16)	Cambrian-Ordovician
Cambrian	Upper	Trempealeau Group Tunnel City Group	Potosi Dolomite Franconia Fm	Potosi Dolomite Franconia Sandstone	Knox Dolomite	Trempealeau Fm Franconia Fm	Prairie du Chien-Franconia (16)	Cambrian-Ordovician
Cambrian	Upper	Wonewoc Fm	Ironton Sandstone Galesville Sandstone	Ironton Sandstone Galesville Sandstone	Kerbel Fm	Galesville Sandstone	Ironton-Galesville (17)	Cambrian-Ordovician
Cambrian	Upper	Eau Claire Fm	Eau Claire Fm	Eau Claire Sandstone	Eau Claire Fm	Eau Claire Fm	Eau Claire (18)	Cambrian-Ordovician
Cambrian	Upper	Mount Simon Formation	Mount Simon Sandstone	Mount Simon Sandstone of Dresbach Group	Mount Simon Sandstone	Mount Simon Sandstone	Mount Simon (19-20)	Cambrian-Ordovician
Precambrian		Keweenawan Supergroup	Crystalline Basement Complex	Crystalline Basement Complex	Crystalline Basement Complex	Jacobsville Sandstone Crystalline Basement Complex		Jacobsville
References		Wisconsin Geological and Natural History Survey, 2006	Buschbach, 1964 Kolata and Graese, 1983 Kolata, 1990 Mikulic and others, 1985 Willman and others, 1975 Young and Siegel, 1992	Gray and others, 1985	Hull, 1990	Catacosinos and others, 2001		

[1]Rocks of the Pennsylvanian System were grouped with the Mississippian-Devonian hydrogeologic unit for Illinois

EXPLANATION

- Aquifer
- Aquifer/confining unit
- Confining unit
- ——— Depositional surface
- ∿∿∿ Erosional surface
- Gr, Group
- Fm, Formation
- Ls, Limestone

Figure 4. Hydrostratigraphy for the Lake Michigan Basin and adjacent region used in the groundwater-flow model developed in this project (from Lampe, 2008).

is aquifers on the Canadian part of the basin; however, the storage in these aquifers is not known (Riveria, 2005). One example from a Canadian system that has been the focus of much study is that of the Oak Ridges Moraine, an important aquifer system north of Toronto: storage in those deposits is estimated to be 0.05×10^{14} ft^3 (Riveria, 2005). Estimates of groundwater storage require assumptions regarding the depth of freshwater available in aquifers basinwide; geometries, storage coefficients, and specific yields of aquifer materials; and approximate heads (water levels) in the major aquifers. Therefore, storage estimate can vary widely depending on the values used in these estimates; for example, Weist (1978) cites an unpublished report for an estimate for storage in the entire basin of 0.35×10^{14} ft^3. The Great Lakes Commission (1976) preferred not to make an estimate of groundwater in

storage and used annual base-flow estimates as an indicator for groundwater availability.

Flows and Processes

Under predevelopment conditions, the only inputs to the basin were precipitation driven: direct precipitation to the lakes and direct precipitation to the land surface. The latter becomes either direct runoff to the lakes, direct groundwater discharge to the lakes, indirect groundwater discharge to the lakes, or runoff to streams and stream input to the lakes. Historically, the only outputs from the basin were the St. Lawrence River, direct evaporation from the lakes, and evaporation and transpiration from the land area of the basin. Direct

Table 3.   Predevelopment generalized water budget

[Numbers in brackets are either alternate values reported in the literature or component values already included in other table entries and not included in the reported total flows. ft^3/s, cubic feet per second]

	Volume, in cubic feet	Source	Comments
Surface-water storage (Great Lakes)	8.0×10^{14}	Government of Canada and U.S. Environmental Protection Agency, 1995	
Groundwater storage	1.4×10^{14}	Coon and Sheets, 2006	U.S. side of the basin only.
Flows in			
	Rate, in thousand cubic feet per second	Source	Comments
Direct precipitation to Great Lakes	229 [223]	Croley, 2003; Neff and Nicholas, 2005	1950–99 simulation.
Precipitation to land area	505	Croley, 2003	1950–99 simulation.
Surface-water runoff	[220]	Croley, 2003	Surface runoff is equal to precipitation minus evapotranspiration; it is internal to regional budget and not included in "total in" calculation.
Base flow to streams (approximately aquifer recharge)	[151]	Neff and others, 2005	Average of several base-flow-separation techniques and included in surface-water runoff. This value is internal to the budget and not included in "total in" calculation.
Surface water diverted into basin	0		
Groundwater from outside basin	Unknown		The Lake Michigan Basin groundwater-flow-model estimate for the Lake Michigan Basin is 400 ft^3/s, which is less than 2 percent of total flow to groundwater system.
Total in	*734*		

precipitation to the lakes and evaporation from the lakes are major factors and are difficult to quantify. Neff and Nicholas (2005) report that these quantities are currently estimated from data at land-based stations, and they cite the lack of direct over-lake weather monitoring as the greatest data gap contributing to the uncertainty in estimates of the Great Lakes water balance and accounting of water in the system.

Streamflow input to the lakes is generated from surface runoff to streams and groundwater discharge to streams, and it is generally dominated by groundwater discharge to streams. Holtschlag and Nicholas (1998) estimate that the average groundwater component of streamflow for streams in the Great Lakes basin ranges from 25 to 96 percent, and the resulting "indirect" groundwater discharge to the Great Lakes ranges from 22 and 42 percent of the supply to the

lakes. (Indirect groundwater discharge is the volume of water that moves through the groundwater system at some point in its travel, is discharged to a stream, and is subsequently discharged to a Great Lake: it is the base-flow component of streamflow discharged to the lakes.) Thus, although direct groundwater discharge to the Great Lakes is generally neglected in water-balance estimates for the lakes (Neff and Nicholas, 2005), groundwater plays an important role in moving water from precipitation on the land surface to the Great Lakes.

The Great Lakes form the headwaters of the St. Lawrence River, and quantification of the groundwater flows into the system depends on the definition of the basin used in the analysis. If the basin is defined by the surface-water divide, then there is potential for groundwater input from outside the basin

Table 3. Predevelopment generalized water budget.—Continued

[Numbers in brackets are either alternate values reported in the literature or component values already included in other table entries and not included in the reported total flows. ft³/s, cubic feet per second]

	Flows out		
	Rate, in thousand cubic feet per second	Source	Comments
Groundwater out of the basin	0		
Surface water out the St. Lawrence River	271 [251] [246]	Government of Canada and U.S. Environmental Protection Agency, 1995; Croley, 2003; Neff and Nicholas, 2005	Flow out of 251,000 ft³/s given by Government of Canada and U.S. Environmental Protection Agency, 1995; flow of 246,000 ft³/s given by Neff and Nicholas, 2005; 271,000 ft³/s from Croley, 2003, balances the net-basin-supply estimate.
Surface water diverted outside basin	0		
Groundwater transferred outside basin	0		Assumed; groundwater divides and relation to surface-water divides not well known for the entire basin.
Direct evaporation from Great Lakes	178	Croley, 2003	1950–99 simulation.
Evapotranspiration from land area of basin	284	Croley, 2003	1950–99 simulation.
Total out	*733*		

in areas where the groundwater divide extends beyond the surface-water divide away from the Great Lakes. The location of groundwater divides, the response of divides to changes in stresses, and the flux of water through aquifer into the surface-water basin, however, are not well known (Sheets and Simonson, 2006). Regional groundwater-flow modeling of the entire basin would be required to generate an estimate of this flux, but it is expected to be only a minor input to the lakes (Neff and Nicholas, 2005). For example, in the groundwater-flow model of the Lake Michigan Basin developed for this project, the net groundwater import across the surface-water divide

under predevelopment conditions is approximately 440 ft³/s, which less than 2 percent of the total input to the groundwater system (Feinstein and others, 2010).

Recharge to the groundwater system balances the discharge to streams (indirect discharge to the lakes), direct discharge to the lakes, and loss of groundwater within the basin; for example, via transpiration by vegetation that taps groundwater. A variety of methods may be used to estimate recharge at different scales (Delin and Risser, 2007). Neff and others (2006) provide a regional estimate for recharge in the Great Lakes Basin based on base-flow estimates at streamgages and

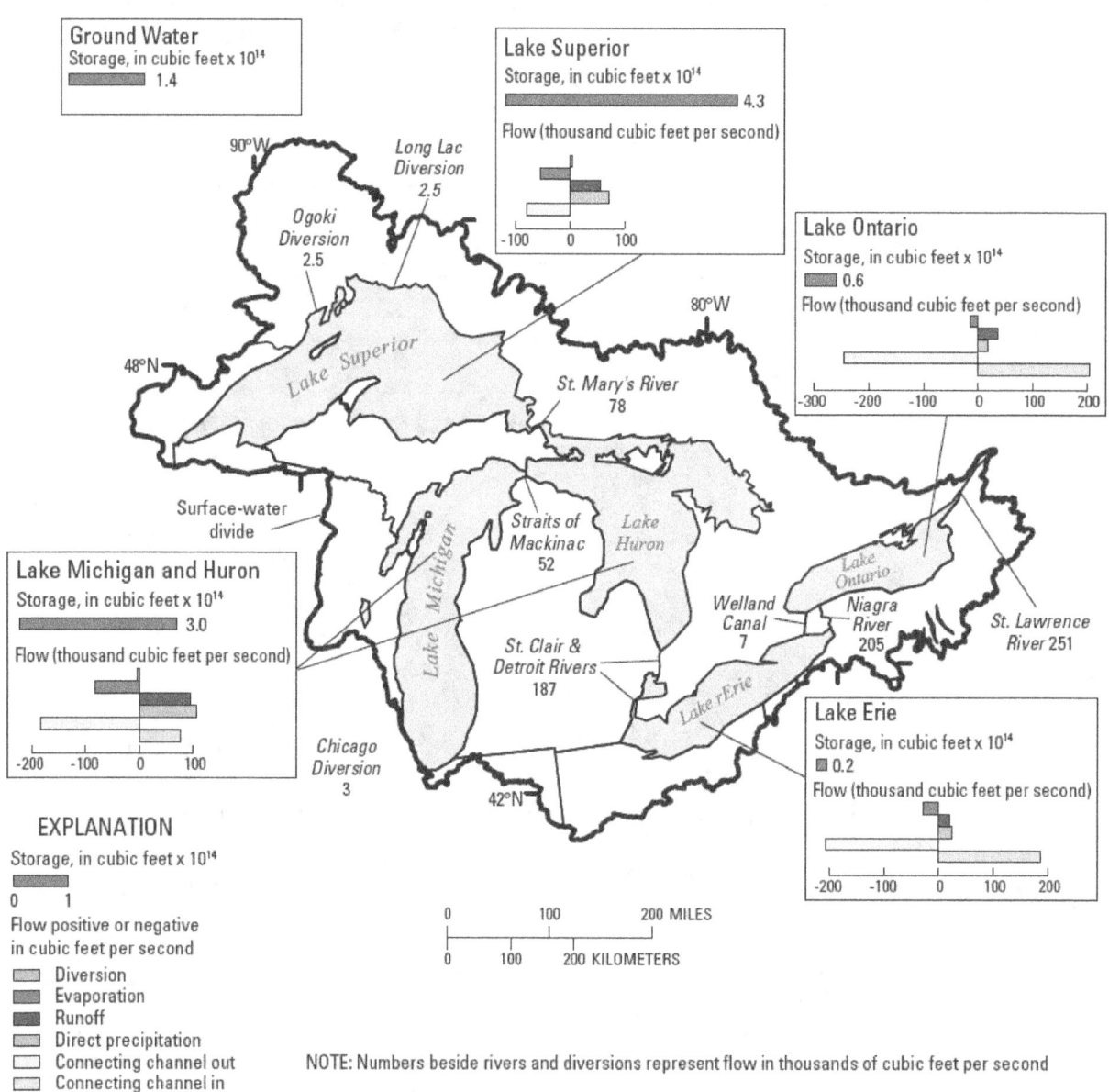

Figure 5. Summary of storage, in cubic feet, and flows, in thousands of cubic feet per second, for the Great Lakes (data from Government of Canada and U.S. Environmental Protection Agency, 1995; Neff and Nicholas, 2005; Coon and Sheets, 2006).

the assumption that long-term recharge is equal to average base flow (fig. 6). These estimates were computed on a fairly coarse spatial scale but reveal variation in recharge rates across the region, from less than 4 in/yr to more than 16 in/yr. To estimate recharge at a more resolved spatial scale and to account for the mechanisms generating recharge from precipitation, a soil-water-balance approach (Westenbroek and others, 2010) was used to estimate recharge for the Lake Michigan Basin groundwater-flow model (fig. 7). Because these estimates were calibrated by using a subset of streamgage data, the average estimate of regional recharge generated by the methods is expected to be similar. The advantages of the soil-water-balance approach are that it calculates components of the water balance on a daily basis, it can be scaled to produce estimates on a spatial scale consistent with the application, its data requirements include commonly available tabular and gridded types, and its data and formats are designed to work with widely available geographic information system (GIS) datasets and file structures (Westenbroek and others, 2010).

Postdevelopment Conditions

The water budget in the Great Lakes Basin has changed from predevelopment conditions because of diversions of water into and out of the Great Lakes Basin and because of humans' use of water within the basin (table 4). Water withdrawals and return flows have changed flow paths, timing, and, potentially, quality of water moving through the basin. Consumptive water use removes water from the basin, although the amount of water lost through consumptive use is difficult to quantify (Shaffer and Runkle, 2007). Consumptive water use is the amount of water evaporated, transpired, incorporated into products or crops, consumed by humans or livestock, or otherwise removed from the immediate water environment. Consumptive use is estimated in relation to human activities; evaporation and transpiration from the system that occurs without human intervention is not typically included in the estimate. For example, the water used by rain-fed agriculture is not included as a consumptive use: this

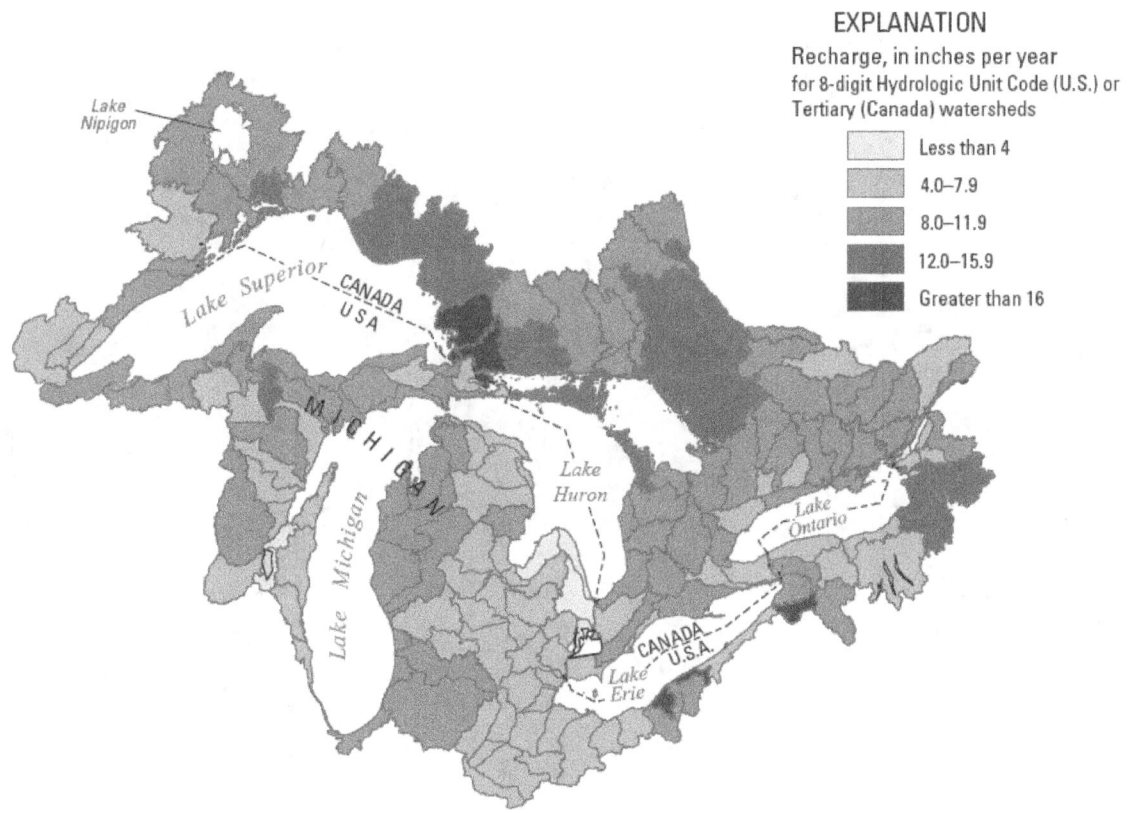

Figure 6. Shallow ground-water recharge estimated from base-flow-separation techniques (Neff and others, 2005).

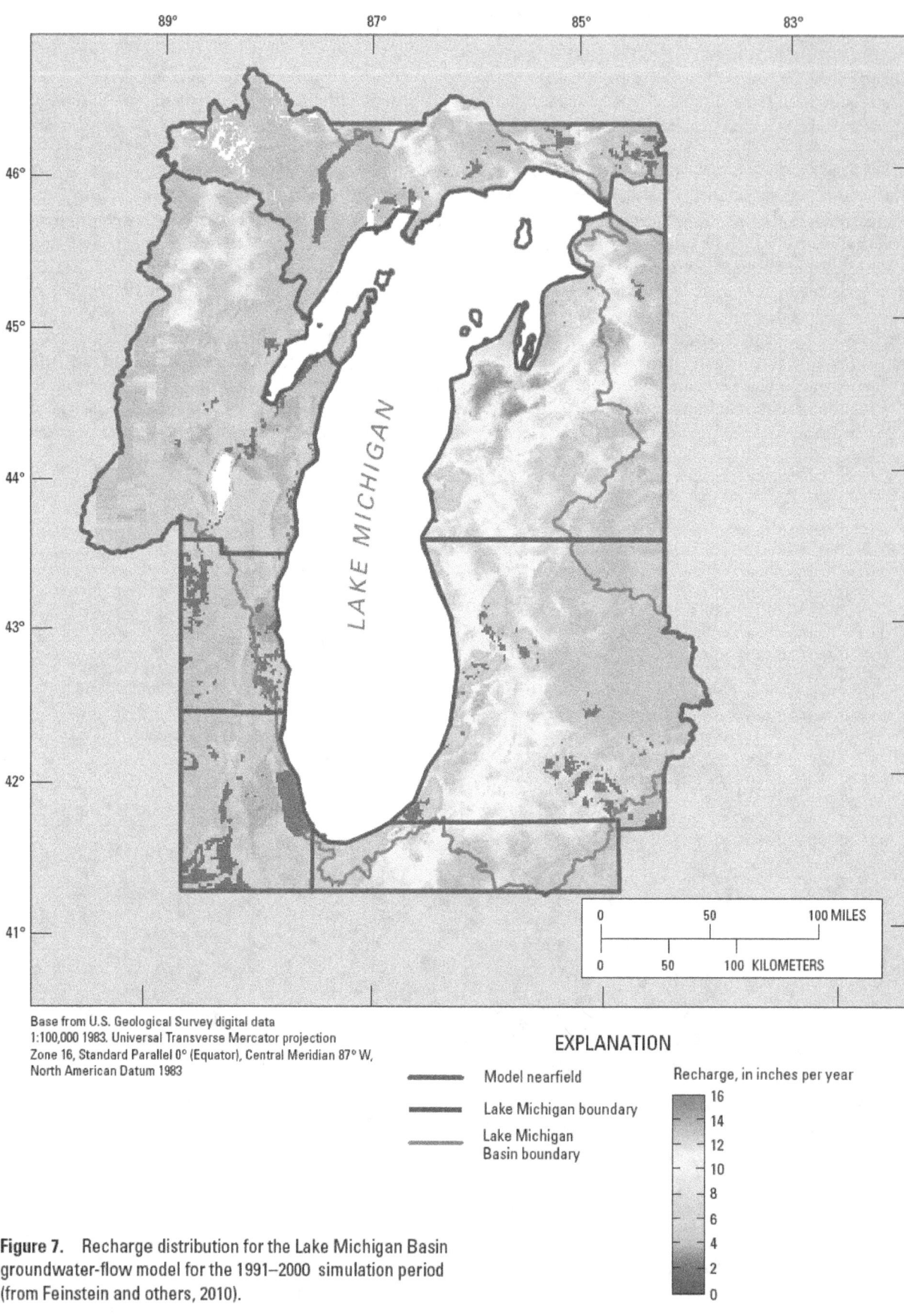

Figure 7.   Recharge distribution for the Lake Michigan Basin groundwater-flow model for the 1991–2000 simulation period (from Feinstein and others, 2010).

water is accounted for in the estimates of evapotranspiration from the land surface. The distinction is important in water-use accounting: water withdrawn by humans is either returned to the basin or lost as consumptive use. Land-use changes may have altered the distribution of precipitation on the land surface and runoff characteristics from the land surface. Part of this water moves through the groundwater system as recharge to the aquifer and discharge to streams (as base flow). These changes, however, are internal to the basin and do not affect the overall budget. Change in storage of water in the Great Lakes in response to annual and decadal variations in climate is less under developed conditions than under predevelopment conditions because control structures have dampened variations in lake levels (Wilcox and others, 2007). Temporal variations in the regional water budget are discussed in subsequent paragraphs, following presentation of a time-averaged budget.

Surface-Water Diversions Into and Out of the Great Lakes Basin

The major diversions are the Ogoki and Long Lac diversions (into the basin) and the Chicago diversion (out of the basin). (For more discussion on these diversions, see International Joint Commission, 1985; Neff and Killian, 2003; and Neff and Nicholas, 2005.) Major intrabasin diversions are the Welland Canal and the New York State Barge Canal. Both of these intrabasin diversions transfer water from Lake Erie to Lake Ontario to allow shipping between these lakes that otherwise would be blocked by Niagara Falls in the natural connecting channel, the Niagara River, between the two Great Lakes.

Regional Water Withdrawals and Water Use

Understanding water withdrawals, transfers, and consumptive uses is important in the context of water availability because one potential constraint on future development is adverse impacts on current users. Examining the effects of withdrawals, transfers, and consumptive uses on the system also provides information required to predict the potential effect of new or expanded uses. By including water-use analysis, water-availability studies can illustrate to decisionmakers that there "is no unused water": new or expanded water withdrawals, transfers, and consumptive uses have effects on surface-water and groundwater system dynamics (Hunt, 2003). The water-use-related activities within the Great Lakes Basin Pilot included four main tasks: assessment of methods to estimate consumptive use and review of typical consumptive-use coefficients for the region (Shaffer and Runkle, 2007; Shaffer, 2008), assessment of seasonal and monthly variation in water withdrawals and consumptive use (Shaffer, 2009), historical water-withdrawal estimates for a groundwater-flow model of the Lake Michigan Basin (Buchwald and others, 2010),

and compilation of water withdrawals by watershed in the U.S. Great Lakes Basin (Mills and Sharpe, 2010).

The Great Lakes-St. Lawrence River Basin Water Resources Compact (Council of Great Lakes Governors, 2005b) sets water-withdrawal limits in terms of consumptive use, so estimates of consumptive use for various water-use sectors are required for proper implementation of the compact and envisioned water-resource management. Theoretically, consumptive water use could be determined by measuring water supplied and water returned for each user. In practice, however, direct determination of consumptive water use is complicated by unknown basin transfers, water returned to the basin through loss in distribution systems, and—most significantly—lack of data regarding the volume of water supplied and the volume of water returned by most sectors. For these reasons, consumptive use is usually estimated by multiplying the volume of water supplied, or withdrawn by self-supplied users, by a consumptive-use coefficient that varies by water-use sector (table 5) or, rarely, by the specific use within a sector (Shaffer and Runkle, 2007; Horn and others, 2008).

Use of simple coefficients to estimate consumptive water use can be problematic because more accurate water use accounting is desired for either water management or future water-withdrawal projections (Horn and others, 2008). For example, the median consumptive-use coefficient for irrigation for the region is 90 percent; but many crops and delivery systems are used across the region. Irrigated crops include corn and soybeans, and Michigan ranked third in the nation (in sales value) in floriculture and nursery products as of 2008 (Kleweno, 2009). Although high consumptive-use coefficients, 90–100 percent, are both the target for efficient irrigation and the most conservative value for water managers, little data are available demonstrating that irrigation reaches this level of efficiency for all sectors across the region. In more arid regions of the county, irrigation by imported surface water represents a major source of groundwater recharge through irrigation return flow and loss of water during distribution through unlined canals and irrigation ditches (Dickinson and others, 2006). For systems that lack data on water delivery and estimated evapotranspiration, an estimated consumptive use coefficient of 70 percent has been used for irrigated cropland (Hanson and others, 2003; Dickenson and others, 2006). In the same way, variation is expected in the commercial and industrial sectors in the Great Lakes region, as was described for a smaller area in New Hampshire (Horn and others, 2008). Techniques to account for water by using more detailed census data, as demonstrated by Horn and others (2008), may be necessary at the regional scale for more accurate water-use accounting. Additionally, because water-use reporting and accounting has traditionally been done by each state or province independently, different sector definitions, estimation methods, and consumptive-use coefficients have been used among the various jurisdictions. As a result of the Great Lakes-St. Lawrence River Basin Water Resources Compact and the Great Lakes-St. Lawrence River Basin Sustainable Water Resources Agreement, increased consistency in water-use reporting has been proposed (Council of Great Lakes Governors, 2009).

The USGS has published summaries of water use for the United States every 5 years since 1950 (U.S. Geological Survey, 2009). Until 2000, these reports included summaries of water use by hydrologic region (2-digit HUC). For the 2000 and subsequent reports, aggregation of water-use data collected from the states by hydrologic cataloging unit (8-digit HUC) became optional, and the 5-year reports have not included summaries by watershed (Kenny, 2004). Because presenting water-use data by watershed may be useful for water managers and may improve the analysis of water availability, the 2005 water-use data from the Great Lakes Basin was aggregated by 8-digit HUC for the Great Lakes Basin Pilot. Mills and Sharpe (2010) discuss the methods used to generate this compilation and limitations of the analysis. The data from 2005 used in the report were compiled from state and local agencies with assistance from other Federal agencies and nongovernmental entities. Water-use estimates for each state are stored in the USGS Aggregate Water Use Data System (AWUDS), and, after final approval of data from all the states, these data will be accessible at *http://water.usgs.gov/watuse/*. In addition to compiling the data by cataloging unit, the data also are summarized by state area included in the Great Lakes Basin and by the drainage area to each of the five Great Lakes (Mills and Sharpe, 2010) (fig. 8).

Basinwide and across all types or sectors of water use, use of surface water dominates, especially surface water directly from the Great Lakes (fig. 8). Great Lake surface water is the dominant supply because the sector with the largest water use in the Great Lakes Basin is thermoelectric power generation, and nearly all water is used for once-through

Table 4. Postdevelopment generalized water budget.

[Numbers in brackets are either alternate values reported in the literature or component values already included in other table entries and are included in the tabulated total flows. ft^3/s, cubic feet per second]

	Volume, in cubic feet	Source	Comments
Surface-water storage (Great Lakes)	8.0×10^{14}	Government of Canada and U.S. Environmental Protection Agency, 1995	See discussion on temporal variability.
Groundwater storage	1.4×10^{14}	Coon and Sheets, 2006	U.S. Great Lakes Basin only; also see discussion on temporal variability.

	Flows in		
	Rate, in thousand cubic feet per second	**Source**	**Comments**
Direct precipitation to Great Lakes	229 [223]	Croley, 2003; Neff and Nicholas, 2005	1950–99 simulation.
Precipitation to land area	505	Croley, 2003	1950–99 simulation.
Surface-water runoff	[220]	Croley, 2003	Surface runoff is equal to precipitation minus evapotranspiration; it is internal to regional budget and not included in "total in" calculation.
Base flow to streams (approximately aquifer recharge)	[151]	Neff and others, 2005	Average of several base-flow separation techniques and included in surface-water runoff. This value is internal to the budget and not included in "total in" calculation.
Surface water diverted into basin	5.0 [5.4]	Government of Canada and U.S. Environmental Protection Agency, 1995; Neff and Nicholas, 2005	
Groundwater from outside basin	Unknown		The Lake Michigan Basin groundwater-flow-model estimate for the Lake Michigan Basin is 500 ft^3/s, which is less than 2 percent of total flow to groundwater system.
Total in	*739*		

cooling of powerplants. An estimated 72 percent of all withdrawals in the basin in 2005 were for power generation. The Lake Michigan and Lake Erie Basins supply most of the water for U.S. water withdrawals. The distribution of withdrawals by state follows the expected pattern based on land area within the basin, although withdrawal for Illinois is large compared to its very small area in the basin because of the use associated with the Chicago metropolitan region. Note that water used for hydroelectric power generation was only reported as an instream use in USGS water-use reports prior to 2000, and it is not included in the estimates herein or in the report by Mills and Sharpe (2010).

The spatial pattern of source for public supply, self-supplied domestic, and irrigation sectors reveal reliance on groundwater and the importance of sources other than the Great Lakes. Most large municipal water systems rely on surface water from one of the Great Lakes, and, as a result, 88 percent of withdrawals for public supply are from surface water (fig. 9). Conversely, self-supplied groundwater is the source for almost all the domestic water for the population in the U.S. Great Lakes Basin outside of municipal areas (fig. 10). Overall, most people in the Great Lakes Basin live in municipal areas served by public supply, whereas most of the area of the basin relies on groundwater for water supply. The source for irrigation water is almost equally split between surface water and groundwater (fig. 11) but, unlike for public water supply, the surface-water sources for irrigation tend to be inland surface water rather than surface water directly from a Great Lake.

Table 4.   Postdevelopment generalized water budget.—Continued

[Numbers in brackets are either alternate values reported in the literature or component values already included in other table entries and are included in the tabulated total flows. ft³/s, cubic feet per second]

	Flows out		
	Rate, in thousand cubic feet per second	**Source**	**Comments**
Groundwater out of the basin	0		
Surface water out the St. Lawrence River	271 [251] [246]	Government of Canada and U.S. Environmental Protection Agency, 1995; Croley, 2003; Neff and Nicholas, 2005	Flow out of 251,000 ft³/s given by Government of Canada and U.S. Environmental Protection Agency, 1995; flow of 246,000 ft³/s given by Neff and Nicholas, 2005; 271, 000 ft³/s from Croley, 2003, balances the net-basin-supply estimate.
Surface water diverted outside basin	3. [3.2]	Government of Canada and U.S. Environmental Protection Agency, 1995; Neff and Nicholas, 2005	
Direct evaporation from Great Lakes	178	Croley, 2003	1950–99 simulation.
Evapotranspiration from land area of basin	284	Croley, 2003	1950–99 simulation.
Surface-water withdrawal	[63]	Great Lakes Commission, 2006a	Great Lakes and inland surface waters, 2004 withdrawals. Only consumptive use is used in the "total out" estimate.
Groundwater withdrawal	[2.3]	Great Lakes Commission, 2006a	2004 withdrawals, only consumptive use is used in the "total out" estimate.
Consumptive water use	3 [3.4]	Great Lakes Commission, 2002, 2006	3,000 ft³/s from 2004 data, 3,400 ft³/s from 1998 data. Destination of return flow is not specified.
Total out	*739*		

Table 5. Consumptive-use-coefficient statistics for the Great Lakes Basin and climatically similar areas, by water-use category (from Shaffer and Runkle, 2007; Shaffer, 2008).

[Minimum (min), median, and maximum (max), 25th percentile, and 75th percentile are in percent and rounded to the nearest whole number. N is the number of references used in the statistical analysis. References are only from publications after either 1975 (mining and commercial), 1980 (industrial, irrigation, thermoelectric, livestock) or 1985 (domestic and public water supply)]

Geographical area	Summary statistics of consumptive-use coefficients, by indicated water-use category					
	Min	**25th**	**Median**	**75th**	**Max**	**N**
Domestic and Public Supply						
Great Lakes Basin	0	10	12	15	74	161
Climatically similar areas	6	10	15	20	70	68
Industrial						
Great Lakes Basin	0	7	10	14	35	122
Climatically similar areas	0	4	10	13	34	97
Thermoelectric						
Great Lakes Basin	0	1	2	2	21	141
Climatically similar areas	0	0	2	4	75	75
Irrigation						
Great Lakes Basin	70	90	90	96	100	95
Climatically similar areas	37	90	100	100	100	75
Livestock						
Great Lakes Basin	[1]0	80	83	90	100	85
Climatically similar areas	[2]10	86	100	100	100	73
Commercial						
Great Lakes Basin	4	8	10	15	26	29
Climatically similar areas	3	8	10	13	33	61
Mining						
Great Lakes Basin	0	7	10	25	58	58
Climatically similar areas	0	10	14	20	86	83

[1]The livestock low coefficient minimum (0 percent) is from the Great Lakes Commission (2002), in which Minnesota reported 0.25 Mgal/d total withdrawn in 1998 and 0 Mgal/d consumptive use. The next lowest coefficient for the Great Lakes Basin was 66 percent.

[2]The livestock low minimum coefficients are from Solley and others (1988) and may be the result of their adding animal specialties, including fish farming, into the livestock water-use category. In previous and subsequent USGS reports, fish farming was in different water-use categories.

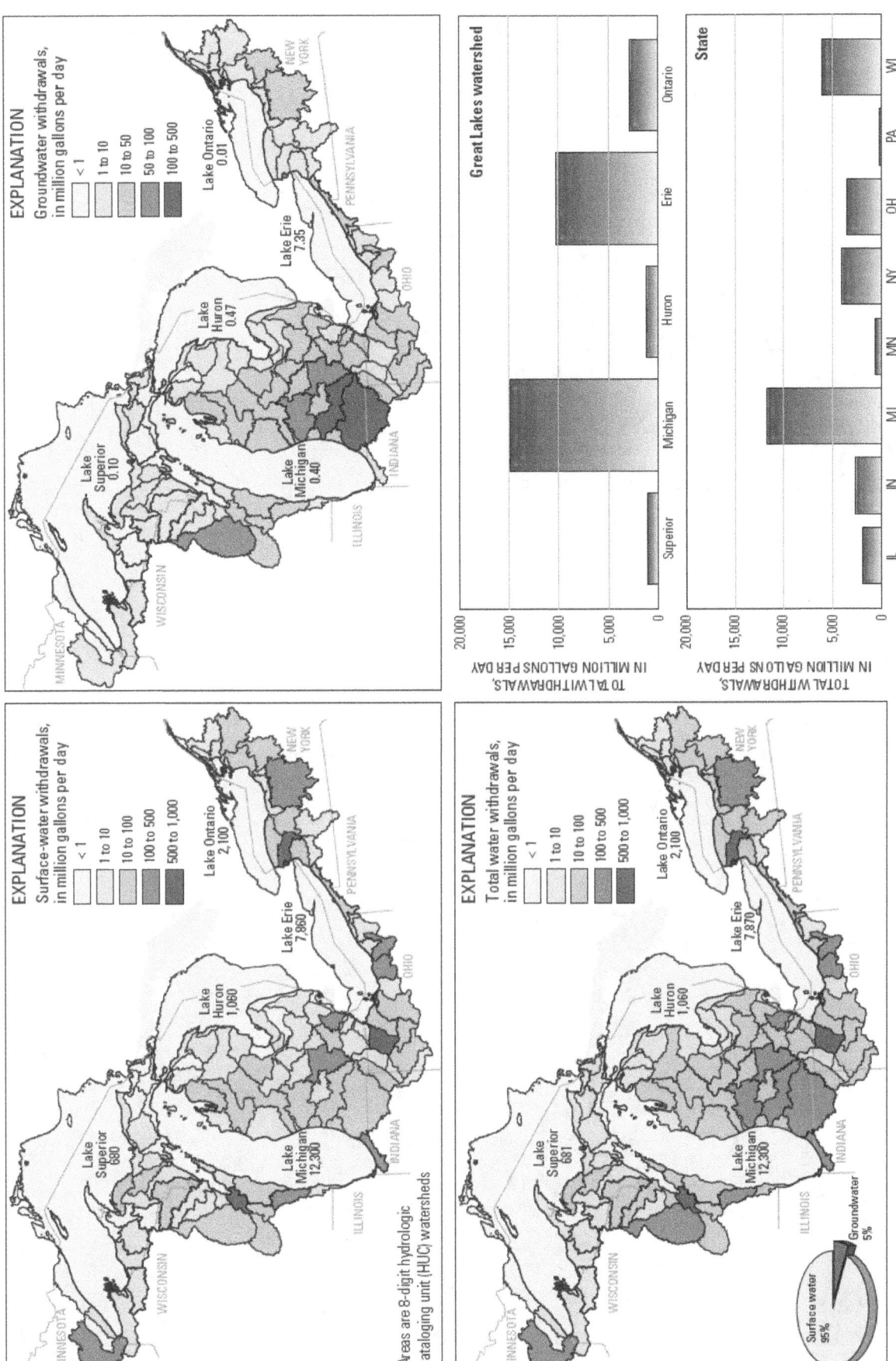

Figure 8.   Surface-water, groundwater, and total withdrawals in the Great Lakes Basin by source, hydrologic cataloging unit (8-digit HUC watershed), Great Lakes watershed, and state area within Great Lakes Basin, 2005 (from Mills and Sharpe, 2010).

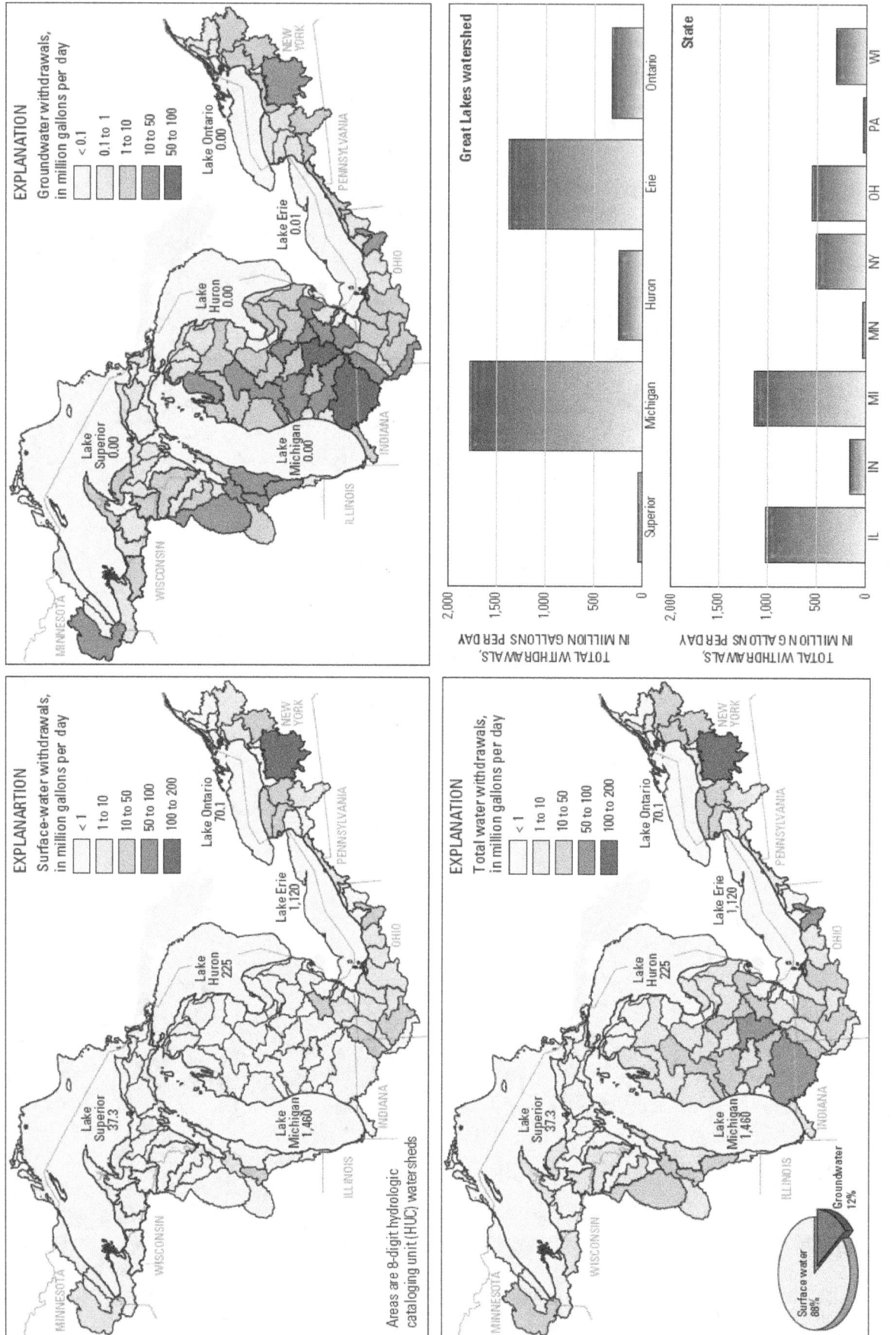

Figure 9. Public-supply withdrawals by source, hydrologic cataloging unit (8-digit HUC watershed), Great Lakes watershed, and area of state within the Great Lakes Basin in 2005 (from Mills and Sharpe, 2010).

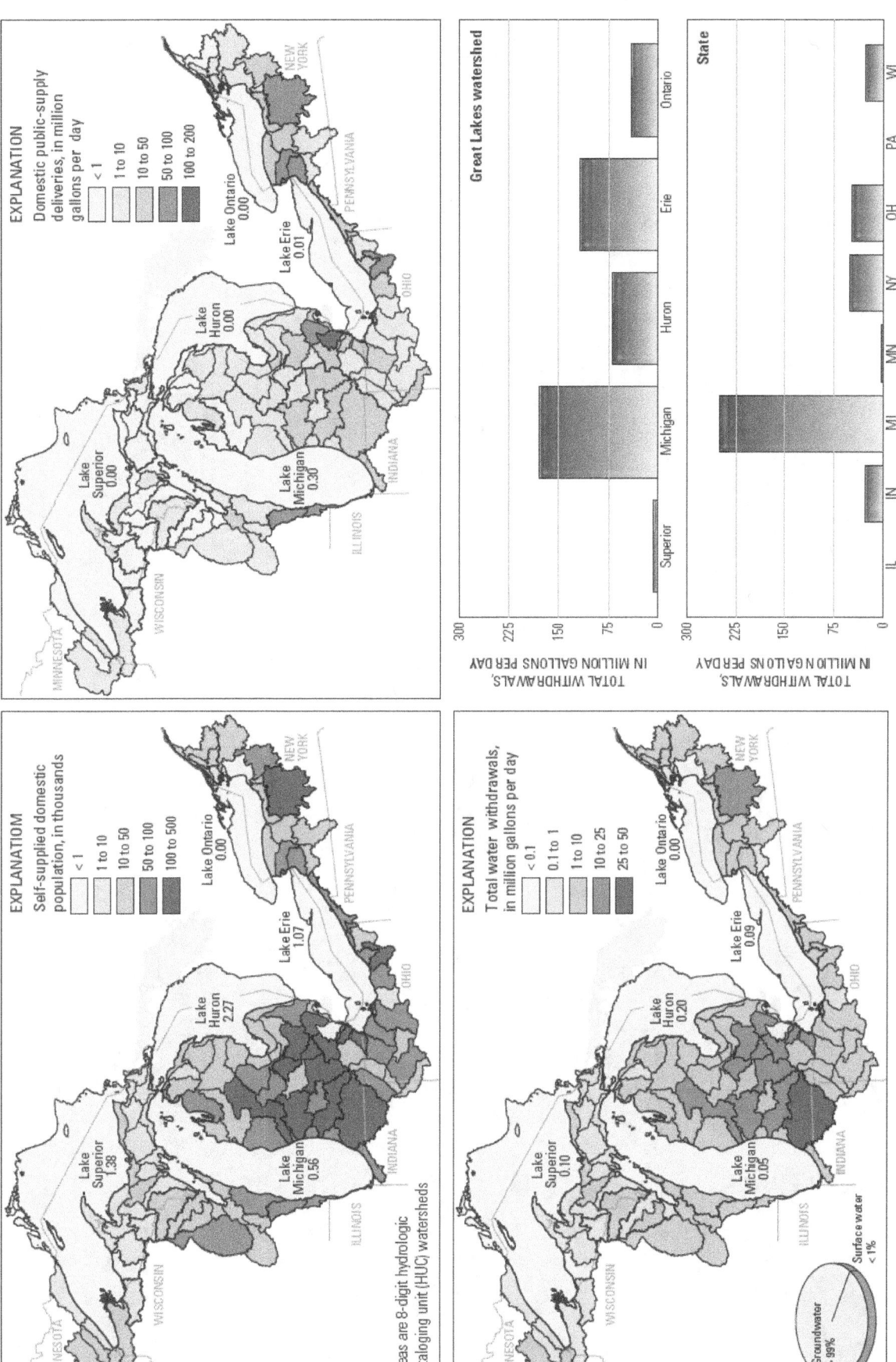

Figure 10. Self-supplied domestic water withdrawals by source, hydrologic cataloging unit (8-digit HUC watershed), Great Lakes watershed, and area of state within the Great Lakes Basin in 2005 (from Mills and Sharpe, 2010).

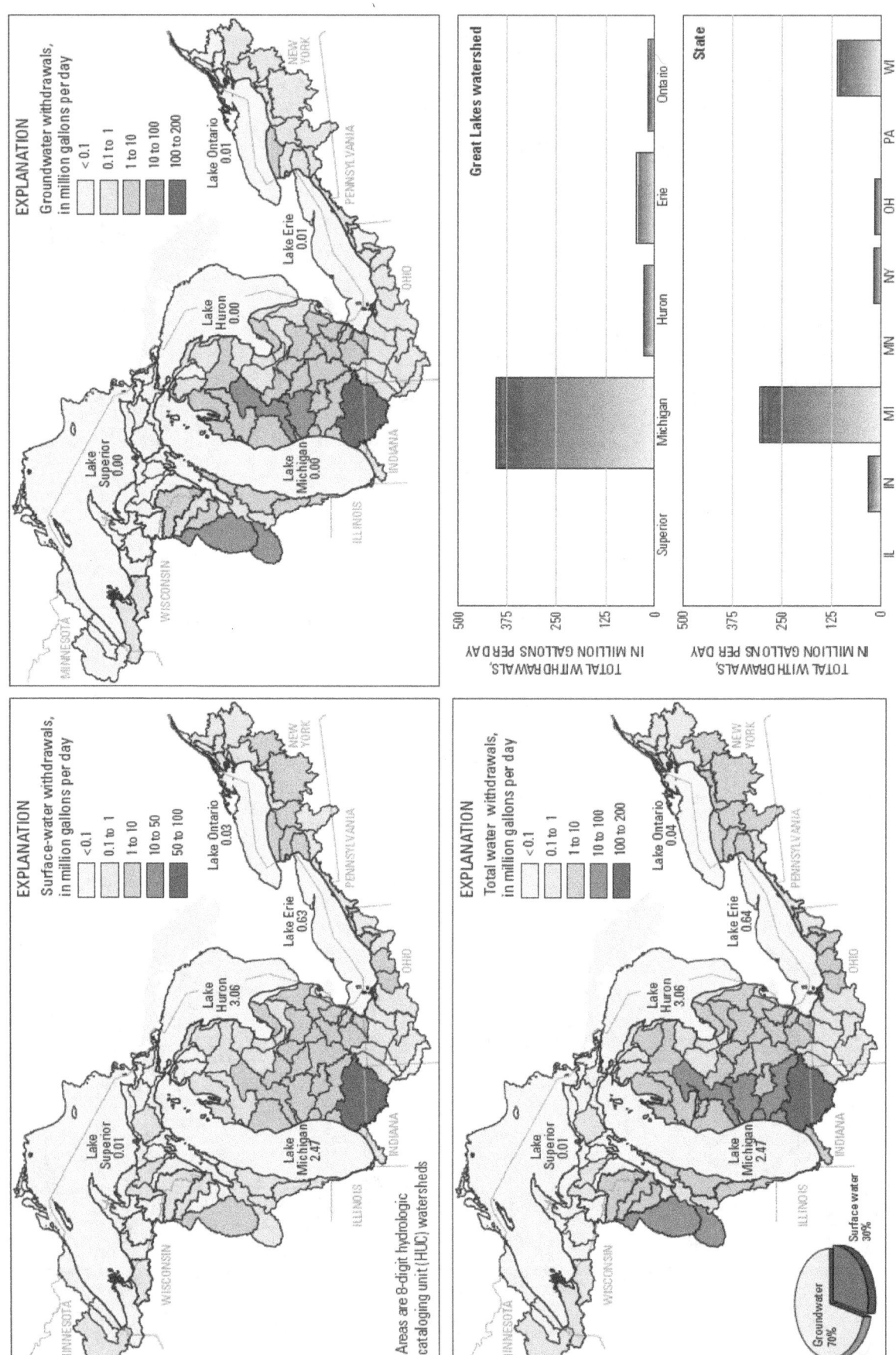

Figure 11. Irrigation-water withdrawals by source, hydrologic cataloging unit (8-digit HUC watershed), Great Lakes watershed, and state area within Great Lakes Basin in 2005 (from Mills and Sharpe, 2010).

Regional Water Budgets Through Time

The water budget in the Great Lakes Basin changes with time primarily because of climate variations. Periods of higher precipitation or lower evaporation lead to increases in lake levels, and periods of lower precipitation or increased evaporation can lead to decreased lake levels (Assel and others, 2004). Climate also has affected streamflow, and trends in precipitation and streamflow are both discussed in this section. Groundwater levels appear to be less influenced by short-term climate variability, but longer droughts are evident in water-level records. Groundwater pumping has led to large drawdowns in some areas of the Great Lakes region.

Water storage in the Great Lakes Basin is dominated by the Great Lakes; therefore, storage in the system is much more variable seasonally, and over longer time periods, than storage for groundwater-dominated systems. The average annual variation in storage for the lakes, from summertime high to wintertime low, is 2.2×10^{12} ft^3 (Wilcox and others, 2007). Expressed as a rate (2.2×10^{12} ft^3 in 6 months = 1.4×10^5 ft^3/s), this change is approximately two orders of magnitude greater than the estimated consumptive-use rate in the basin (3.0×10^3 ft^3/s, table 4). The annual variation is driven by cycles of precipitation, which delivers more water to the basin in the spring and early summer, and evaporation, which removes more water from the lakes in fall and early winter. Winter evaporation from the lakes is critical to lake levels. Lack of ice cover on the lakes can lead to increased winter evaporation and lowering of Great Lake water levels (Wang and others, 2010). Wilcox and others (2007) discuss long-term lake level variations and the mechanisms that have controlled lake levels in the past 4,500 years. These authors show that more variation in lake levels has been observed directly in the past 150 years, and inferred from other indicators for the past 4,500 years, than has been typical from year to year since postdevelopment (fig. 12). The difference in the volume of water in storage from relatively high to relatively low lake levels is several times greater than the average annual change in volume.

In addition to lake-level records, precipitation and streamgage records exhibit both interannual variation and trends over the past 50 to 90 years (Hodgkins and others, 2007). Precipitation and runoff both appear to have increased with time for most monitoring stations within the U.S. Great Lakes Basin, and Hodgkins and others (2007) detail these changes in terms of monthly and annual averages. In summary, mean annual runoff increased during 1955–2004 by 2.6 in. based on the average of records from 43 streamgages; however, there was significant variability in both time and space. Runoff was lower higher from 1970 until 2004 than it was from 1955 to 1970. Some increase in runoff was evident at most stations, exceptions being a few gages near and in the Upper Peninsula of Michigan (fig. 13A). Fewer gages were available with streamflow records extending from 1935 to 2004; but trends at these 16 gages were similar to those in the set available for 1955–2004 (fig. 13B). The analysis also showed increases in mean monthly runoff for most months based on records from 28 streamgages; groups of gages showed decreases in March, April, and May, with an evident decrease in mean monthly runoff values in April at most gages (Hodgkins and others, 2007). Overall, low flows in the basin increased over much of the basin, as illustrated by widespread general increase in the mean annual 7-day low runoff (the lowest annual average of 7 consecutive days of runoff) (fig. 14). The average increase in the mean annual 7-day low runoff from 1955 to 2004 was 0.048 (ft^3/s)/mi^2 based on the average of records at 27 gages.

Estimation of the change in groundwater storage in the system in response to development is complicated by two factors: (1) natural variations in groundwater storage are estimated to be larger than the change in storage resulting from pumping, and (2) groundwater divides have moved in response to pumping. On the regional scale, at averaged or long-term temporal conditions, water moves into and out of storage in response to climate variations. In dry years, or for several years during dry periods, average groundwater levels decline and water is released from storage. Conversely, during wet years, or for several years during wet periods, average water levels rise and water is returned to storage. The large cone of depression in the deep bedrock aquifer in southeast Wisconsin and northern Illinois near Chicago resulting from extensive pumping in the region does not release enough water from storage compared to the regional behavior of the system to significantly affect the regional water budget.

The effect of the movement of groundwater divides in response to pumping on groundwater in storage is more difficult to quantify. Quantification depends on the conceptual model used to define the system. In one view, the groundwater basin is defined by the existing groundwater-flow divides so that pumping may essentially enlarge the basin at the same time that water is removed from storage (Coon and Sheets, 2006). For the Great Lakes groundwater basin, the increase in storage resulting from the westward shift of the groundwater divide in southeast Wisconsin since predevelopment was estimated to be approximately 3 percent of the total groundwater in storage in the basin. Despite the very large cone of depression caused by groundwater pumping in southeast Wisconsin and near Chicago, the estimated decrease in volume of water from storage in the system is relatively small, less than 0.1 percent. This apparent contradiction is because of the relatively low specific storage coefficient for the confined bedrock aquifers used for water supply. An alternate viewpoint would be to fix the groundwater basin to its predevelopment boundaries. Changes in groundwater divides, such as the westward shift of the divide in southeast Wisconsin, would be represented by changes in the lateral flux across the fixed predevelopment boundary. By this second viewpoint, pumping does not change the size of the groundwater basin, and, therefore, it cannot change the volume of aquifer material contributing to groundwater in storage.

For the generalized regional water budgets, no change in groundwater storage is given; these issues are explored in more detail through the subregional groundwater-flow model developed for the Great Lakes Basin Pilot (Feinstein and others, 2010) and discussed later in this report.

Water withdrawals in the region have changed as population has increased in the basin. The total withdrawals tend to reflect the national trend that, despite increasing population, total water withdrawals either decreased or increased only slightly from 1980 to 2005 (Hutson and others, 2004). In the Great Lakes Basin, water withdrawals for thermoelectric

power decreased by 4 percent and public-supply withdrawals decreased by 14 percent from 1985 to 2005. These decreases were offset somewhat by increased withdrawal for self-supplied domestic use, 16 percent, and irrigation, 57 percent, over this same time period (fig. 15). The net decrease in withdrawals in the U.S. Great Lakes Basin during 1995–2005 is estimated to have been 2.2 billion gallons per day, about a 7-percent decrease over this time period (Mills and Sharpe, 2010).

One of the more interesting trends in the water-use data is that withdrawals for public water supply have decreased despite an increase in population in the region. As discussed

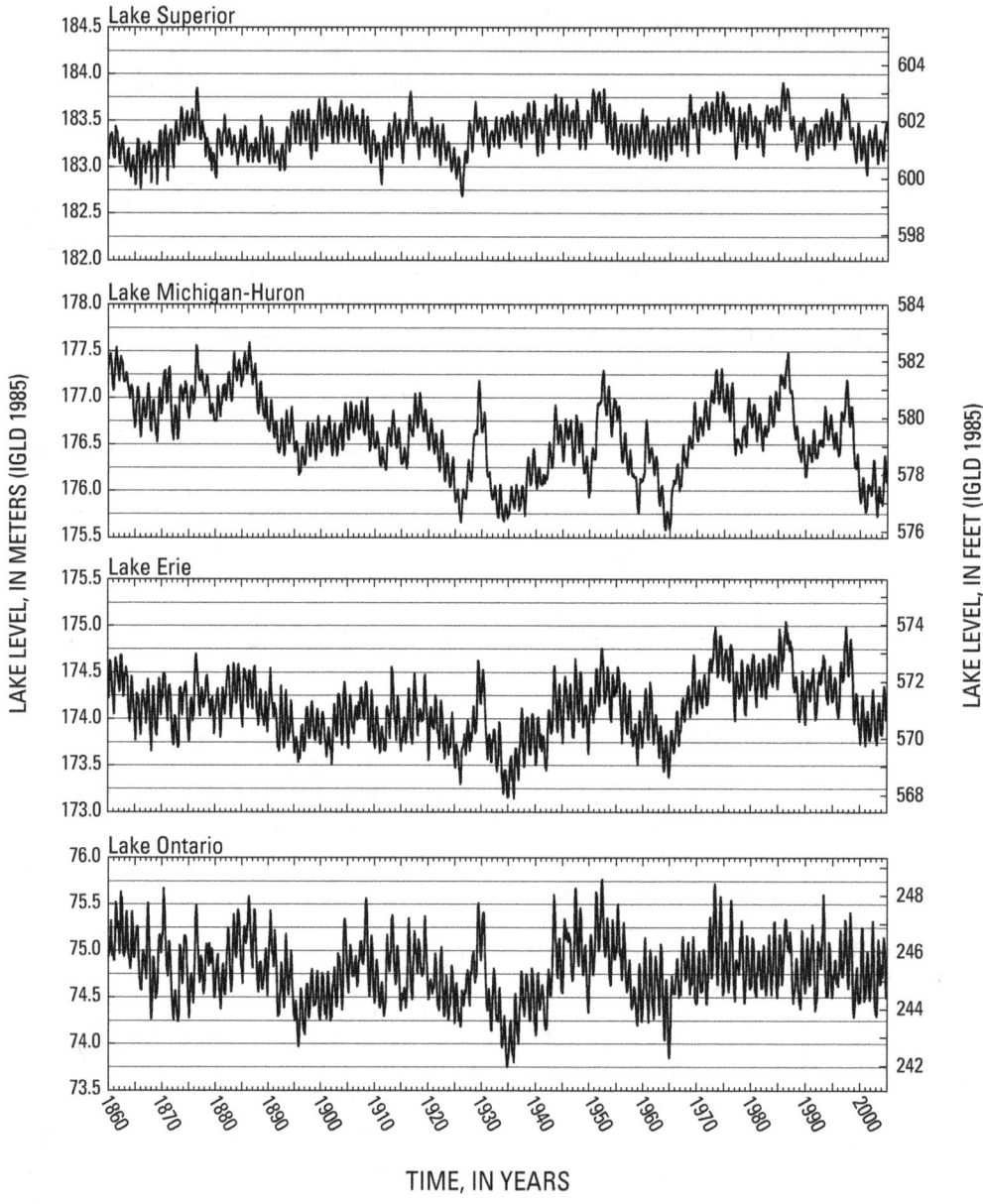

Figure 12. *A,* Historical lake levels for the Great Lakes, 1860–2005.

by Mills and Sharpe (2010), this trend may be caused by increased efficiency or conservation, reductions in delivery of water from public-supply systems to industrial users, or shifts in overall domestic water use away from public supply to self-supplied domestic sources as population increases in areas outside those served by public supply. Uncertainty in estimation, changes in reporting, and changes in water accounting over the time period also may explain some of the observed trends (Mills and Sharpe, 2010).

In the context of water availability, natural variation in the system dominates changes in storage and flows, and effective water-resources planning must recognize the natural variability in the system. The importance of natural variability, however, does not discount human impact on the water resources at the Great Lakes Basin scale. As mentioned, dredging in the 1960s has been suggested as a mechanism leading to permanently lowered lake levels for Lakes Michigan and Huron (W.F. Baird Associates, 2005). Wilcox and others (2007) discuss how regulation of the levels of Lakes Superior and Ontario has affected the ecological and beach-building effects of natural variation in levels.

These trends and the temporal variability of the system are important for water management because long-term averages often are used to base decisions. If the hydrologic system does not vary about a constant long-term average, then the nature of the trend and its implications on future development should be studied (Milly and others, 2008). Water-management decisions need to be tempered by an understanding of the natural variability of the system and long-term trends in the region. Development may have occurred in areas during times when the lakes were naturally lower or higher than average, and the impact of changing lake levels on this development may not be feasibly mitigated because natural variation appears to be much greater than human-influenced variation. Use of models developed for subregional and local spatial scales within the Great Lakes Basin as part of the Pilot project to evaluate potential effects of climate change are presented in this report.

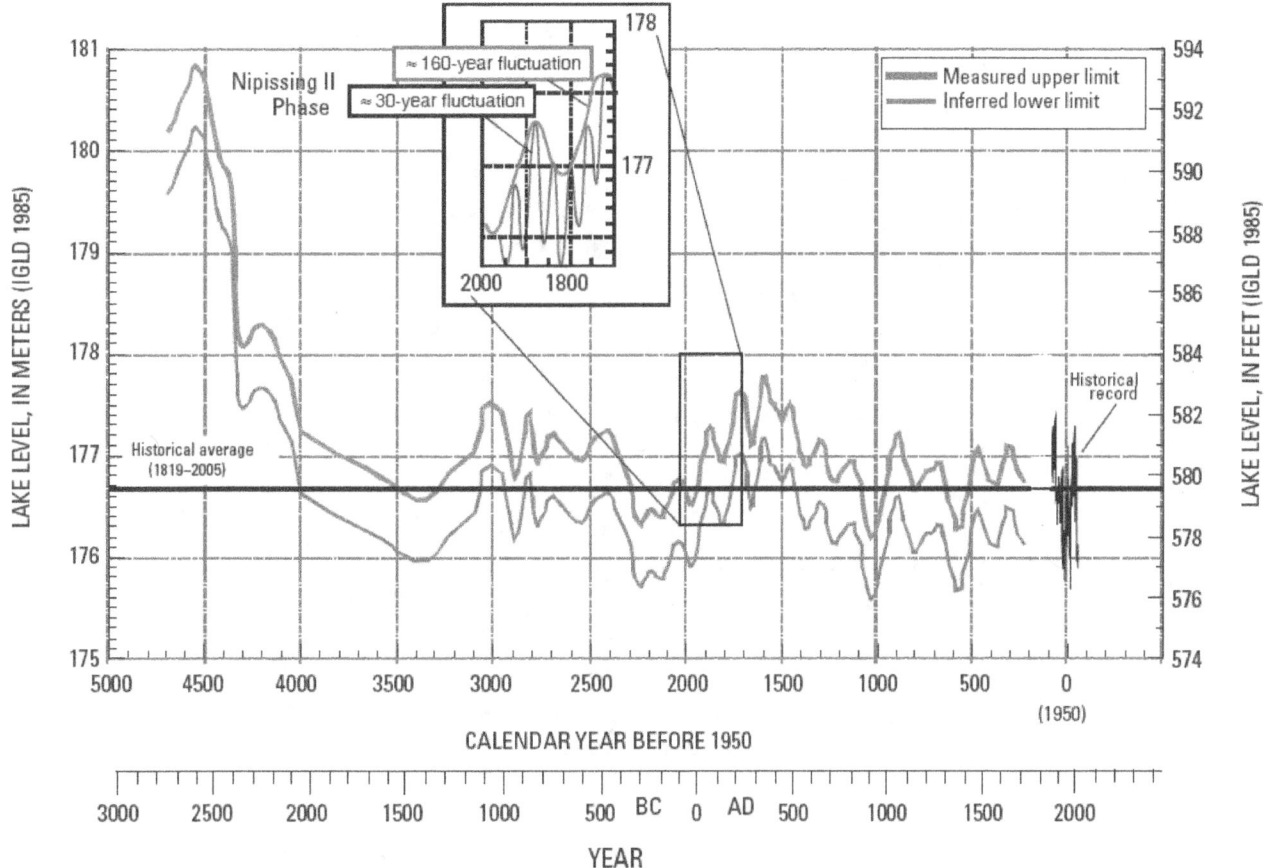

Figure 12. *B*, Late Holocene and historical level for Lake Michigan-Huron; red line is interpreted from beach-ridge studies, and lower black line is an inferred lower limit based on the range of historical record (from Wilcox and others, 2007).

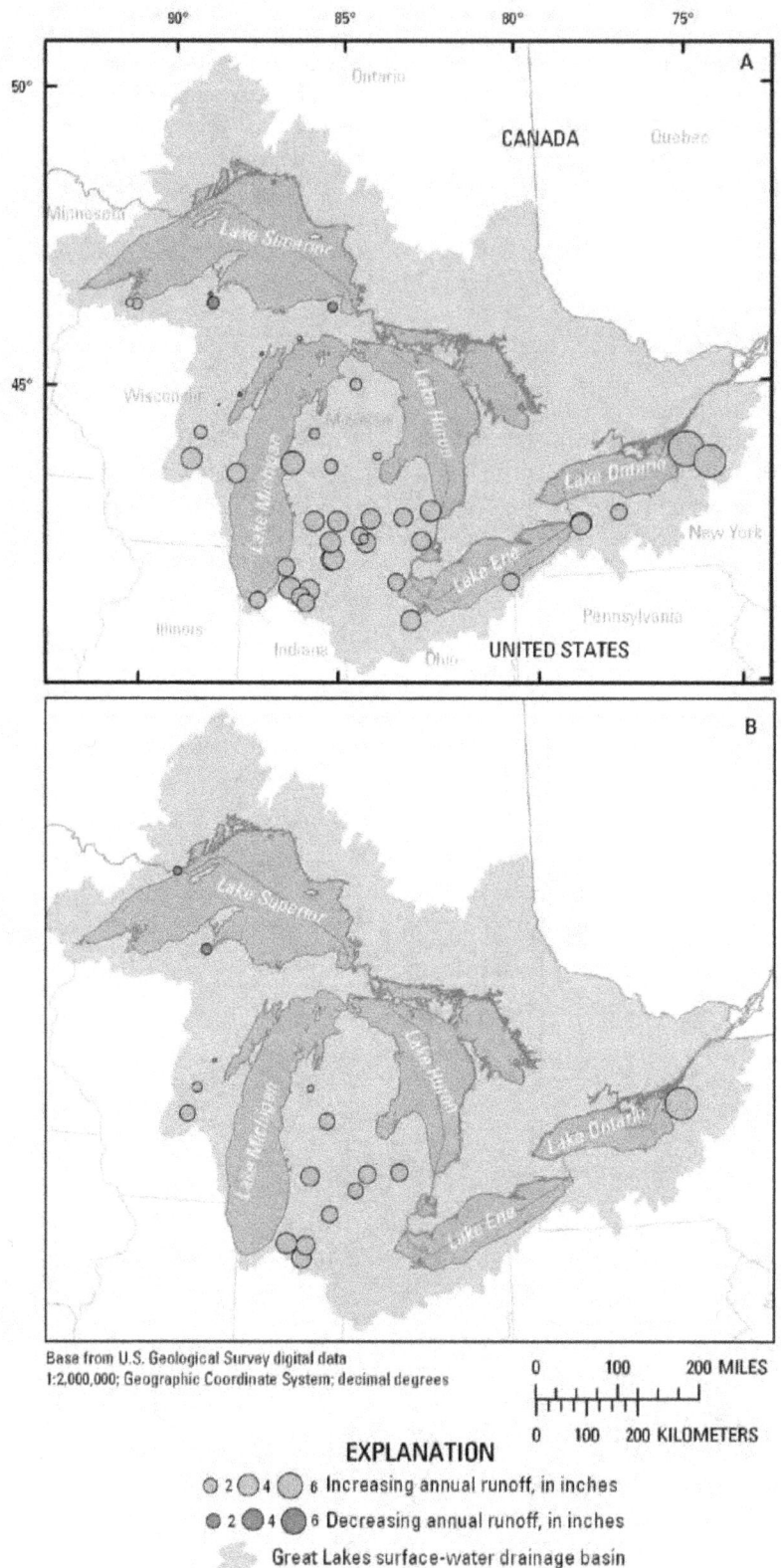

EXPLANATION

⦿ 2 ◯ 4 ◯ 6 Increasing annual runoff, in inches

⦿ 2 ⬤ 4 ⬤ 6 Decreasing annual runoff, in inches

Great Lakes surface-water drainage basin

Figure 13. Changes in annual runoff at selected long-term streamgages. *A*, 1955–2004. *B*, 1935–2004. Circle sizes are proportional to increases or decreases (from Hodgkins and others, 2007).

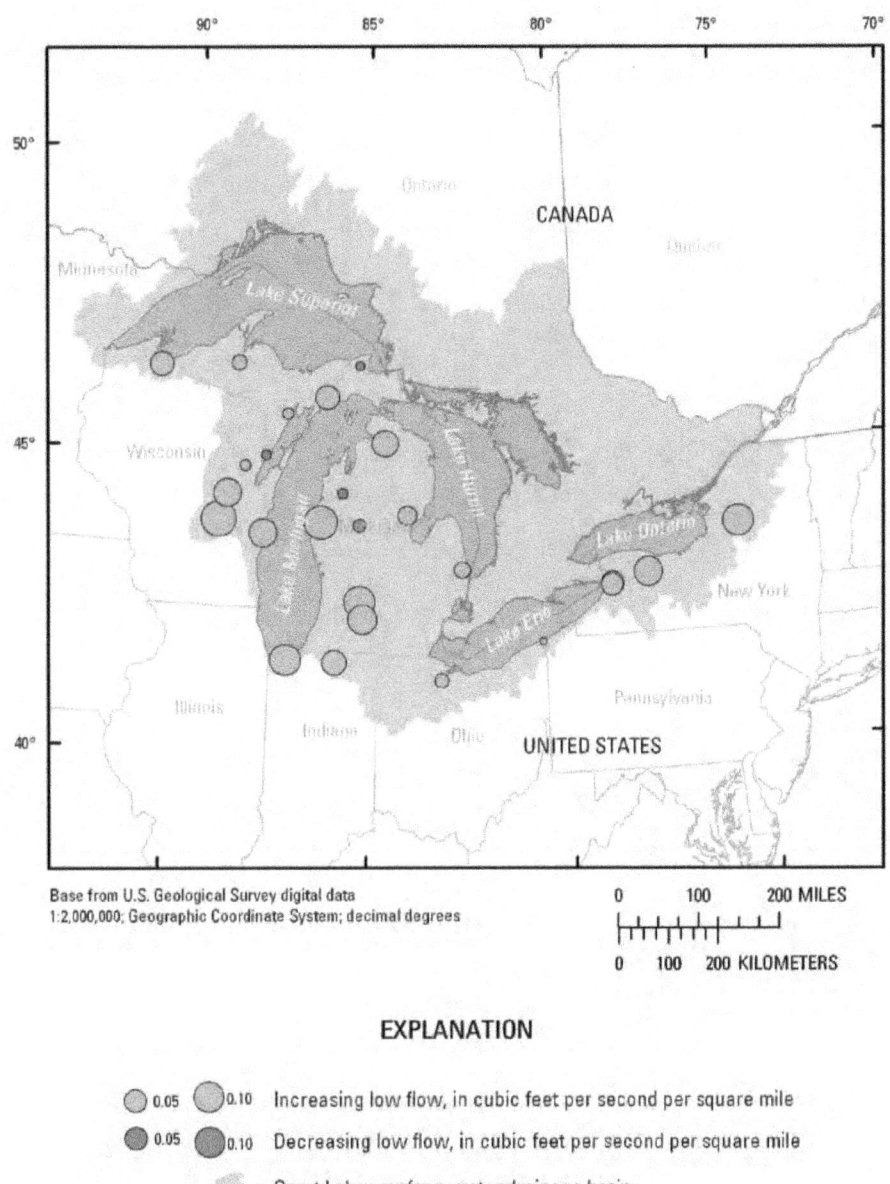

Base from U.S. Geological Survey digital data
1:2,000,000; Geographic Coordinate System; decimal degrees

0   100   200 MILES

0   100   200 KILOMETERS

EXPLANATION

0.05 0.10   Increasing low flow, in cubic feet per second per square mile

0.05 0.10   Decreasing low flow, in cubic feet per second per square mile

Great Lakes surface-water drainage basin

Figure 14.   Changes in annual 7-day low runoff at selected long-term streamgages, 1955–2004. Circle sizes are proportional to increases or decreases (from Hodgkins and others, 2007).

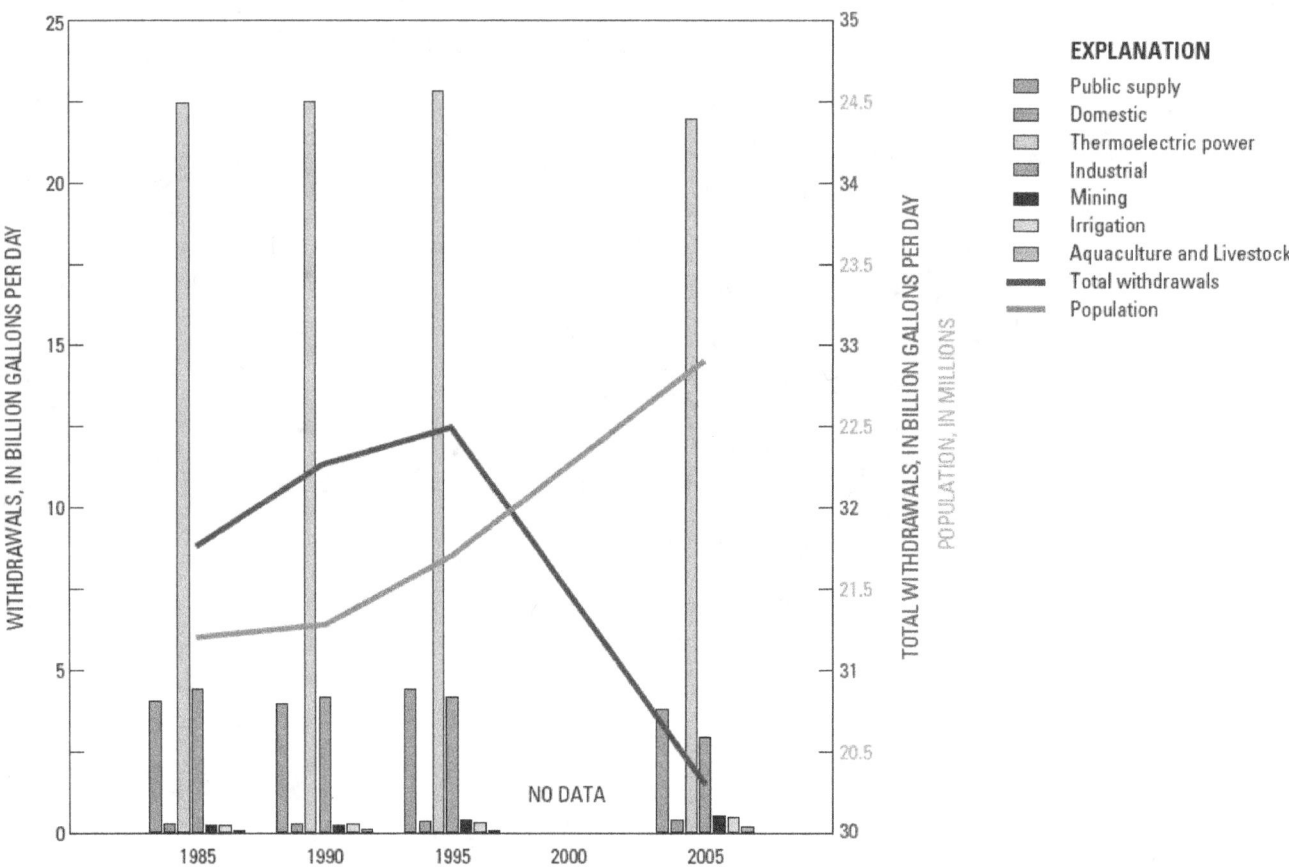

Figure 15.   Trends in total water withdrawal by water-use sector in the Great Lakes Basin, 1985–2005 (from Mills and Sharpe, 2010).

Regional Indicators

The basic indicators of water availability include stream-flows, lake levels, groundwater levels, water quality, and water withdrawals. These data may be combined and distilled to yield a smaller set of indicators that may be helpful for decisionmakers and the public because they condense a great deal of information into a few values. Trends in time or spatial comparisons can be made clearer by way of these more refined indicators. Application of refined indicators at the Great Lakes regional scale emphasizes both the large storage volume and the large flux of water through the system. The indicators proposed by Vörösmarty and others (2000, 2005) and Weiskel and others (2007) are straightforward to apply for the Great Lakes Basin.

The index of relative water demand, *RWD* (Vörösmarty and others, 2000, 2005), is defined as the ratio of water use for the domestic sector (*D*), the industrial sector (*I*), and the agricultural sector (*A*) relative to the flux of water through the system. This flux may be quantified by the estimated predevelopment mean annual streamflow, *Q*, from the basin. The denominator also may be interpreted as the net water available

for use, and it may be adjusted for required instream flow or for streamflow that is otherwise inaccessible (see for example, Postel and others, 1996). The *RWD* may be expressed as

$$RWD = \frac{D+I+A}{Q} \qquad (1)$$

Scale of application is important to recognize in interpreting the meaning of a computed indicator. Indicators may be estimated for regional basins, smaller watersheds, or arbitrary areas of any size. For example, in order to map relative water stress for Africa, Vörösmarty and others (2005) computed a local relative water demand for 8-km (26,000-ft) grid cells across Africa by estimating local water use and local flux through each grid cell,

$$RWD_n = \frac{(D+I+A)_n}{Q_{Cn}} \qquad (2)$$

where

RWD_n is the index of local relative water demand for grid cell n, dimensionless,

$(D+I+A)_n$ is the water demand in grid cell n for domestic, industrial and agricultural sectors, as volume per time, and

Q_{Cn} is the river-corridor discharge entering cell n from upstream cells, as volume per time.

On a regional scale for the Great Lakes Basin, a relative water demand may be determined by combining the total freshwater-withdrawal information for 2005 presented by Mills and Sharpe (2010) with an estimated mean annual flow of the St. Lawrence River:

Total freshwater withdrawal in 2005 = 30,305 Mgal/d = 47,000 ft³/s

Mean annual outflow of the St. Lawrence River (tables 3 and 4) = 271,000 ft³/s

$$RWD = \frac{(47{,}000\ \text{ft}^3/\text{sec})}{(271{,}000\ \text{ft}^3/\text{sec})} = 0.17 \qquad (3)$$

Of this, the major withdrawal is for thermoelectric power generation, and the withdrawn water is largely returned to the basin. The estimated consumptive use in the basin in 2004 was approximately 1,900 Mgal/d (2,950 ft³/s) (Great Lakes Commission, 2006).

$$RWD = \frac{(2{,}950\ \text{ft}^3/\text{sec})}{(271{,}000\ \text{ft}^3/\text{sec})} = 0.011 \qquad (4)$$

High stress on water resources of an area are indicated by index values greater than 0.4 (Vörösmarty and others, 2000; Vörösmarty and others, 2005), and the Great Lakes Basin is well below this threshold, especially if the RWD is computed with consumptive use. This computation was done on the highest estimate of mean annual flow out of the basin in table 3. Use of a lower estimate or adjustment to account for instream flow requirements would increase the estimated RWD indicators, but the RWD for the Great Lakes Basin would still be quite small.

Weiskel and others (2007), who built on the work by Vörösmarty and others (2000, 2005) to develop indicators of human impact on hydrologic systems, state that the RWD does not fully capture the full range of human impacts because it does not incorporate return flow or water imports. Return flow and imports can lead to a system that is dominated by human activity while having a relatively low RWD. Weiskel and others (2007) propose examining the net flux for a basin that includes estimates of return flow and water import to the basin. Normalizing the human-induced inflows and outflows (shown below) by the net flow of water through the system produces two new indices, h_{in} and h_{out}, that can be graphed to illustrate the dominant water-use regime for a basin. Endpoints on such a plot can be used to classify the regimes

into four types: (1) natural-flow dominated, (2) withdrawal dominated, (3) return-flow dominated, and (4) human-flow dominated (fig. 16).

The normalized flows, h_{in} and h_{out}, also were combined to form two additional indices: (1) the human water balance index, HWB, and (2) the water-use intensity index, WUI (Weiskel and others, 2007). These two new indices may be written as

$$HWB = h_{in} - h_{out}, \qquad (5)$$

$$WUI = (h_{in} + h_{out})/2, \qquad (6)$$

where

h_{in} normalized human-induced return flows into a basin, $H_{in}/NetFlux$,

h_{out} normalized human-induced withdrawals out of a basin, $H_{out}/NetFlux$,

H_{in} human-induced flux into a basin (returns), and

H_{out} human-induced flux out of a basin (withdrawals).

The NetFlux normalizing human return flows and withdrawals may be defined for the whole basin or for just the aquifer, depending on the system of interest. These basin and aquifer expressions for net flux can be written as follows (Weiskel and others, 2007):

$$
\begin{aligned}
NetFlux_{basin} &= (P - ET) + (GW_{in} + SW_{in}) + H_{in} - \Delta S/\Delta t \\
&= (GW_{out} + SW_{out}) + H_{out} \\
NetFlux_{aquifer} &= R_{net} + (R_{GW} + R_{SW}) + H_{in} - \Delta S/\Delta t \\
&= (D_{GW} + D_{SW}) + H_{out}
\end{aligned}
$$

The flux components are the following.
Flows into the basin:

P precipitation,

GW_{in} groundwater inflow from adjacent basins,

SW_{in} surface-water inflow from adjacent basins,

R_{net} net aquifer recharge ($R_P - D_{ET}$),

R_P aquifer recharge from precipitation,

D_{ET} water lost from aquifer by evapotranspiration,

R_{GW} aquifer recharge by leakage from adjacent aquifers, and

R_{SW} aquifer recharge by leakage of surface water.

Flows out of the basin:

ET evapotranspiration,

GW_{out} groundwater outflow to adjacent basins,

SW_{out} surface-water outflow to adjacent basins,

D_{GW} aquifer discharge to adjacent aquifers, and

D_{SW} aquifer discharge to surface water.

Change in storage:

$\Delta S/\Delta t$ net rate of change of storage in the basin or aquifer.

The HWB ranges from -1 to 1, and the WUI ranges from 0 to 1. The HWB indicates the type and magnitude of human alteration of the water-resources system. Positive values of HWB indicate that the human impacts result in a net import of water to the system, and negative values of HWB indicate net withdrawals from the system. The magnitude of the *HWB* indicates the relative magnitude of the net import or withdrawal from the basin, but low values of *HWB* may be caused by a balance between human-induced imports and exports. The *WUI* also indicates the relative importance of human-induced flows to natural flows; however, its magnitude includes both import and withdrawal. As *WUI* approaches 1, the system becomes entirely dominated by human-induced flows (fig. 16).

Estimating these summary indicators for the Great Lakes Basin confirms that the overall basin has low values for both the *HWB* and the *WUI* and is classified as natural-flow dominated. The reason for this classification is because the large natural flow that divides the values of h_{in} and h_{out}, yielding low values.

$$h_{in} = 0.02$$
$$h_{out} = 0.02$$
$$HWB = -0.003$$
$$WUI = 0.023$$

The values are computed without taking into account the amount of water used for hydroelectric power generation, which was 809,120 Mgal/d for 2004 (Great Lakes Commission, 2006). If this volume is included in the calculation, the system is dominated by human use because hydroelectric-power-generation volumes exceed the natural flow rate from the system by approximately a factor of 5. Another confounding issue is importation of groundwater from outside the surface-water basin, either because the natural groundwater divide is, in some places, outside the surface-water divide used for the calculation or because pumping near the basin divide has, in some places, captured water from beyond the divide that is returned to the Great Lakes Basin. This volume is unknown, but it is thought to be small relative to other fluxes in the system, and it is not included in the estimates of the indices.

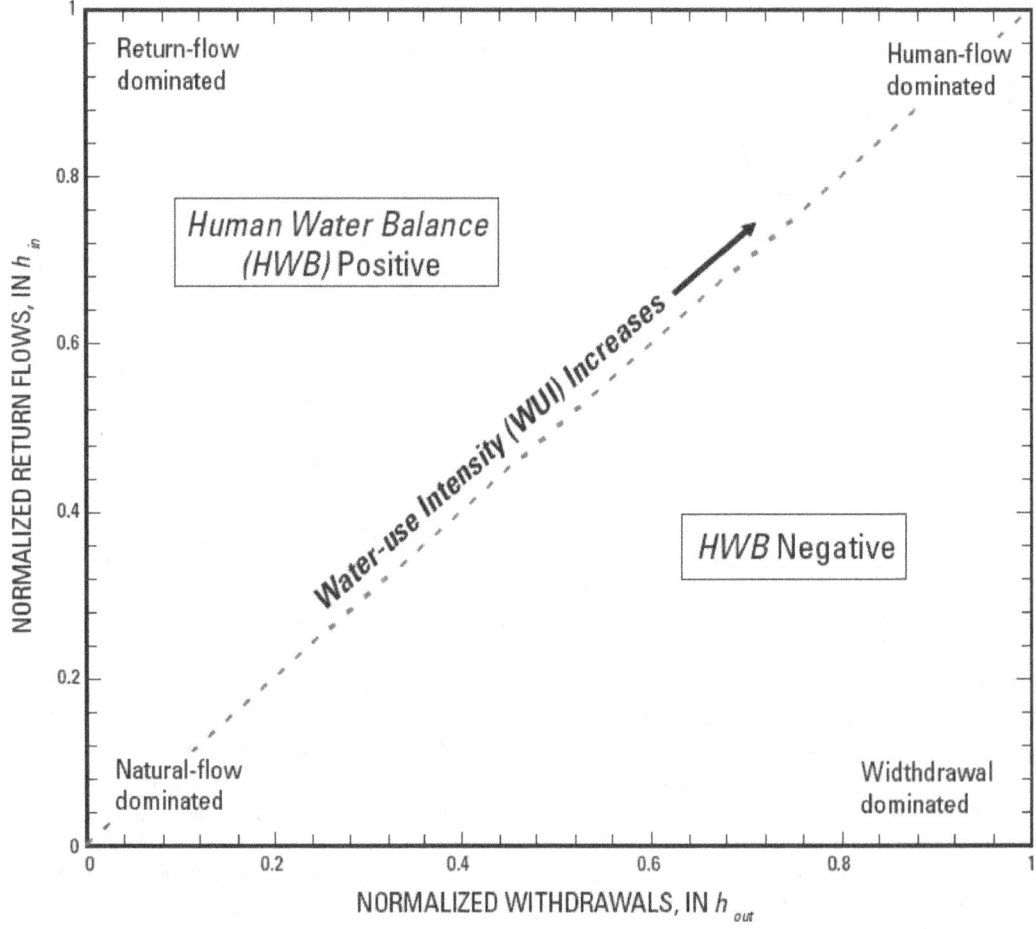

Figure 16.   Human water-use regimes defined by normalized human withdrawals, h_{out}, and normalized human return flows, h_{in}.

HWB and *WUI* for the Great Lakes Basin (−0.003, 0.023) are lower than any of those reported for selected stream basins by Weiskel and others (2007) and are substantially lower than for developed basins such as the South Platte River Basin in Colorado, Nebraska, and Wyoming, which drains approximately 24,300 mi² (−0.30, 0.76), or the Yellow River in China, which drains 334,000 mi² (−0.73, 0.52).

Other indicators that may help illustrate the storage and flow in the Great Lakes Basin and relate flux through the system to storage within the basin. For the entire basin, the ratio of storage volume to flow through the system serves as an average retention time in the basin and is approximately 100 years (Government of Canada and U.S. Environmental Protection Agency, 1995). This ratio often is inverted and cited as a water-renewal rate in the basin of 1 percent. This low renewal rate is used to illustrate the vulnerability of the system to pollution or to changes in climate (for example, Williamson and others, 2009). If each lake is examined individually, then the retention time ranges from 2.6 years for Lake Erie, because of its relatively small volume and its more downstream location in system resulting in large flow through it, to 191 years for Lake Superior, because of its large storage volume and relatively lower flow (Government of Canada and U.S. Environmental Protection Agency, 1995). These indicators imply that the lakes are relatively resistant to short-term changes or stresses because of their storage. The long retention time and large storage also imply that once adverse conditions are observed in the system, many years may be required for corrective action to produce desired results.

Summary and Importance of Regional Analysis

Generalized predevelopment and postdevelopment water budgets presented in tables 3 and 4 may be summarized schematically (fig. 17). These summaries emphasize the importance of surface-water storage in the Great Lakes Basin. This situation is unique, especially on the large scale of the basin, in that surface-water storage exceeds groundwater storage. In most large areas, groundwater storage is dominant. Also notable are the large storage volumes compared to the flow rates through the basin and the large volumes and flows compared to water withdrawal and return in the system. Figure 17 and related summary tables 3 and 4 include fluxes that are not quantified very well: direct groundwater discharge to the lakes, groundwater flow to or from adjacent basins (outside the surface-water divide), and consumptive use. The proportion and location of return flows have not been well documented for many uses. Overlake precipitation and evaporation, which are major contributors to the water budget, have not been directly measured (Neff and Nicholas, 2005). Important temporal variability in the system also is not reflected in these summaries. On the whole, water in storage and water flux through the system are very large compared to observed and estimated water withdrawals.

Need for Subregional and Local Analyses

The Great Lakes Basin hydrologic setting contains such a great deal of freshwater that the overall water availability of the system may not be in question. The appropriate question for this system may be, "Is water available in the basin for human and ecological needs *where* it is needed and *when* it is needed?" Answering this question, and managing resources in light of this question, requires information and analysis at more local scales than that of the whole basin and at timeframes shorter than historical long-term annual averages. Closer examination of hydrologic processes and water use in the system also is required. The Great Lake Basin Pilot stressed the analyses at various spatial and temporal scales, and results of these multiscale analyses are summarized in the remainder of this report.

Subregional Water-Availability Analysis Within the U.S. Great Lakes Basin

Water-availability results from individual subregional studies within the Great Lakes Basin Pilot are summarized in this section. These studies included examinations of groundwater availability, surface-water availability, and water withdrawal in different subregions within the U.S. Great Lakes Basin. In keeping with the pilot nature of the project, studies included water-availability assessments, methods development, and methods testing. The results are presented by topic rather than subregion to help clarify the presentation.

Groundwater

The need for hydraulic analysis to evaluate of the effect of new or increased withdrawals on groundwater has been clearly articulated by Bredehoeft and others (1982), Bredehoeft (1997, 2002), and Alley and others (1999). The overall water budget for the groundwater system, expressed in terms of long-term recharge, for example, provides little information regarding the response of the system to increased pumping. The pumping will initially remove water from storage and will lower the hydraulic head in the aquifer. At some time, however, the increased pumping will be balanced by either an increase in recharge to the pumped aquifer or a decrease in discharge from the pumped aquifer. Groundwater availability depends on the response of the aquifer to pumping. Groundwater-availability constraints may arise either from undesired lowering of the hydraulic head in the aquifer (excessive removal from storage) or from undesired reduction in streamflow or other surface-water capture, which in turn may lead

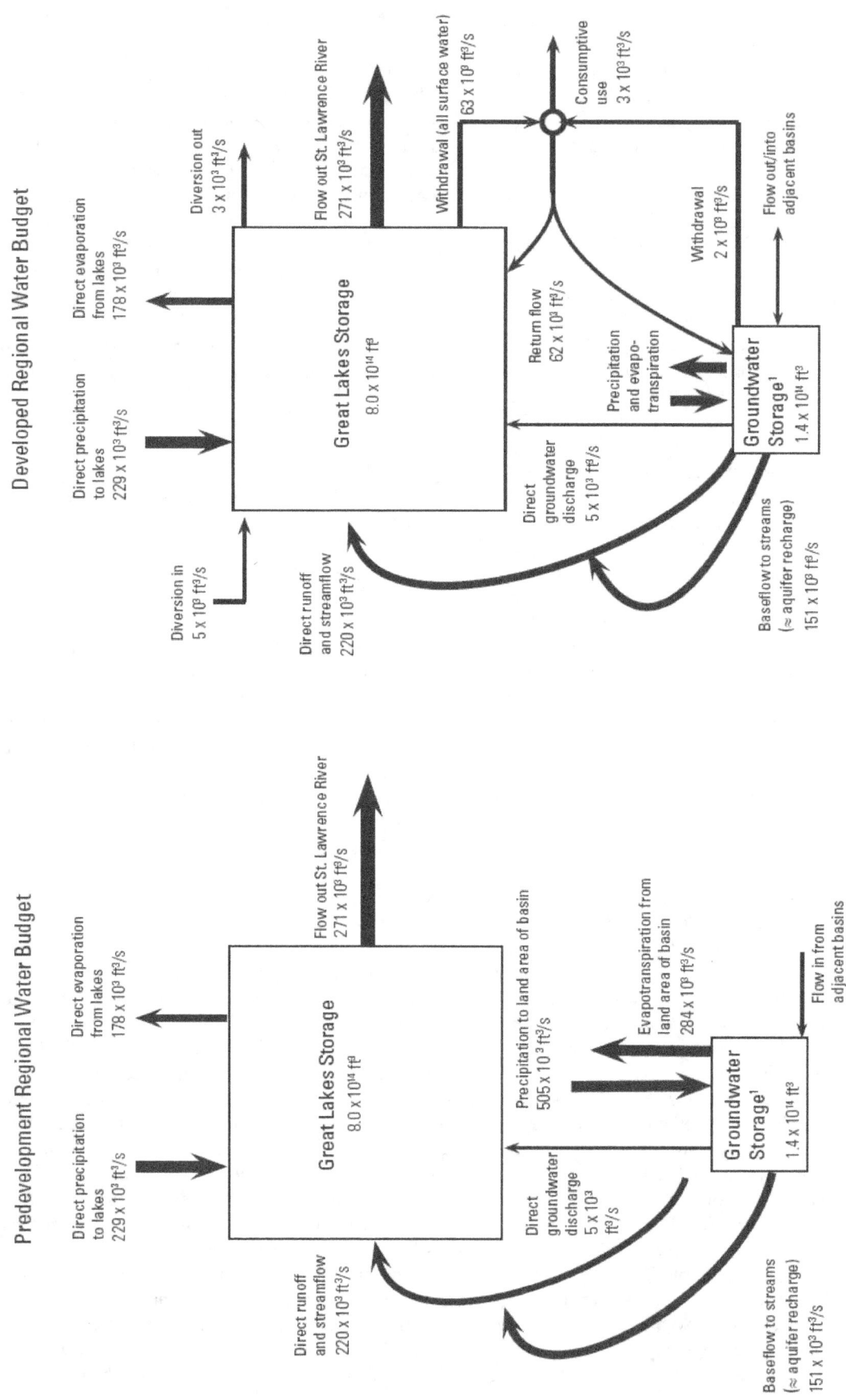

Figure 17.   Predevelopment and postdevelopment long-term average water budgets for the Great Lakes Basin.

to ecological impact or conflict over surface-water resources (excessive capture of discharge). Given that groundwater is such a large component of streamflow in the U.S. Great Lakes Basin (Holtschlag and Nicholas, 1998) and given the difficulty in increasing recharge to the aquifer by groundwater pumping (Bredehoeft and others, 1982; Bredehoeft, 1997), the dominant process in the Great Lakes Basin is likely to be reduction in discharge of groundwater to surface water. The rate at which the system transitions from removal of storage to capture of streamflow or other surface water is important in understanding the effect of groundwater withdrawals. Local analysis to assess the source of water to wells and the transient behavior of the system is required to understand the dynamics of the groundwater system. Therefore, a groundwater-flow model for the Lake Michigan Basin was developed to examine subregional groundwater availability.

Groundwater-Flow Model

A groundwater-flow model was developed for the Lake Michigan Basin to analyze subregional groundwater availability. The size of the entire basin, lack of data or previous modeling efforts in eastern parts of the basin, and challenges posed by modeling an international groundwater system precluded development of a regional model for the entire Great Lakes Basin. The subregional scale of the Lake Michigan Basin model is commensurate in size with other regional groundwater-availability studies being done by USGS (Reilly and others, 2008); the subregional scale also yielded important water-availability information for much of the Great Lakes Basin and allowed for methods development and testing within the pilot project for use in other projects nationwide. The groundwater-flow model for the Lake Michigan Basin is described in a series of reports (Arihood, 2009; Lampe, 2009; Buchwald and others, 2010; Feinstein and others, 2010).

Feinstein and others (2010) summarize the Lake Michigan Basin groundwater-flow model as

- a simulator providing an opportunity for refining quantitative methods in support of groundwater modeling, developing indicators of sustainability of water resources in the Lake Michigan Basin, illustrating groundwater-system response to pumping, and quantifying current groundwater availability in the Lake Michigan Basin;

- a platform for development of embedded, refined models needed to address water-management issues at the local scale;

- an integrator of data from numerous sources at a variety of scales regarding hydrogeology, hydrologic observations, and water use for future water-availability studies; and

- a forecasting tool that can be used to address the effects of future changes in water use and in climate for the western part of the Great Lakes Basin and adjacent areas.

Model results also help frame the analysis for issues that have high uncertainty and are difficult to describe, such as (1) the location and movement of aquifer divides (Sheets and Simonson, 2006), (2) groundwater storage and the change in storage in response to changing conditions (Coon and Sheets, 2006), and (3) direct and indirect groundwater discharge to Lake Michigan (Holtschlag and Nicholas, 1998; Neff and Nicholas, 2005).

The groundwater-flow model was developed by using the computer programs MODFLOW-2000 (Harbaugh and others, 2000) and SEAWAT-2000 (Langevin and others, 2003). It is a finite-difference model with 391 rows oriented west to east and 261 columns oriented north to south. The rows and columns are both nonuniform, but the area of greatest interest of the model has the smallest cells, with uniform cell sizes of 5,000 ft by 5,000 ft. This area of uniform cell sizes is centered on Lake Michigan and extends from row 10 to row 381 and from column 12 to column 248. The area of the model domain is 180,963 mi^2. Less than half of this area falls within the Lake Michigan Basin, and Lake Michigan itself has an area of approximately 22,000 mi^2 (Government of Canada and U.S. Environmental Protection Agency, 1995). Twenty numerical layers were used to discretize the subsurface from the land surface to Precambrian bedrock. The three upper layers of the model represent glacial deposits over most of the land area, and the model extends vertically through several bedrock aquifers that form the Wisconsin Arch and structural Michigan Basin (figs. 4 and 18). To aid in presentation of model results, the area of the model with uniform cell spacing of 5,000 by 5,000 ft and some nonuniform cells within the Lake Michigan Basin are referred to as the model nearfield (fig. 19). Model results are reported for the nearfield. In order to simulate groundwater conditions in the area, boundary conditions and stresses are applied to both the nearfield and remaining part of the model (farfield).

Feinstein and others (2010) described in detail the boundary conditions and stresses imposed on the numerical model, and they analyzed the sensitivity of model results to changes in these boundary conditions and stresses. The farfield boundary conditions include no-flow boundaries along the outer edges of the model area. Two zones of model cells in the northwest and northeast corners of the model where thin glacial materials overlie Precambrian bedrock also are assigned as no-flow boundaries. Head-dependent flux boundaries are applied to cells that represent areas under the major lakes in the farfield of the model domain: Lake Superior, Lake Huron, Lake Erie, and Lake St. Clair. For these lakes, the lake stage and lakebed conductance is specified. The flux between the model and each lake varies in accordance with the difference between estimated head in the finite-difference cell with the boundary condition imposed and the lake stage assigned

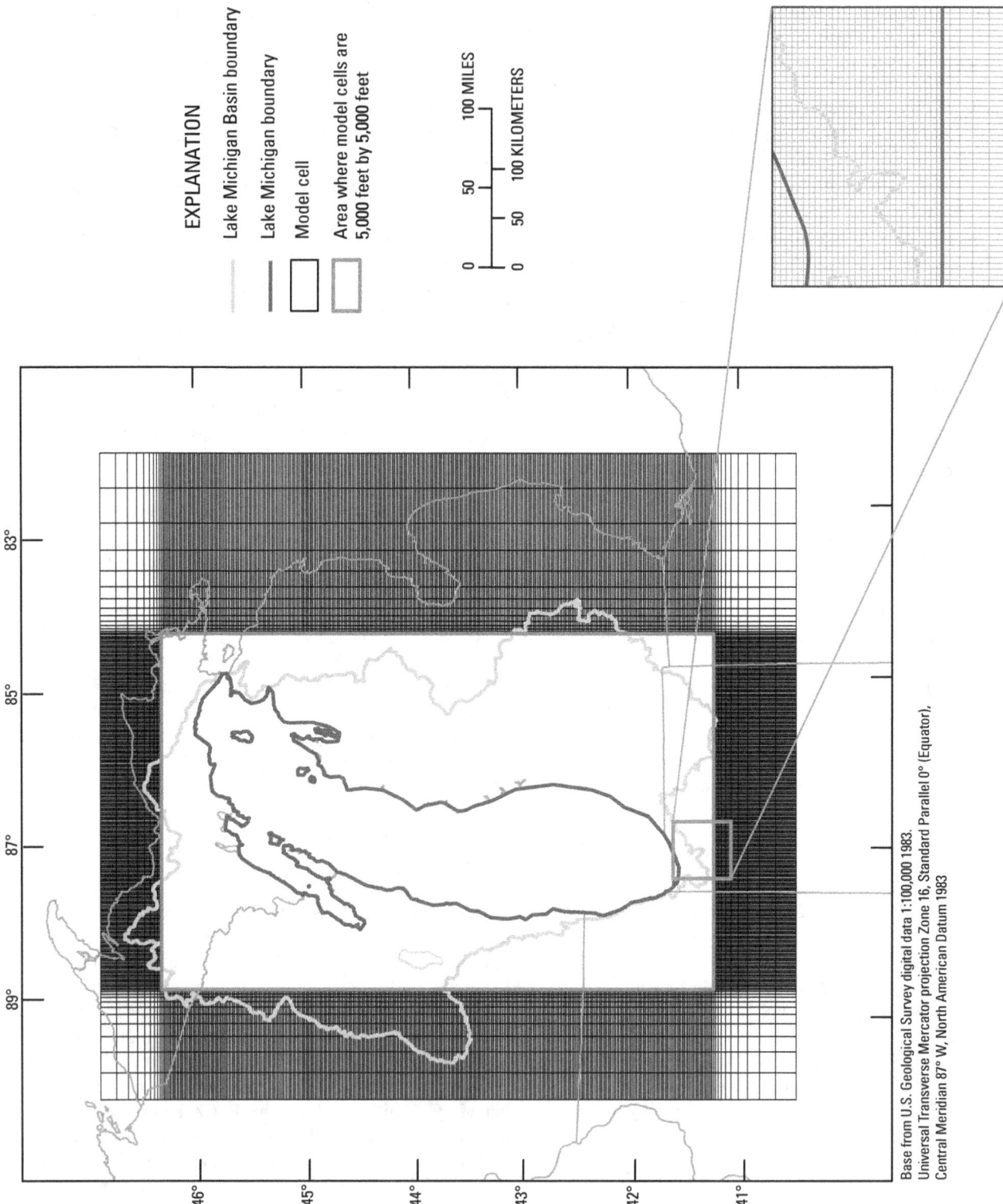

Base from U.S. Geological Survey digital data 1:100,000 1983.
Universal Transverse Mercator projection Zone 16, Standard Parallel 0° (Equator),
Central Meridian 87° W, North American Datum 1983

Figure 18.   Model grid, Lake Michigan Basin drainage basin, and area where model cells are 5,000 feet by 5,000 feet (from Feinstein and others, 2010).

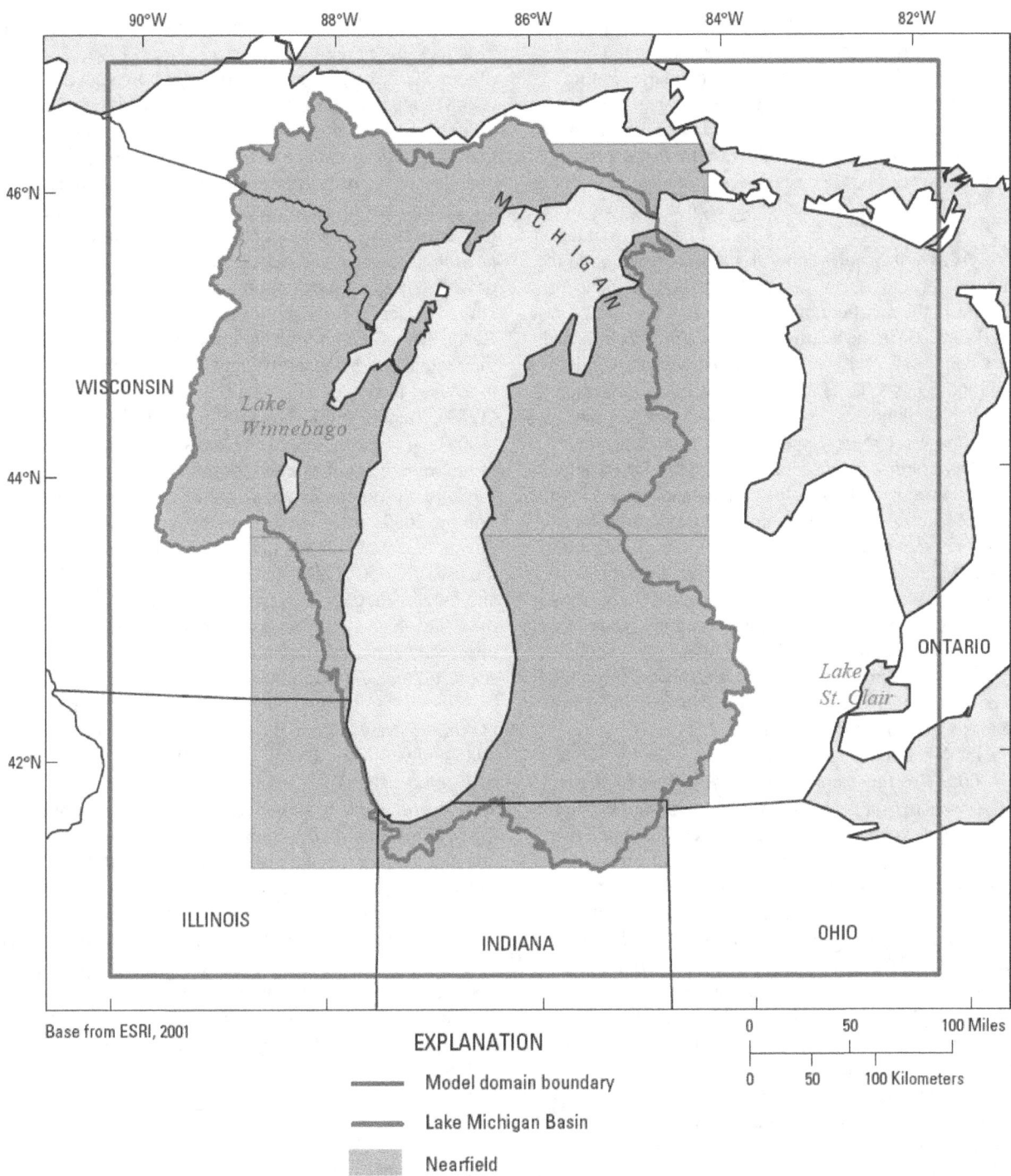

Figure 19.   Nearfield area of Lake Michigan Basin groundwater-flow model.

to the cell. Specified-flux boundary conditions are applied in the southwest corner of the farfield to allow the model to account for water that moves across the boundaries in the southwest part of the model farfield in response to pumping within the model. The fluxes specified were estimated by using results from a numerical model of northeastern Illinois (Meyer and others, 2009). Constant-head boundary conditions were assigned to the topmost active layer of the farfield of the model to fix the water table in these cells to an approximation of the observed water table; doing so fixes the recharge to the system in the farfield and allows model calibration focus on the behavior in the nearfield of the model domain.

Surface water in the nearfield is represented as imposed boundary conditions on the model. These boundary conditions represent major lakes (Lake Michigan and Lake Winnebago), smaller lakes, wetlands, and streams. Lake Michigan and Lake Winnebago are represented by using head-dependent-flux boundary conditions in a similar fashion to the farfield Great Lakes. For farfield lakes, the conductance values used to simulate the lakebeds were quite high so that the lakebed itself offers little resistance to flow. The upper layers of the model under Lake Michigan, however, were designed to represent the sediments under the lake and more accurately reflect the exchange of water between the two lakes and the groundwater system (Feinstein and others, 2010). Smaller lakes, wetlands, and streams were represented in the model, and approximately 60 percent of the nearfield cells had some surface-water feature imposed as a boundary condition.

The model simulates groundwater conditions from 1864 through 2005. This timespan was subdivided into 13 stress periods: a stress period is an interval of time during which the conditions imposed on the model are held constant, and five time steps are used within the simulation of each stress period except the first. The first stress period produced a steady-state approximation to conditions prior to 1864 and required only one time step. Pumping, boundary conditions, and recharge were held constant for each stress period. The withdrawals by pumping are summarized by Feinstein and others (2010) and detailed by Buchwald and others (2010). Recharge to the model was estimated by developing computer code for a modified Thornthwaite-Mather soil-water-balance approach (Westenbroek and others, 2010). The Soil-Water-Balance (SWB) model performs an accounting of water in the soil zone by using daily time steps to estimate water delivered through the soil zone to the water table, which is recharge to the aquifer. Climate variables, including temperature and precipitation, and landscape and soil characteristics are required inputs for the SWB model (Westenbroek and others, 2010). Water is added to the soil zone through precipitation and snowmelt and is removed through evapotranspiration and recharge to the aquifer. The daily estimates of recharge produced by the model were aggregated to produce long-term average recharge values that were applied to the 13 stress periods (fig. 20). Recharge imposed on the model varies with stress period and is generally higher after 1970, which is consistent with general increases in precipitation and changes in land-use practices,

particularly improvement in land-conserving agricultural practices, in the region (Gebert and Krug, 1996; Hodgkins and others, 2007; Juckem and others, 2008). Juckem and others (2008) state that climate variation appears to control the overall trends in base flow (which is tied to groundwater recharge), and agricultural-practice changes have magnified the recharge changes in part of Wisconsin outside of the Great Lakes Basin.

Indicators of the condition of the groundwater system and its response to development included the simulated hydraulic head in the system and associated change in head (drawdown). A major cone of depression, one of the largest in the United States, is adjacent to and extends into the Great Lakes Basin. The importance of the Cambrian-Ordovician aquifer to the region and the observed drawdowns in this aquifer have motivated many studies, including those by Young and others (1989), Mandle and Kontis (1992), and Feinstein and others (2005). Because these earlier results indicated that the cone of depression could extend into saline parts of the Michigan Basin (data sources for the saline-water input are detailed by Lampe, 2009), the effect of salinity and density-dependent flow was included in the Lake Michigan Basin model through the use of the SEAWAT-2000 computer program (Feinstein and others, 2010). The drawdown is caused by pumping in the Chicago and Milwaukee metropolitan regions, and the observed behavior is reproduced by the flow model (fig. 21; see also Feinstein and others, 2010).

Observations and analysis of model results reveal that the maximum drawdown in the system occurred in approximately 1985 and was approximately 1,000 ft. In the 1980s, Chicago, Milwaukee, and other communities near Lake Michigan shifted from wells to Lake Michigan water for public supply. This shift decreased the demand on the groundwater system and led to a recovery of approximately 400 ft (fig. 22). Between 1970 and 1990, the locus of the cone of depression moved westward in response to decreased demand from wells near the lake and increased development in western suburbs of Chicago and Milwaukee. Between 2000 and 2005, the drawdown stabilized, primarily because new development has focused on shallower wells or wells in the Cambrian-Ordovician aquifer outside the major cone of depression because of water-quality concerns associated with radium in the Cambrian-Ordovician aquifer (Kay, 1999).

Groundwater Budget

Simulation results from the model can be analyzed to show the water budget through time for the Lake Michigan Basin (fig. 23*A*,*B*). This analysis shows that despite large drawdowns due to pumping in the Chicago and Milwaukee metropolitan areas, the overall effect of development on the groundwater system is small compared to fluctuations caused by climate variation. The major components of the groundwater budget are recharge into the system and discharge to local surface-water features (streams out) (fig. 23*A*). The next most important fluxes are input from losing surface-water features

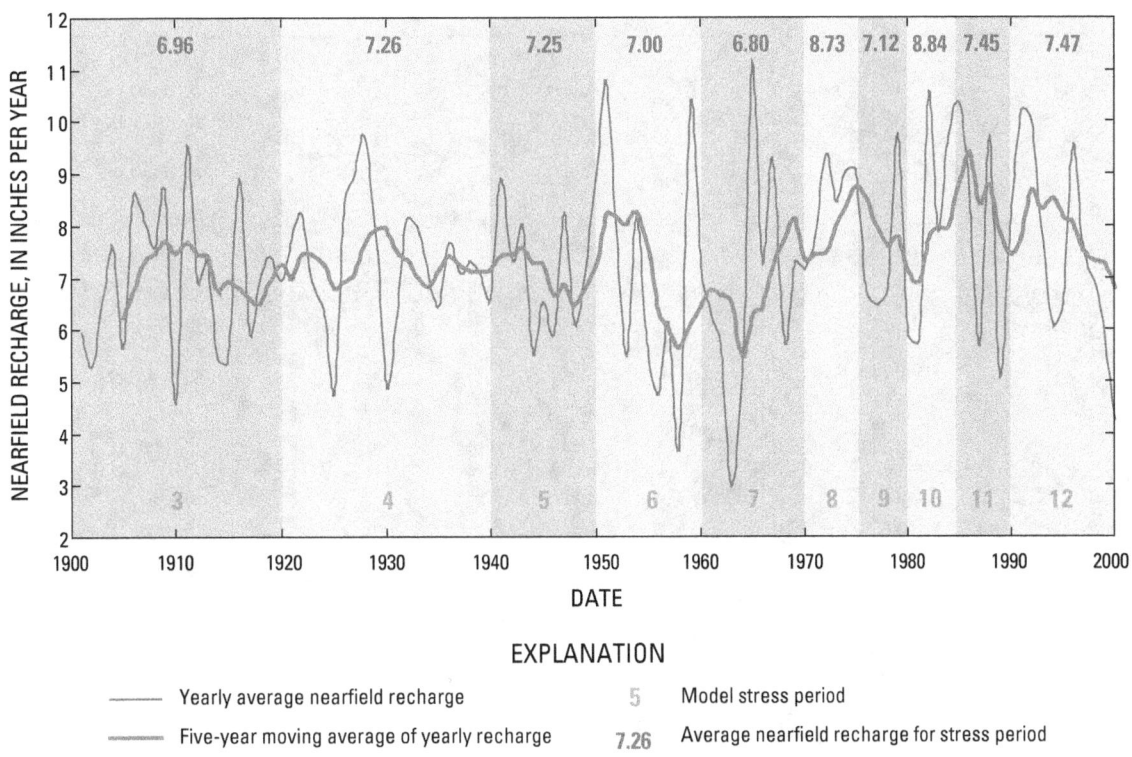

Figure 20. Recharge values assigned to stress periods for the Lake Michigan Basin groundwater-flow model with yearly and 5-year moving averages of recharge, as estimated by using the Soil-Water-Balance model (from Feinstein and others, 2010).

and flow out to inland lakes. Least important to the budget, but perhaps most visible and of interest to users in the area, are the fluxes out of the system to wells and directly to Lake Michigan, and the fluxes into and out of storage as heads in the aquifers change in response to pumping and changes in recharge. The role of pumping and storage changes can be noted in this type of figure only if changes in time are emphasized by highlighting the changes in budget components. Even when the changes in the budgets are emphasized, the major components are (1) changes in recharge arising from climate variability and (2) associated responses of outflow to inland surface water and groundwater levels determining water in storage. This pattern is especially true for the four stress periods during 1970–90 (stress periods 8–11; see also fig. 20); the changes in imposed recharge because of climatic changes from one period to the next cause water to move in and out of storage as the system responds to the change from the lowest imposed recharge in stress period 7 (1960–70) to high recharge in stress period 8 (1970–75) followed by lower recharge in stress period 9 (1975–80) (fig. 23B).

An alternative analysis that illustrates the source of water to wells is generated by using particle tracking to identify the potential pathways water moves through the system (Feinstein and others, 2010). Through this analysis, the starting point for particles that are discharged to wells within principal aquifers in the system are identified (fig. 24). These starting points

represent locations where water that eventually is removed by a well originates in the shallow aquifer system. The purpose of this analysis is twofold: first, it reinforces and illustrates the notion of capture discussed by Bredehoeft (2002) and, second, it shows interaction between major pumping centers and Lake Michigan, which is of interest in the area (see, for example, Cherkauer and others, 2006). Wells pumping water from the bedrock aquifer capture water from the surface-water system and interact with Lake Michigan on very long time scales. A large area within Lake Michigan is simulated to supply water to wells, but most of the particles that begin in the lake travel longer than 10,000 years to reach the pumping wells.

The discharge of groundwater to Lake Michigan should be recognized as occurring either as direct discharge from the groundwater system to the lake or indirect discharge of groundwater to streams that then discharge into the lake. Regionally, indirect discharge is far more important to the water budget of the lake (Holtschlag and Nicholas, 1998; Neff and Nicholas, 2005). Groundwater-budget results for the Lake Michigan Basin (fig. 23) indicate that direct discharge to the lake ("Lake Michigan out") under predevelopment conditions was 1.2 percent of the total input to the groundwater system and that indirect discharge to the lake ("Streams out") under predevelopment conditions was 98.8 percent. Simulation results from the end of the 2000–2005 stress period indicate that 96.9 percent of the inflow to the groundwater

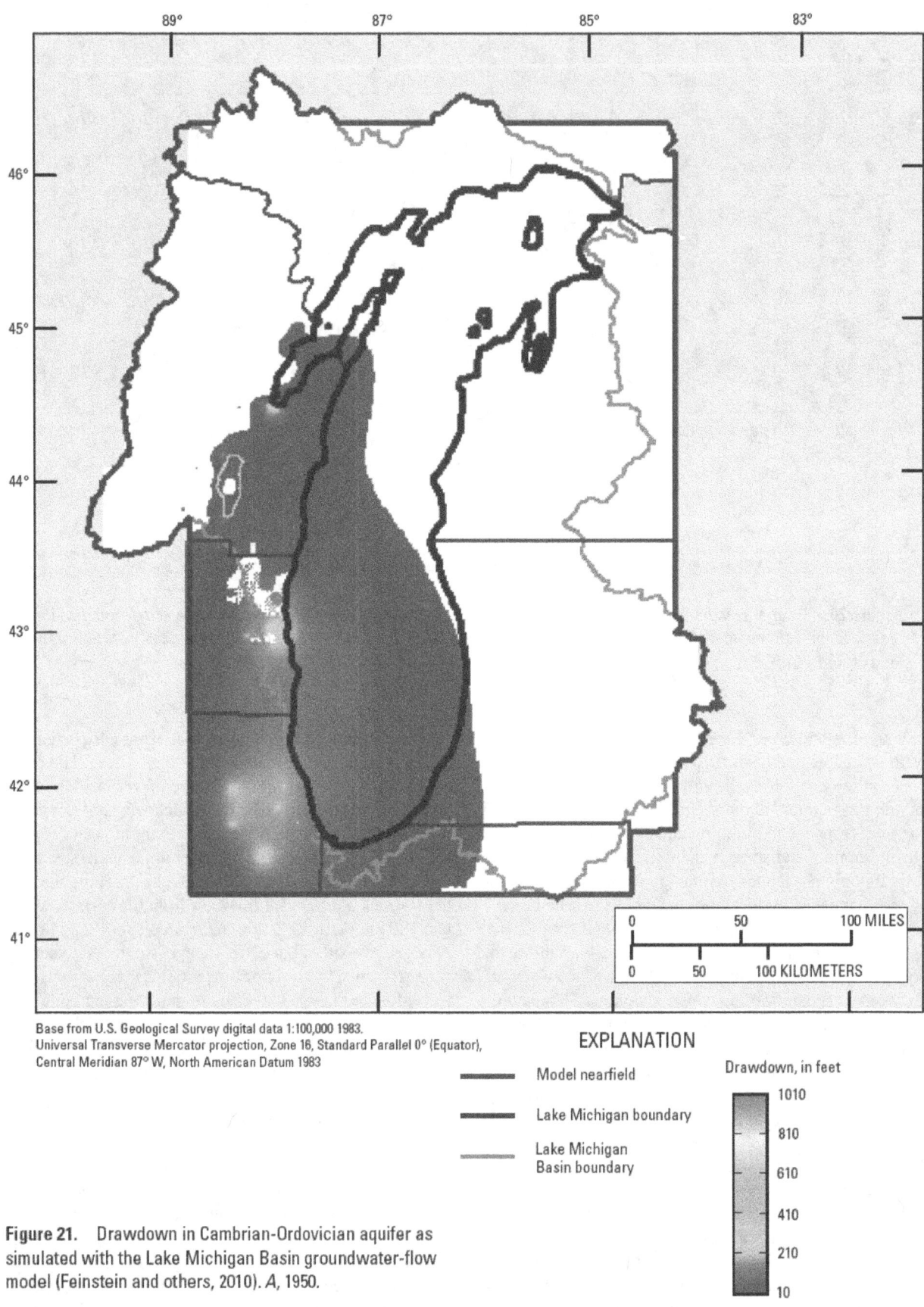

Base from U.S. Geological Survey digital data 1:100,000 1983.
Universal Transverse Mercator projection, Zone 16, Standard Parallel 0° (Equator),
Central Meridian 87° W, North American Datum 1983

EXPLANATION

—— Model nearfield

—— Lake Michigan boundary

—— Lake Michigan
     Basin boundary

Drawdown, in feet

1010
810
610
410
210
10

Figure 21.   Drawdown in Cambrian-Ordovician aquifer as
simulated with the Lake Michigan Basin groundwater-flow
model (Feinstein and others, 2010). *A*, 1950.

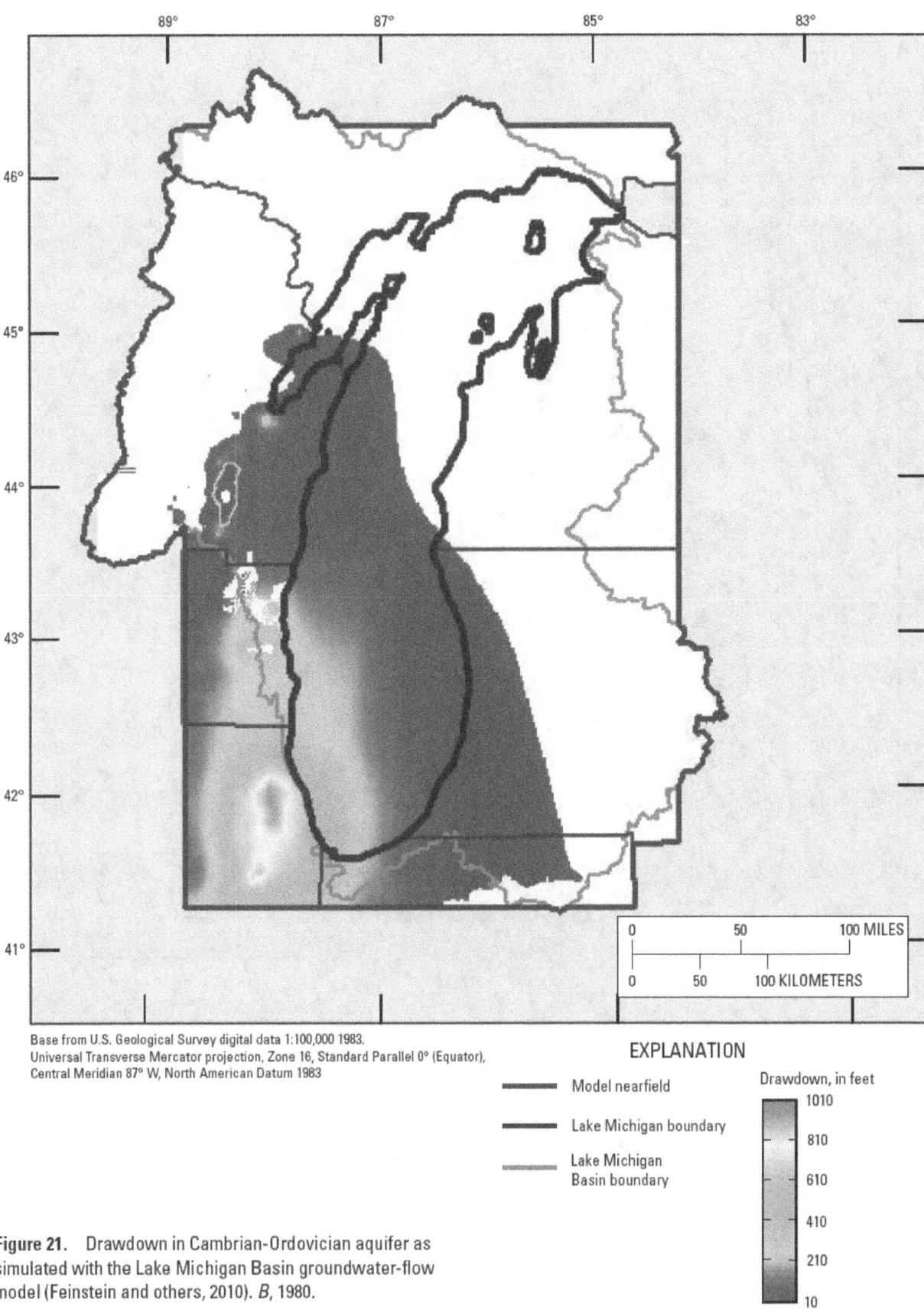

Base from U.S. Geological Survey digital data 1:100,000 1983.
Universal Transverse Mercator projection, Zone 16, Standard Parallel 0° (Equator),
Central Meridian 87° W, North American Datum 1983

EXPLANATION

——— Model nearfield

——— Lake Michigan boundary

——— Lake Michigan
Basin boundary

Drawdown, in feet

1010
810
610
410
210
10

Figure 21. Drawdown in Cambrian-Ordovician aquifer as
simulated with the Lake Michigan Basin groundwater-flow
model (Feinstein and others, 2010). *B*, 1980.

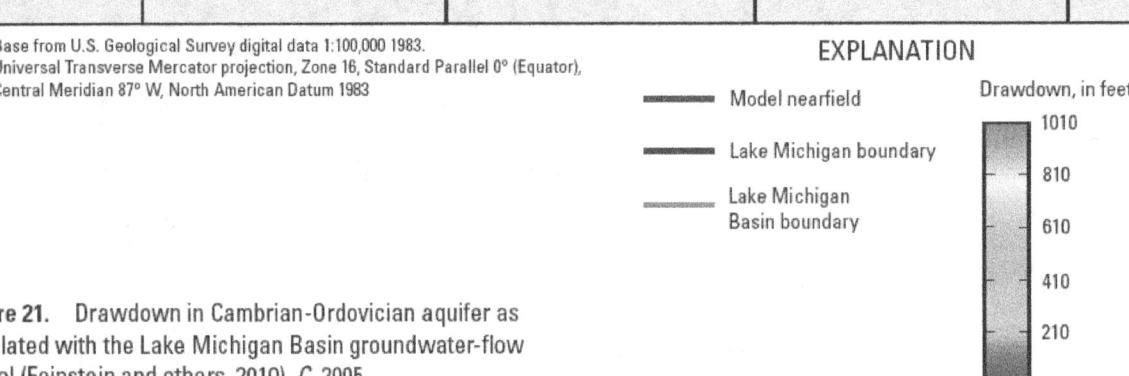

Base from U.S. Geological Survey digital data 1:100,000 1983.
Universal Transverse Mercator projection, Zone 16, Standard Parallel 0° (Equator),
Central Meridian 87° W, North American Datum 1983

EXPLANATION

——— Model nearfield

——— Lake Michigan boundary

——— Lake Michigan
Basin boundary

Drawdown, in feet

1010
810
610
410
210
10

Figure 21. Drawdown in Cambrian-Ordovician aquifer as
simulated with the Lake Michigan Basin groundwater-flow
model (Feinstein and others, 2010). *C*, 2005.

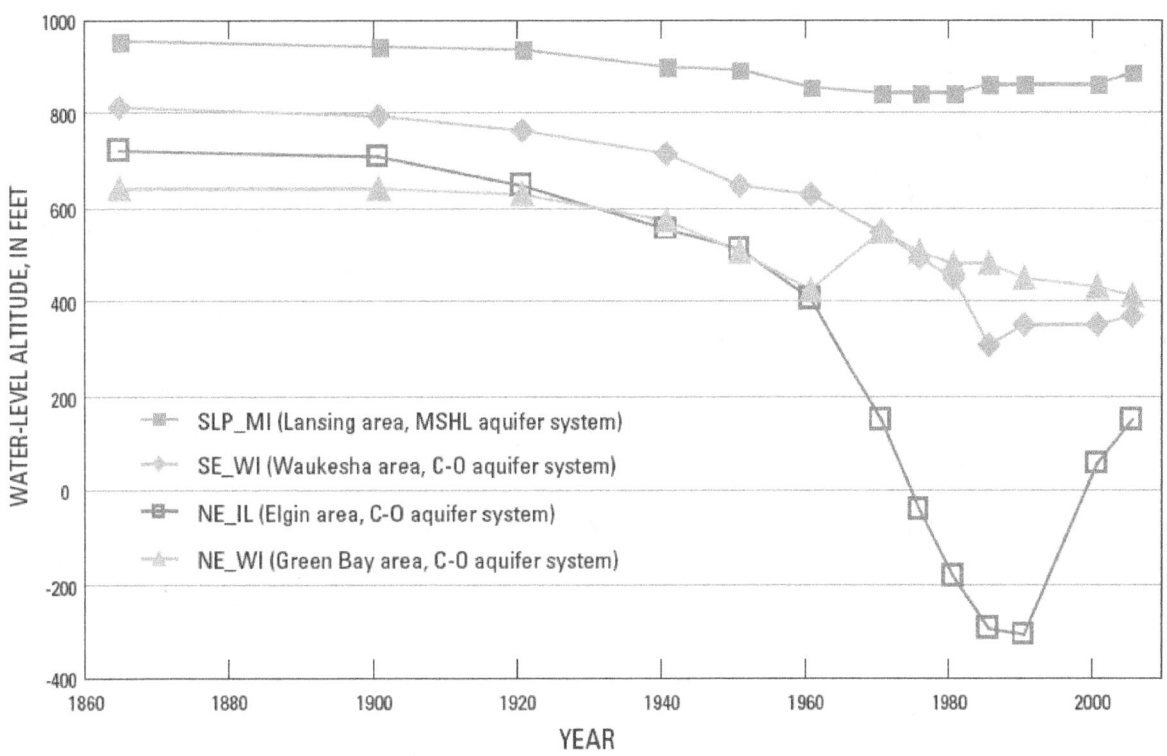

Figure 22. Simulated water-level hydrographs at pumping centers within water-budget zones of the Lake Michigan Basin groundwater-flow model (from Feinstein and others, 2010).

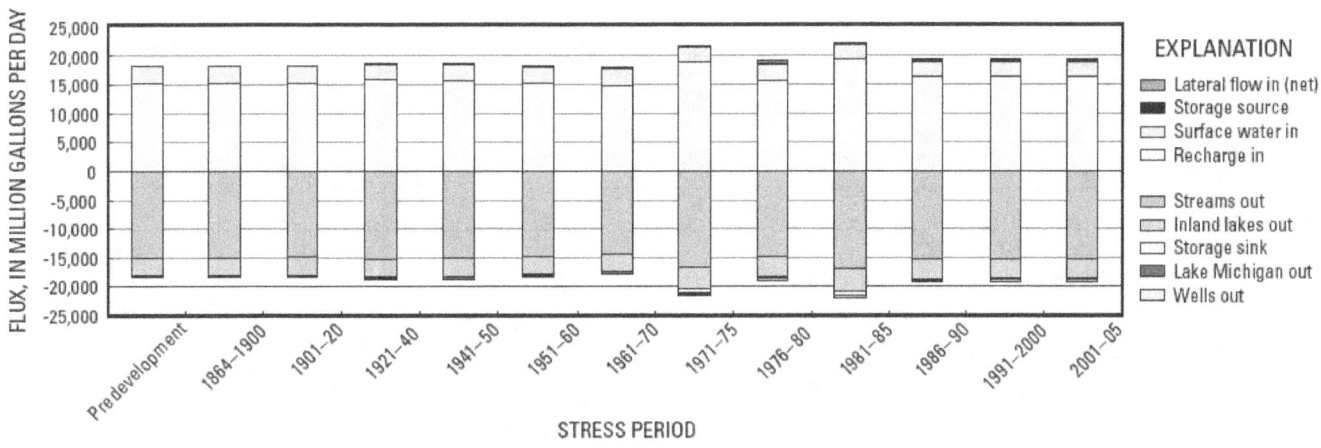

Figure 23. Water budget for the Lake Michigan Basin from groundwater-flow model showing proportions of water-budget components for each modeled stress period (from Feinstein and others, 2010).

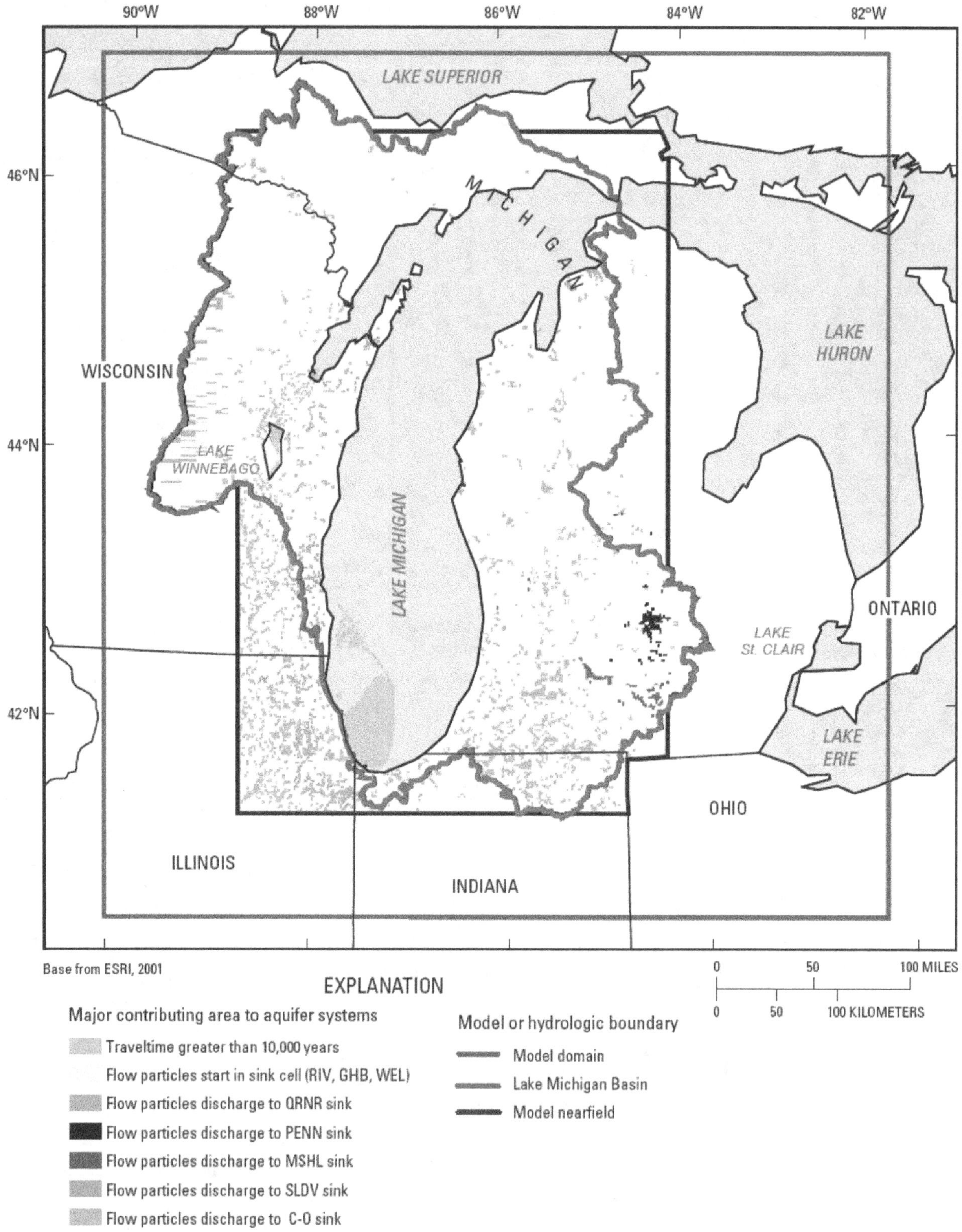

Figure 24. Contributing areas to wells in principal aquifers (from Feinstein and others, 2010).

system was delivered to Lake Michigan through indirect discharge ("Streams out"), 3.1 percent of the inflow to the groundwater system was removed by pumping ("Wells out"), and 1.1 percent of the inflow to the groundwater system was discharged directly to Lake Michigan ("Lake Michigan out"). The rate of direct discharge estimated with the Lake Michigan Basin model ranged from approximately 0.08 to 8 ft³/s per 5,000 ft of shoreline. The overall average direct discharge rate was an average of 0.33 ft³/s per 5,000 ft of shoreline. More detailed analysis and grid refinement of the model near the lake suggested that these estimates slightly underestimated the direct discharge (Feinstein and others, 2010). Refinements to the subregional model, however, yield an estimated value of 0.5 ft³/s per mile of shoreline, with a corresponding increase in the fraction of input to the system discharged directly to the lake such that the direct discharge is approximately 2 percent of the overall water budget for the Lake Michigan Basin (Feinstein and others, 2010). These values are consistent with estimates reported by Neff and Nicholas (2005).

To analyze the water budget in more detail and to contrast different locations within the model, the domain was divided into seven water-budget zones, and the groundwater budget for 1864–2005 was estimated for each zone from the model simulation results (figs. 25 and 26). Additional refinement of the analysis identified shallow and deep aquifer systems. In this context, shallow aquifer systems refer to those above the first major and relatively continuous confining unit, and deep aquifer systems are those below the first relatively continuous bedrock confining unit. Shallow groundwater flow is either unconfined (for example, flow that occurs in coarse-grained glacial deposits or in bedrock that is overlain by coarse-grained glacial deposits) or semiconfined (for example, flow in zones where fine-grained glacial deposits overlie a bedrock aquifer without an intervening bedrock confining unit). Deep groundwater flow is by definition always in bedrock, and it is always either confined or semiconfined as in the example given above. Pumping wells and withdrawals can be described as shallow or deep depending on the open interval of the well and its relation to the uppermost bedrock confining unit.

Examination of the sources of water to shallow and deep aquifer systems for the seven water-budget zones reveals some similarities but also some major differences in behavior between the east and west parts of the study area (fig. 26A, B). For all the water-budget zones, downward leakage from inland surface water is the major source of water to wells for the subregional groundwater-flow model. Storage release, which is the result of changes in hydraulic heads in the aquifers, is more important for aquifers west of Lake Michigan. For 2005 (results in the figure are shown for the end of the 2000–2005 stress period), storage release is less important for shallow pumping than for pumping from deep systems.

Shallow pumping in the Northeast Wisconsin (NE_WI) water-budget zone decreased groundwater levels, and approximately 9 percent of the water produced by wells came from this release in storage. Six percent of the water pumped was from lateral flow into the water-budget zone either from

Lake Michigan (1 percent) or outside of the zone (5 percent). The remaining 85 percent of pumping was captured inland surface water, and it may have been either diversion of water that would have been discharged to streams or induction of inland surface water to the shallow aquifer. To the east of Lake Michigan, the Northern Lower Peninsula of Michigan zone (NLP_MI) behaved much the same for shallow pumping except that lateral flow was not a significant source of water to wells. For this shallow water-budget zone, 9 percent of the water came from storage release, and 91 percent came from captured inland surface water. A decrease in pumping in the Northeast Illinois (NE_ILL) water-budget zone for the 2000–2005 stress period lead to recovery of water levels, and water returned to storage in this water-budget zone. Because water levels recovered from earlier drawdown by pumping, the analysis indicates that the source to water to wells from captured inland surface water is greater than 100 percent. All the water produced by the wells is captured from inland surface water, and the excess (9 percent of the pumping rate in this case) represents the water that is returning to storage in the shallow system. The remaining shallow mass-balance zones all were dominated by capture of inland surface water.

For the deep aquifer system, changes in storage and lateral flow were more important for the Southeast Wisconsin (SE_WI), Northeast Illinois (NE_ILL), and Northern Lower Peninsula of Michigan (NLP_MI) water-budget zones than these sources were for the shallow system. Again, water returned to storage in the NE_ILL water-budget zone, amounting to 18 percent of the pumping rate; sources of water to the wells and to storage were leakage from the overlying aquifers that ultimately is captured inland surface water (68 percent), lateral flow from Lake Michigan (8 percent), and lateral flow from outside the water-budget zone (42 percent). Captured water from Lake Michigan was more important for the deep SW_WI zone (11 percent of pumping) and deep NLP_MI zone (56 percent of pumping). The deep NE_WI and SLP_MI water-budget zones were dominated by leakage from overlying aquifers capturing inland surface water (greater than 95 percent of the pumping rate in both cases).

Groundwater-Availability Summary Indicators

Water-budget information from the groundwater-flow model may be used to calculate summary indicators for the Great Lakes Basin region. To contrast the different budget zones, summary indicators for the deep and shallow aquifer systems in each of the budget zones were computed. Slightly different summary indicators were developed for analysis of model results than were used for the regional water-budget analysis. The normalized water-use components of the *HWB* and *WUI* indicators discussed previously are bounded by 1 (Weiskel and others, 2007). Use of a groundwater-flow model to compute these indicators, however, allows for climate-driven variations in the water budget to be separated from other changes in the system, therefore making it possible to

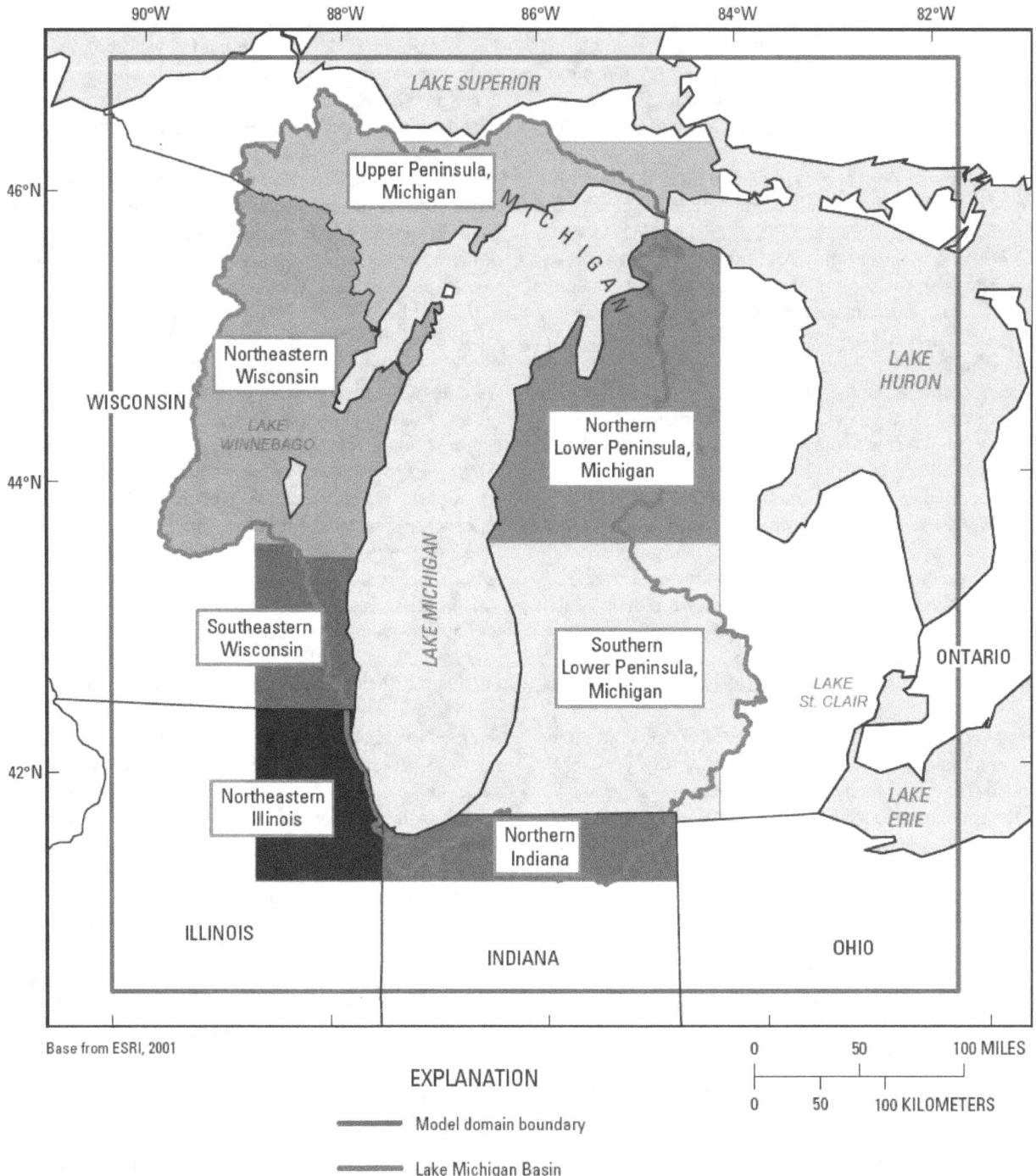

Figure 25. Water-budget zones of Lake Michigan Basin groundwater-flow model used to summarize groundwater-availability results (from Feinstein and others, 2010).

define indicators that further emphasize withdrawal-related differences between areas.

The major source of water to wells is captured surface water from inland sources (fig. 26). Observations and analysis presented by Hodgkins and others (2007), however, suggest that groundwater discharge (base flow to streams), as indicated by the mean annual 7-day low flow, increased during 1970–2005 (fig. 14). This apparent contradiction is reconciled by examination of the imposed recharge on the model (fig. 20). The recharge increase for 1970–2005 delivers more water to the groundwater system than is removed by pumping over this time period (fig. 23). To estimate the effect of pumping on streamflow and to eliminate the effects of climate variability,

the model was run without any pumping stress imposed. The model results with pumping were then subtracted from the model results without pumping to isolate the effect pumping has on the system. Because the recharge to the groundwater system is fixed for each time period and because recharge does not depend on the pumping rate in the simulations, subtracting the results removes the effects of climate variability from the analysis.

Summary indicators were developed in which the water withdrawals and returns were normalized to the estimated net flux through the system in the absence of pumping. The new indicator, HWB', is similar to the Demand-to-Supply Ratio (DSR) discussed by Cherkauer (2009). The difference

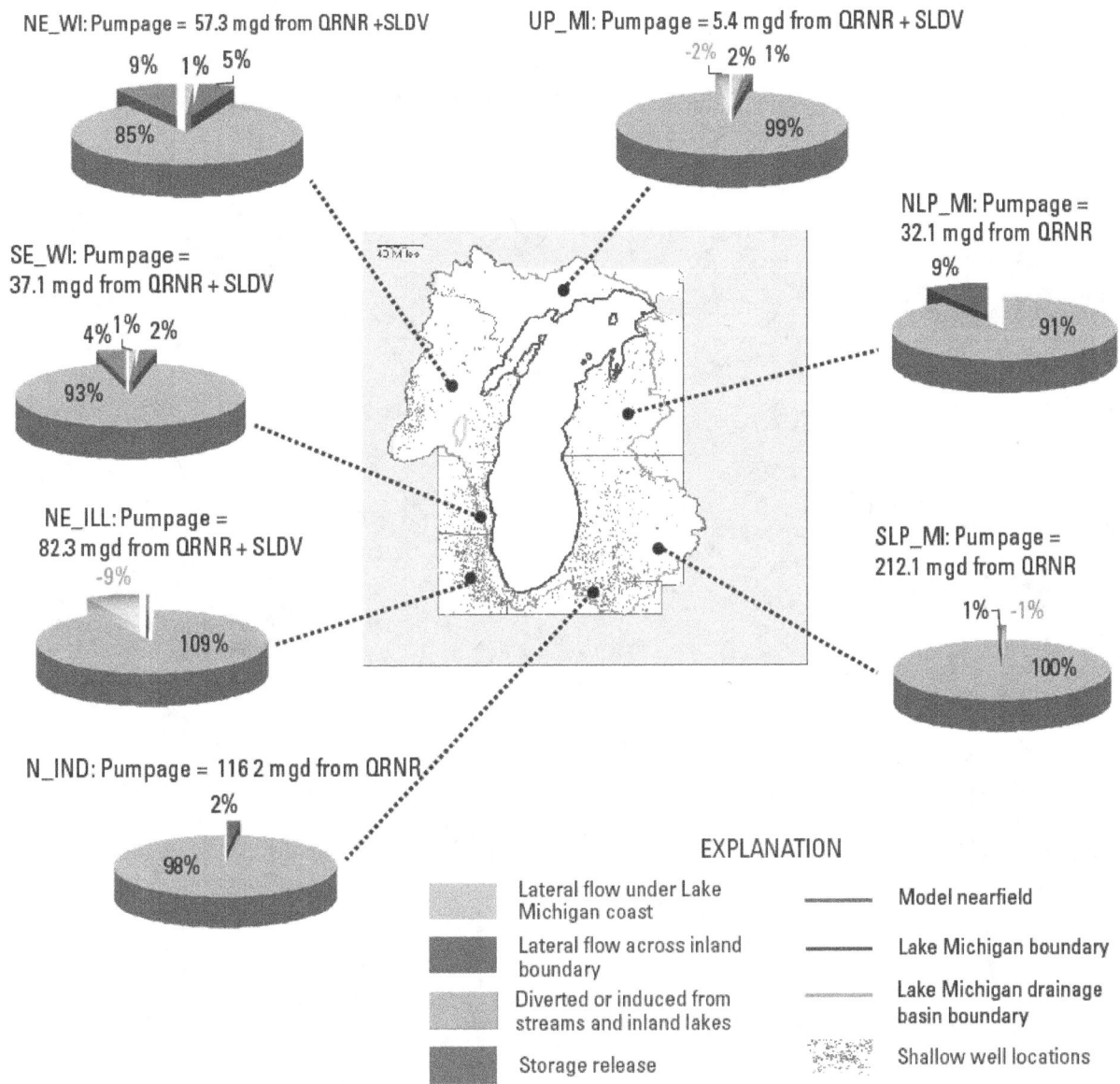

Figure 26. Sources of water to wells by water-budget zone and aquifer system for 2005 from the Lake Michigan Basin groundwater-flow model. *A*, Shallow aquifer systems.

between the new indicator, denoted by either *HWB'* or *DSR'*, and the *DSR* used by Cherkauer (2009) is that in the latter net withdrawal is normalized by predevelopment flows. The *DSR* summary indicator is sensitive to climate variability; and, if climate variability is significant compared to withdrawals, then it will mask the effects of pumping on the analysis.

A modified the water-use intensity index, *WUI'*, also could be defined where human-induced inflows and out-flows are normalized by estimated fluxes computed by using the groundwater-flow model without pumping; for the Great Lakes Basin, however, areas are generally not character-ized by low *HWB* and high *WUI* indicators representative of a human-dominated system (fig. 16), so a modified *WUI* is not considered in this section.

A Base-flow-Reduction Ratio (*BRR'*) defined by the decrease in estimated net base flow to streams for each mass-balance region was estimated by using the difference between

the pumping and no-pumping simulations. Because pumping may induce the capture of surface water from streams to the aquifer, the net base flow may become negative and the ratio may exceed 1. In the same way as the Demand-to-Supply Ratio, *BRR'* differs from the Base-flow Reduction Index *BRI* used by Cherkauer (2009) because the latter normalizes with respect to predevelopment conditions (it also is expressed as a percentage), and in this section the normalization is with respect to a no-pumping condition.

The indicators used in this section are

$$DSR' = HWB' = h'_{in} - h'_{out}$$
$$= \text{(net withdrawal)(net flux without pumping)}$$

$$BRR' = (bf_{nopumping} - bf_{pumping}) \, / \, bf_{nopumping}$$
$$= \text{(change in net base flow due to pumping)/}$$
$$\text{(net flow without pumping)}$$

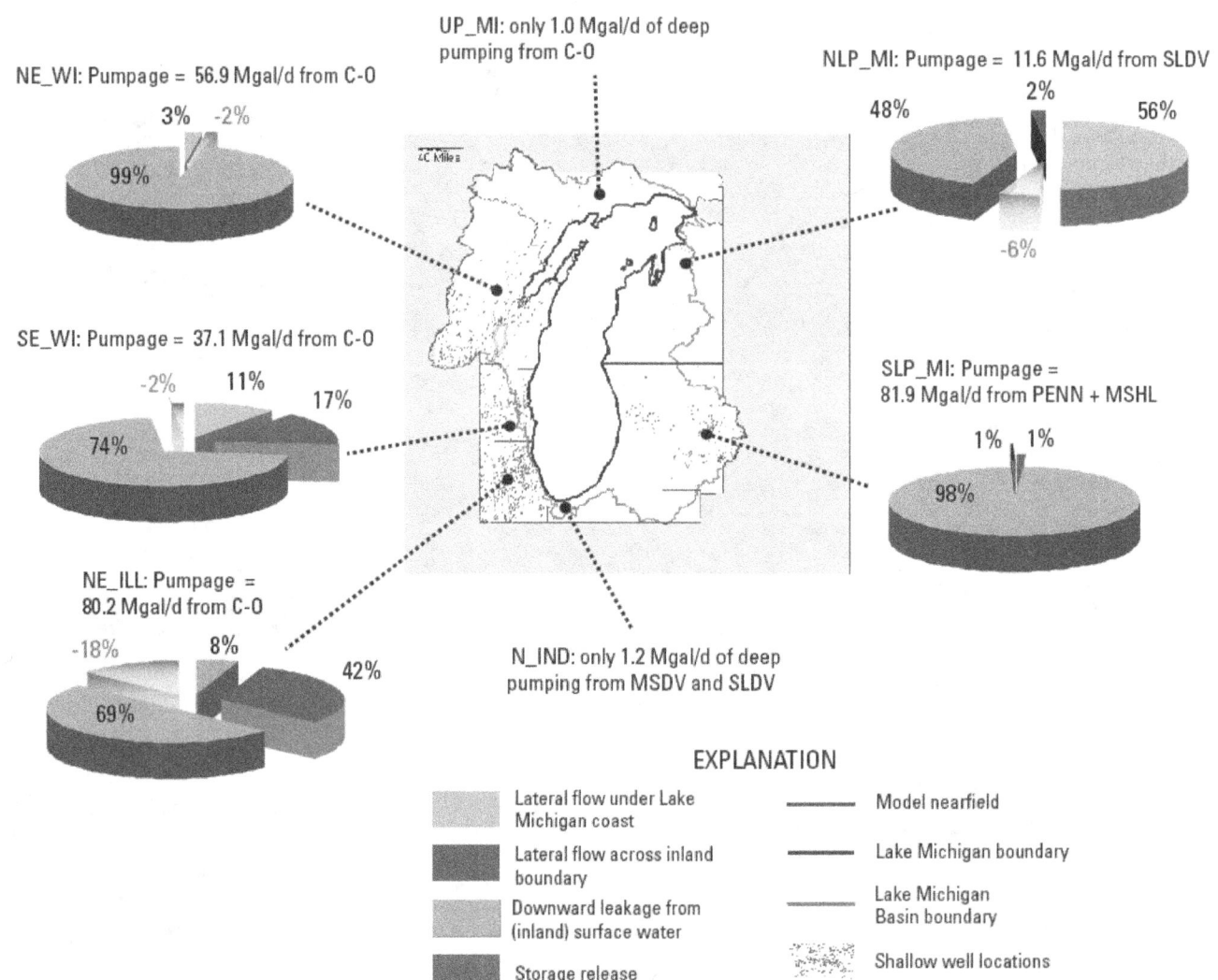

Figure 26. Sources of water to wells by water-budget zone and aquifer system for 2005 from the Lake Michigan Basin groundwater-flow model. *B*, Deep aquifer systems (from Feinstein and others, 2010).

where

h'_{in} normalized human return flows into a basin, $H_{in}/NetFlux'$,

h'_{out} normalized human withdrawals out of a basin, $H_{out}/NetFlux'$,

H_{in} human-induced flux into a basin (returns),

H_{out} human-induced flux out of a basin (withdrawals),

$bf_{pumping}$ net base flow (base flow to streams – flux from streams to aquifers) under pumping conditions, and

$bf_{nopumping}$ net base flow (base flow to streams – flux from streams to aquifers) under no-pumping conditions.

The NetFlux' normalizing human return flows and withdrawals is computed by using the calibrated groundwater-flow model with no human withdrawals imposed on the simulation.

$$NetFlux' = R_{net} + (R_{GW} + R_{SW}) + \Delta S'_{in}/\Delta t$$
$$= (D_{GW} + D_{SW}) + \Delta S'_{out}/\Delta$$

All terms in these equations were defined previously except $\Delta S'_{in}$, which is volume of water released from storage for the time interval computed by the model in the absence of withdrawals by pumping, and $\Delta S'_{out}$, which is the volume of water added to storage for the time interval computed by the model in the absence of withdrawals by pumping. Water is released from storage if water levels in the aquifer decrease, and water is taken into storage if water levels increase.

Water-budget results indicate that withdrawals by pumping are only a small fraction of the overall groundwater budget for the Lake Michigan Basin (fig. 23). The Demand-to-Supply Ratio and Base-flow-Reduction Ratio calculated for the Lake Michigan Basin by using the entire aquifer system also show this result (fig. 27). The DSR' indicator maximum value was approximately 0.03 for the Lake Michigan Basin, and the BRR' was approximately 0.033. These results echo the important theme describing water availability in the region: there is regional abundance of groundwater resources compared to regional demand. By examining the indicators for smaller areas, however, the potential for local conflicts, limitations, or storages can be seen.

For shallow aquifers, the Base-flow-Reduction Ratio is more illustrative of the behavior of the system than the Demand-to-Supply Ratio in the water-budget zones because the natural flux through the shallow system is high compared with the demands on the system. The BRR' increases from zero at predevelopment conditions to maximum values near 19 for in 1985, after which it stabilizes or decreases slightly (fig. 28A). The water-budget zones with the greatest ground-water withdrawals, NE_ILL and SW_WI, have the largest BRR'. On the scale of this model, the base-flow reduction is diffuse and cannot be attributed to significant impacts on certain streams. Local-scale modeling is required to quantify the interaction of wells with individual surface-water features, as shown in a later section of this report. The BRR' is computed only for the shallow aquifers because these aquifers account

for almost all of the base flow to streams in the model. The pumping in these water-budget zones, however, is from both the deep and shallow systems. Shallow pumping dominates local base-flow reduction, but pumping in the deep part of the flow system may increase leakage from the overlying shallow system and thereby cause local base-flow reduction.

The DSR' indicator is less than 0.12 for all water-budget zones for both shallow and deep parts of the flow system except the southeast Wisconsin (SE_WI) and northeast Illinois (NE_ILL) water-budget zones. All the water-budgets zones other than SE_WI and NE_ILL, like the Great Lakes Basin, would be considered within the natural-flow-dominated water-use regime. The two exceptions indicate withdrawals are an important part of the water budget of the respective zone. Exploring the data used to create the indices reveals that, in the absence of pumping, the flux of groundwater in the deep part of the flow systems in SE_WI and NE_ILL is low and that pumping increases the flow through the system as more water is induced into the system and discharged through wells. Examining the DSR' indicator through time indicates that for the deep parts of the SE_WI and NE_ILL flow systems, the pumping flux exceeds the natural flux through the deep aquifer system. In both of these mass-balance areas, pumping has caused large drawdowns (fig. 22) and has induced both lateral and vertical flow through the aquifer system to the pumping centers. For NE_ILL the Demand-to-Supply ratio peaked at approximately 7.5, and for SE_WI it peaked at approximately 3.5 (fig. 28B). The time histories of DSR' also reveal changes in the pumping history for the two zones and emphasize the peak in pumping in the 1980s. These results imply that different management schemes might be necessary in the SE_WI and NE_ILL zones than in the rest of the region and that groundwater availability may be limited by different factors in these zones than in the rest of the region.

Drawdown from four pumping centers within the Lake Michigan Basin was examined in fig. 22. Three of these centers are reexamined here with respect to the Base-flow-Reduction Ratio and Demand-to-Supply Ratio to further illustrate the importance of spatial scale on groundwater-availability analysis. The BRR' for the Green Bay pumping area, Waukesha pumping area, and Lansing pumping area are consistent with the values computed for the larger water-budget zones. The maximum BRR' is for the Green Bay area, at 14 (fig. 29A). The Demand-to-Supply Ratio, however, was much higher for these pumping centers than the larger mass-balance zones, peaking at greater than 12 for the Waukesha pumping area (fig. 29B). High values of DSR' may motivate stakeholders to examine local water-budget components and sources of water to wells in order to learn the dynamics of the groundwater system. Such understanding could lead to improved groundwater-availability planning in the region.

One potential problem with the use of these indicators, especially at local spatial scales, is that self-supplied domestic use is not included in the subregional model. Water use in the groundwater-flow model focuses on high-capacity public-supply, irrigation, and industrial wells. High-capacity wells are defined as those that extract on average more than 70 gal/min (100,000 gal/d) over a pumping period. Domestic wells are typically not included in regional models of this scale because they represent a poorly known, diffuse demand on the model and because much of the water removed by domestic wells is returned to the system through onsite septic systems or similar wastewater disposal methods. Because the accounting for these withdrawals and return flow to the groundwater system is not in place, H_{in} and h'_{in} cannot be estimated very well. The indicators also should be used with caution. Low values of these indicators do not necessarily mean that there are not groundwater-availability issues. For example, the DSR' for the Lansing pumping area is quite low for the entire simulation time, but the Lansing area did experience excessive draw-down leading to degradation of water quality in the 1960s. To mitigate this drawdown, the demands in the area were spread out by the use of additional wells, and system recovered. This episode is not shown through the indicators. Conversely, high values of DSR' may not mean that the pumping is not sustainable. Pumping can induce flow from both the broader

region and adjacent aquifers. The aquifers in the Great Lakes Basin appear to be able to capture enough water to stabilize drawdown fairly quickly, and, although the drawdowns are quite large, they might not pose a major constraint on ground-water availability. The indicator might highlight potential areas of groundwater availability limitations, but the actual dynamics of the system and local effects of withdrawals must be determined.

Despite these caveats, these summary indicators may be useful in contrasting different locations within the modeled area, thereby highlighting differences in the region that might warrant attention for more detailed water-availability analysis. The indicators may reveal areas at risk for water competition, conflict, or shortages from relatively small decreases in the supply of water to the area, increases in use, or changes in how local communities value instream flows or make decisions regarding development and water resources. The indicators also may be more intuitive to decisionmakers or stakeholders than maps showing drawdown or source of water to well-water budgets.

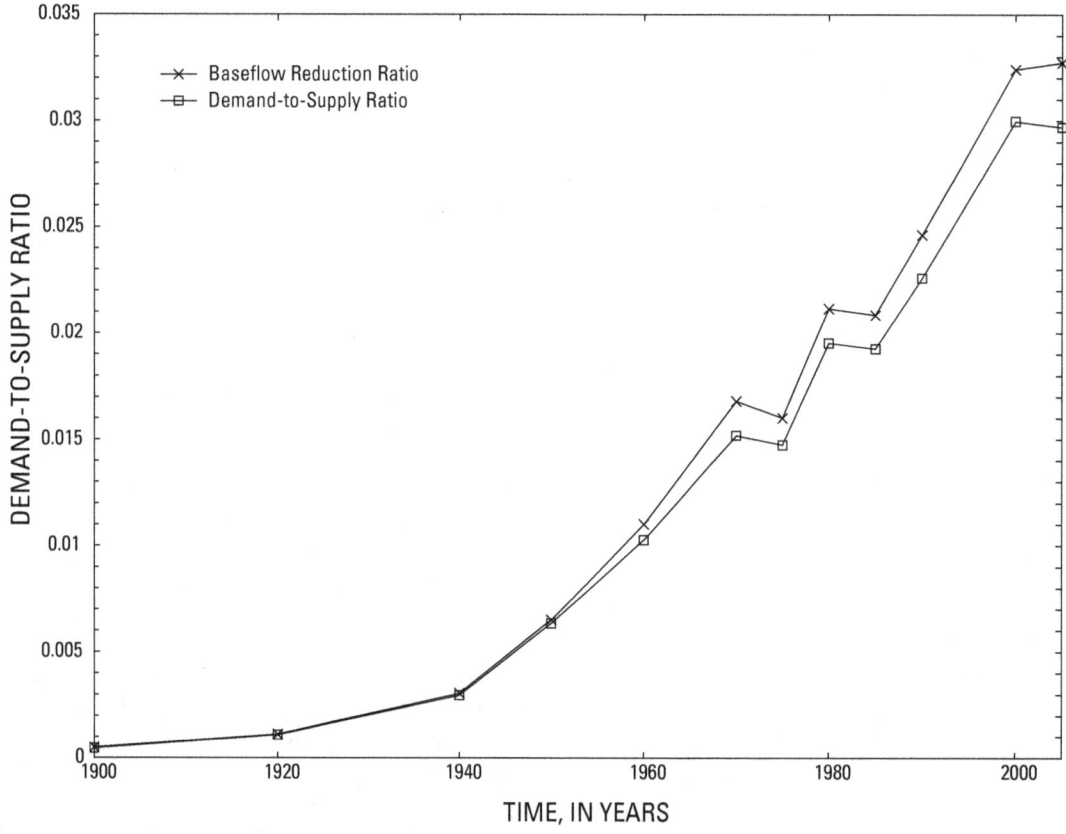

Figure 27. Demand-to-Supply Ratio and Base-flow-Reduction Ratio for the Lake Michigan Basin aquifer system as computed by use of the Lake Michigan Basin groundwater-flow model.

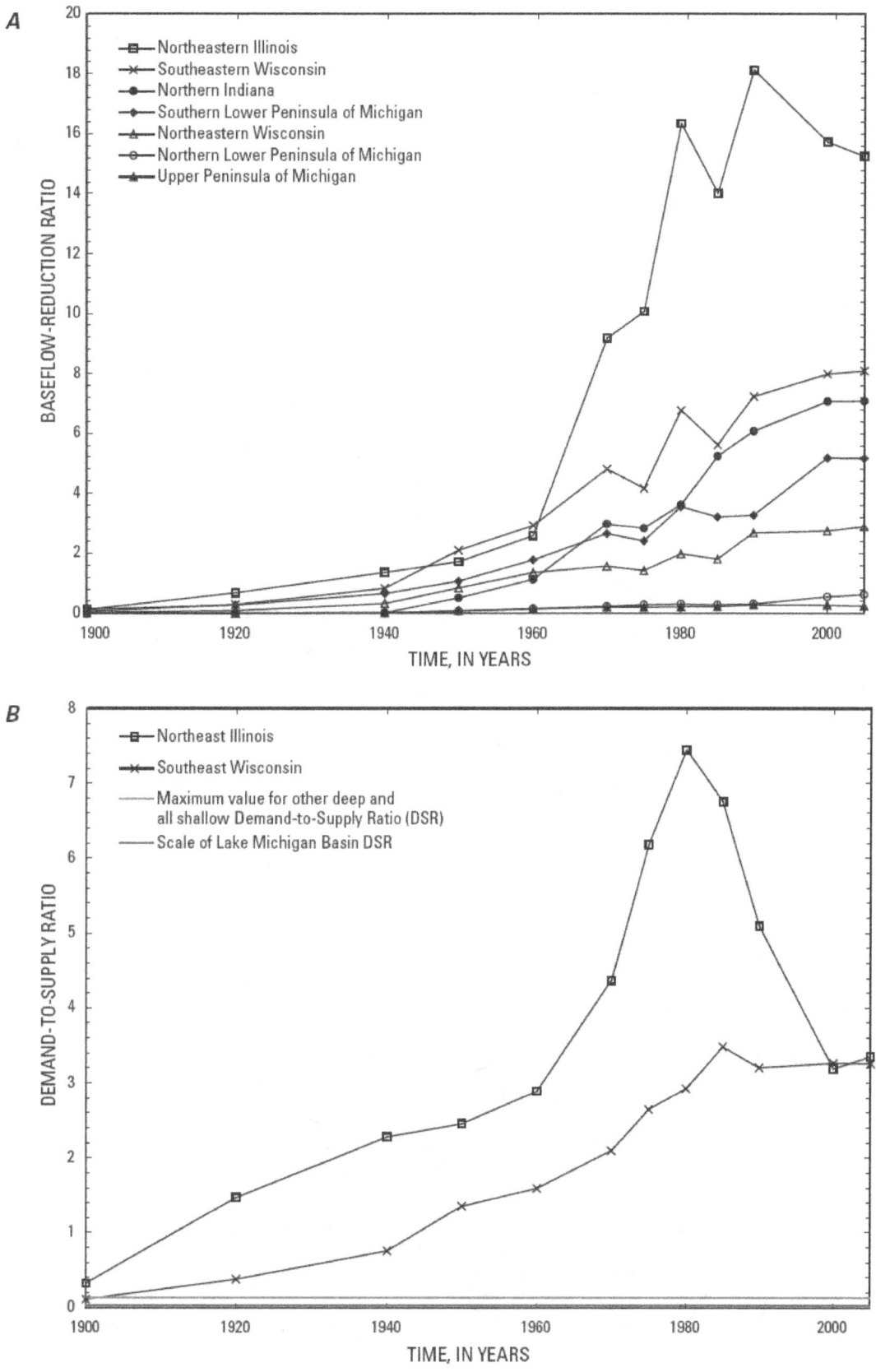

Figure 28. Indictors computed for the water-budget zones for the Lake Michigan Basin groundwater-flow model. *A,* Base-flow-Reduction Ratio for shallow aquifers. *B,* Demand-to-Supply Ratio (DSR) for deep aquifers.

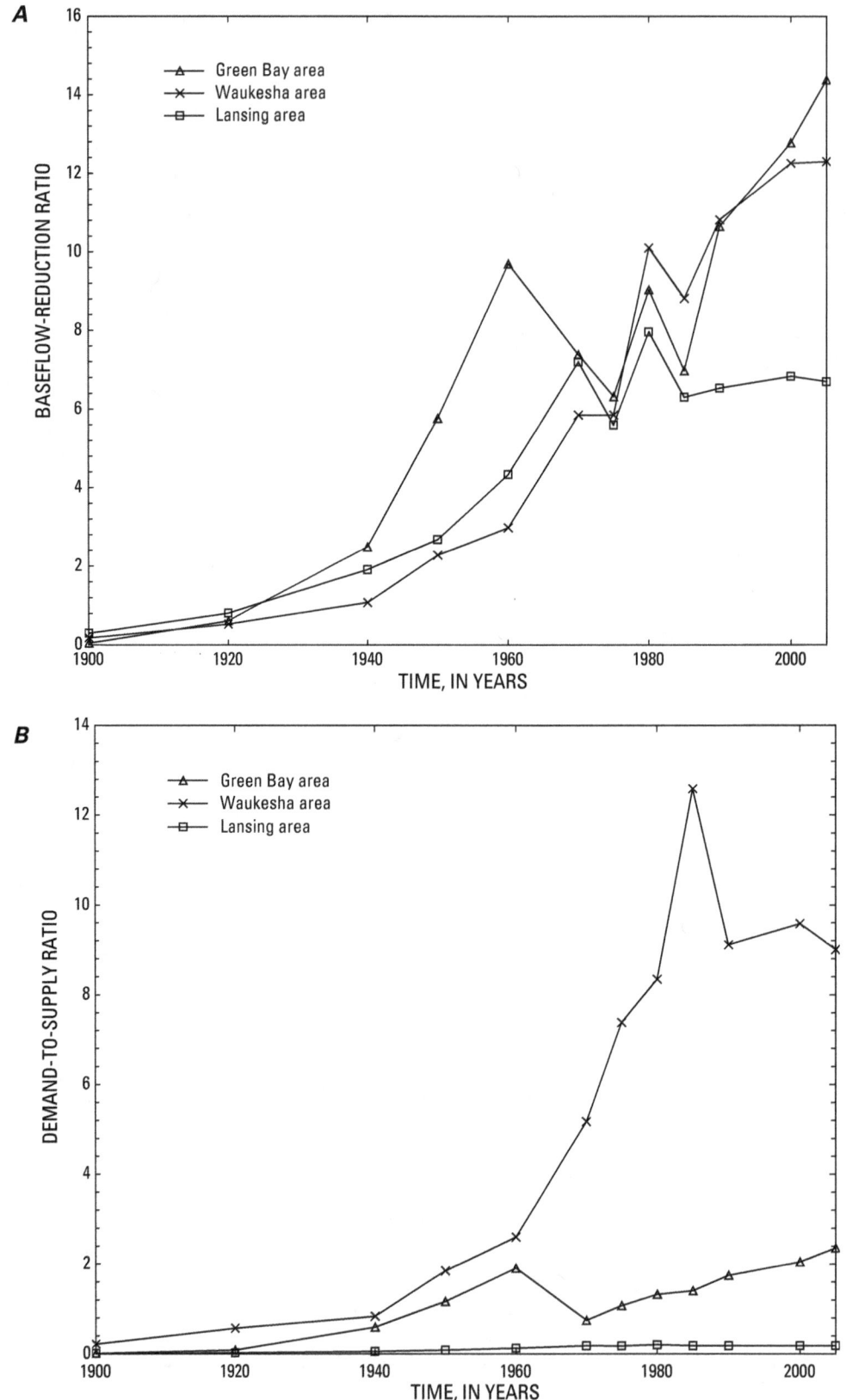

Figure 29.   Indicators computed at selected pumping areas within the Lake Michigan Basin groundwater-flow model. *A*, Base-flow-Reduction Ratio for shallow aquifers. *B*, Demand-to-Supply Ratio for deep aquifers.

Groundwater-Flow Model and Groundwater Availability

Analysis of groundwater-flow model results has illustrated the two major responses of the system that may constrain groundwater availability: drawdown and base-flow reduction. Once identified through field observations and described by applied groundwater-flow modeling, management decisions may be made to mitigate potential negative impacts of these responses. Drawdown can lead to increased energy costs, excessive consolidation of aquifer material leading to undesired land subsidence, interference between high-capacity wells and other users, and migration of poor-quality water into the aquifer (Freeze and Cherry, 1979). Large base-flow reductions can adversely impact ecosystems or other riparian users and may raise issues of sustainability. Drawdown may be shown through maps of model results and field observations or indicated by high values of DSR'. Base-flow reduction may be shown through mass-balance results and the BRR'. Indicators may be helpful in summarizing technical information for stakeholders.

From a management perspective, focusing the analysis on local watersheds within the modeled region to identify those that might have water-availability issues is often necessary. The scale of the modeling, however, precludes such an analysis on local scales. The fluxes estimated for a small number of grid cells will not accurately portray the hydraulic or hydrologic conditions for individual watersheds and, as discussed previously, many local removals and returns are not included in the subregional model. To address this limitation, methods to extend the subregional analysis to the local scale were tested within the Great Lakes Basin Pilot, and these methods and the results of application of the methods are discussed later in this report. The local-scale application also integrates local groundwater analysis with the surface-water analysis discussed in the next section.

A final use of the Lake Michigan Basin groundwater-flow model is as a forecasting tool to examine the potential effects of future changes in water use and climate. The SWB method was used to estimate recharge under a climate-change scenario generated by using an atmosphere-ocean coupled general circulation model (AOGCM) (Maurer and others, 2002; Hayhoe and others, 2008). The particular AOGCM used provided potential temperature and precipitation realizations on a daily basis from 1960 to 2099. The data output from the AOGCM reflects potential conditions under an assumed scenario of high global greenhouse gas emissions (A1fi scenario) (Hayhoe and others, 2008). For the long stress periods relevant to this subregional model, the changes in recharge are not very large, and changes to the system would be akin to the changes observed in the original 13-stress-period simulation. If recharge is varied slightly, the stream base flow received from the aquifer responds fairly quickly, and there is a slight adjustment in the source of water to wells. Climate-change simulations appear to be more relevant in the model domain when local stream response on shorter time scales is considered. Such

simulations are presented later in this report where local-scale issues are discussed.

Two different projections were simulated. The first is a "no future growth scenario," and it is referred to as a "staycast." This scenario is used to simulate how the system will continue to change if 2005 conditions stay constant, and it serves as a useful baseline because accurate predictions of future water use are quite difficult. The staycast shows the potential for the delay in response of the aquifer to pumping as the system shifts from change in storage to capture, and it illustrates how long it could take for the system to reach equilibrium with current imposed conditions. Future water-use projections, referred to as "forecasts", were developed for the model region independent of effects of climate variability or change. These projections were assembled by using information from local and regional planning agencies (Buchwald and others, 2010). The water-use projections were used to develop two new stress periods, 2006–20 and 2021–40, and the model was used to forecast the response of the groundwater system to the projected water use. The recharge used in the both the staycast and forecast simulations was the same as used for the models for the last two model stress periods (1991–2005), thereby omitting climate change as a driver on the system.

Model results for both the staycast and the forecast indicate recovery in parts of the different aquifer systems but additional drawdown elsewhere. Changes in the shallow system are fairly small, 10 ft or less, for the whole model domain (fig. 30). Changes in the deep bedrock aquifer system are greater and more coherent compared to the changes in the shallow, Quaternary system (fig. 31). In the staycast simulations, water levels in the deep bedrock aquifer system are predicted to recover in the Chicago/Milwaukee area of the model because 2005 pumping stress in this area of the model is less than the maximum withdrawals imposed before 2000. Some drawdown is predicted in the deep bedrock aquifer system on the eastern side of Lake Michigan in the staycast. In the forecast, however, future use in Wisconsin from the deep bedrock aquifer system was predicted to decrease or stay at 2005 conditions, but use in Illinois southwest of Chicago was predicted to increase from 2005 levels. These water-use projections lead to forecasted water levels that recover in Wisconsin and decrease in both Illinois and Michigan. In the deep bedrock aquifer system, the predicted recovery or drawdown is much larger than for the Quaternary system, and forecasted changes for this system exceed 100 ft on the western side of Lake Michigan.

Surface Water

The surface-water characteristic of primary interest in the Great Lakes Basin pilot study was streamflow, which is a major component of regional water budgets for the Great Lakes (tables 3 and 4; fig. 17) and a critical factor in assessing water availability on subregional or local scales. Streamflow is commonly characterized by use of a streamflow statistic,

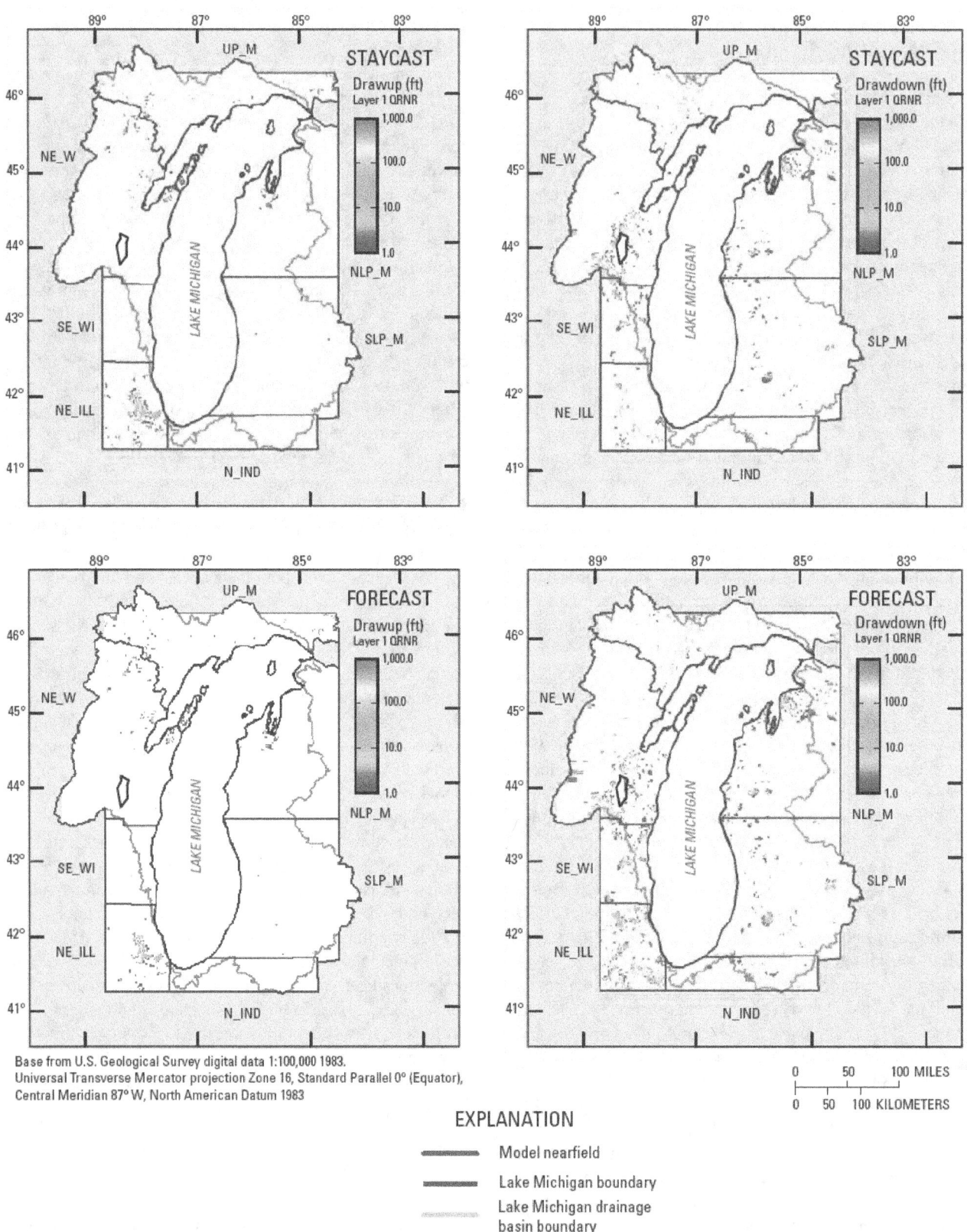

Base from U.S. Geological Survey digital data 1:100,000 1983.
Universal Transverse Mercator projection Zone 16, Standard Parallel 0° (Equator),
Central Meridian 87° W, North American Datum 1983

EXPLANATION

Model nearfield

Lake Michigan boundary

Lake Michigan drainage
basin boundary

Figure 30.   Staycast and forecast simulations for 2005–40 showing recovery and drawdown in the Quaternary aquifer system, in feet, in response to continued pumping at 2005 rates (staycast) and projected pumping rates for 2005–40 (forecast) (from Buchwald and others, 2010).

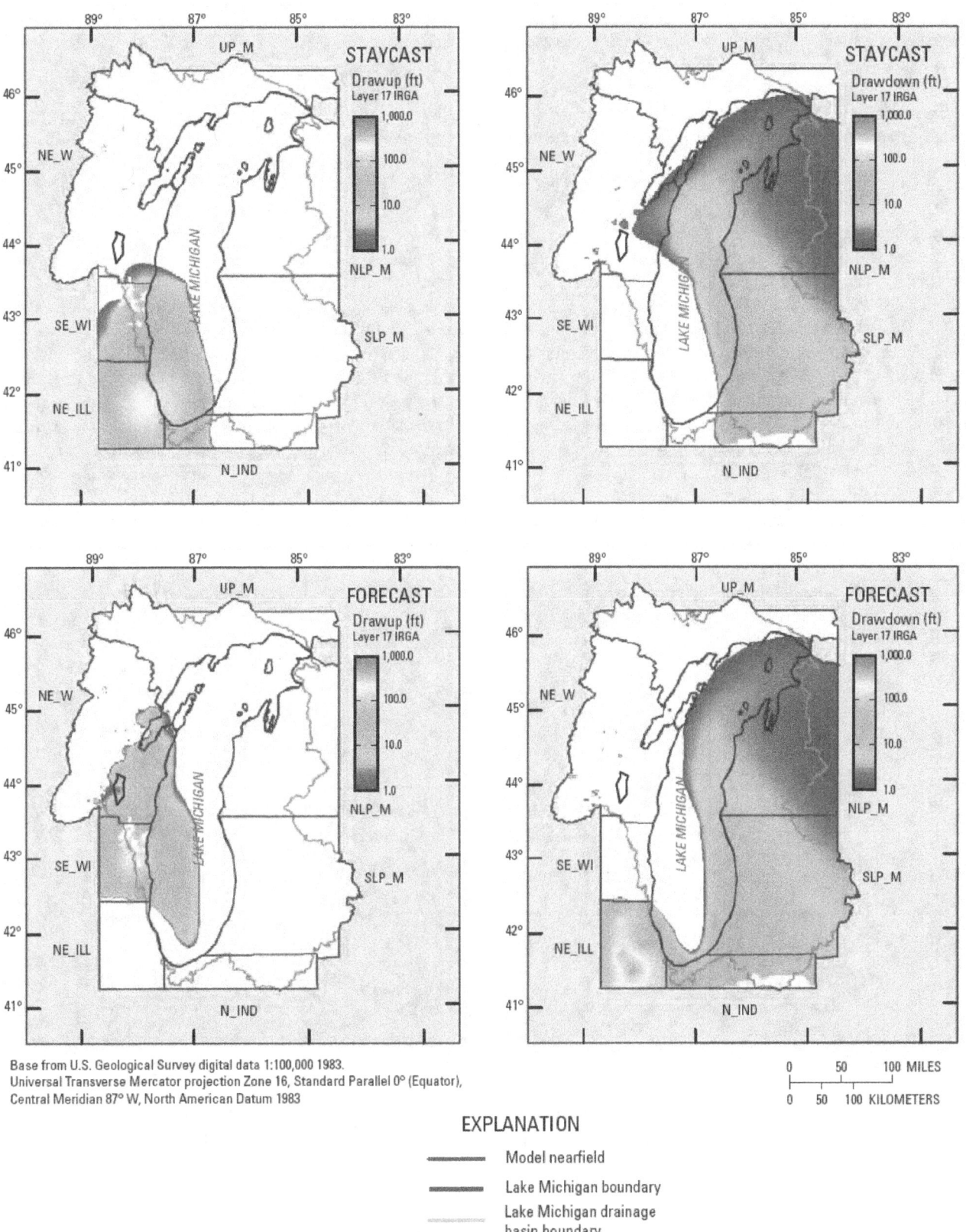

Base from U.S. Geological Survey digital data 1:100,000 1983.
Universal Transverse Mercator projection Zone 16, Standard Parallel 0° (Equator),
Central Meridian 87° W, North American Datum 1983

EXPLANATION

———— Model nearfield

———— Lake Michigan boundary

———— Lake Michigan drainage
basin boundary

Figure 31. Staycast and forecast simulations for 2005–40 showing recovery and drawdown in the Cambrian-Ordovician aquifer system, in feet, in response to continued pumping at 2005 rates (staycast) and projected pumping rates for 2005–40 (forecast) (from Buchwald and others, 2010).

such as monthly mean flow. The difficulty with a streamflow statistic for this study, however, is that a summary statistic fails to characterize the temporal variability in the streamflow resource. In this analysis, therefore, streamflow is character- ized by a time series of monthly flow estimates rather than a summary statistic. For water-availability studies, flow esti- mates are needed to define not only the desired ecological flows at all reaches but also the quantity of water available to attain these ecological flows (Poff and others, 1997; Arthing- ton and others, 2006; The Nature Conservancy, 2008).

Under the Great Lakes Basin Pilot, a new method was developed to estimate monthly streamflow and water yields. The new method, Analysis of Flows In Networks of CHannels (AFINCH; Holtschlag, 2009) produces estimates of monthly flows in reach segments and water yields from catchments defined by the National Hydrography Dataset (NHD) with value-added attributes through the NHD*Plus* suite of data (Bondelid and others, 2006). NHD*Plus* reach segments aver- age about 1 mi in length, and catchment areas average about 1 mi². Water yield is defined as the incremental flow in a reach segment divided by the local drainage area. Yields are used because drainage area explains much of the variation in streamflow: streams with larger drainage areas tend to have higher flows. To explain more of the variability in streamflow in the region and to link landscape characteristics such as land use, land cover, slope or soils to flows, the observed flow in a reach segment is divided by its drainage area and the resulting yield is correlated to landscape characteristics.

In AFINCH, water yields are estimated by user-defined multiple-regression equations on the basis of measured flows at streamgages and monthly climatic data and land-use characteristics. One important feature of AFINCH is that the measured flows may be adjusted for water use if detailed water-use data are available for the area of interest. Estimated water yields are multiplied by corresponding catchment areas to compute estimated streamflows, and these streamflows are accumulated downstream through the NHD*Plus* network. Esti- mated flows at streamgages are constrained to match measured flows by adjusting upstream estimates of water yields. Flows are conserved within AFINCH, and AFINCH also auto- matically adapts to annual changes in the active streamgage network. AFINCH integrates monthly streamflow, water-use, and climatic data with land-use data. Annual changes in the set of active streamgages and the subsequent alterations in the incremental areas and land-use characteristics assigned to each gage and land are incorporated (fig. 32). In the initial development of AFINCH, monthly streamflow data were obtained from USGS streamgages, and monthly climatic data were obtained from PRISM (Parameter-elevation Regressions on Independent Slopes Model) dataset (Daly and others, 2002;

AFINCH Design

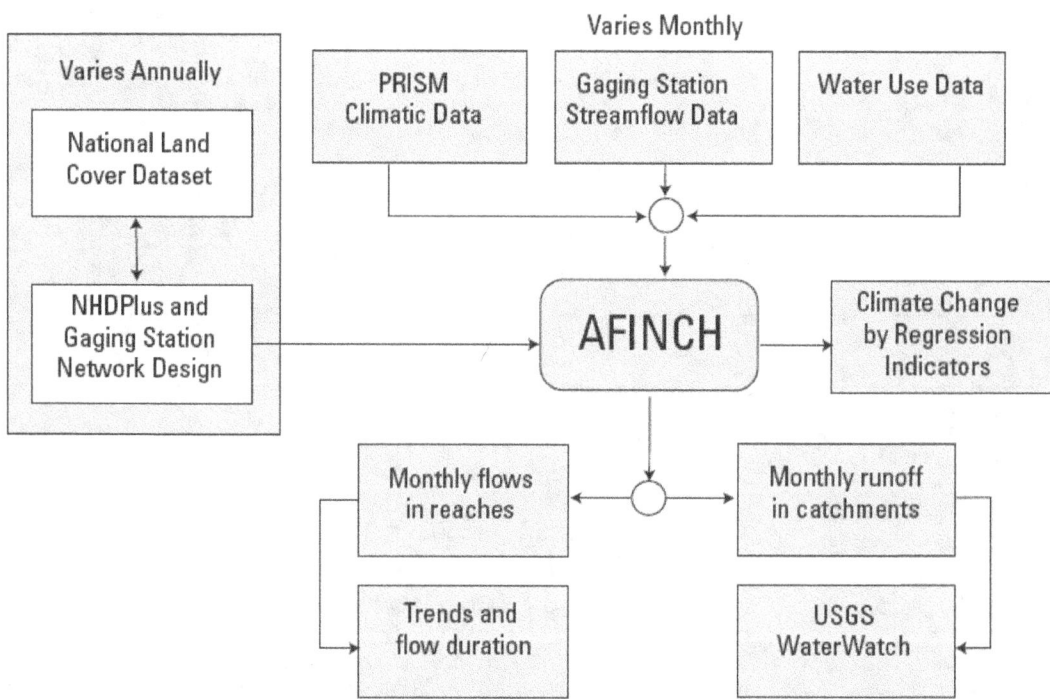

Figure 32.   Schematic of AFINCH data sources and analysis results.

see also *http://www.prism.oregonstate.edu/*). Land-use characteristics, based on the 1992 National Land Cover Database (NLCD), were used for development and initial testing (Vogelmann and others, 2001; see also *http://landcover.usgs.gov*). Limited water-use data were available for the area of study.

Streamgages in a monitoring network commonly measure flows that have been measured previously at one or more upstream gages. This remeasurement creates a spatial correlation structure that is not consistent with the independence among response variables that is assumed in multiple-regression analysis. To reduce this dependence among monthly flows at streamgages, incremental flows and drainage areas are computed. Incremental flows represent the change in flow that occurred since it was last measured at upstream gages. Incremental flows at the most upstream gage in a monitoring network equals the total measured flow. Similarly, incremental drainage areas represent the total drainage area minus the drainage areas of any upstream gages.

Within AFINCH, measured monthly flows at streamgages may be adjusted by specified monthly water-use information at upstream reach segments before the monthly regression equations are developed. Specified monthly water withdrawals are added to measured flows at downstream gages to better reflect natural flows. Similarly, specified flow augmentations, such as interbasin transfers to a stream or wastewater discharges, are subtracted from measured flows at downstream gages. Measured monthly flows at streamgages are termed "apparent flows" in AFINCH; measured flows that have been adjusted on the basis of specified water-use data to better represent natural flow conditions are referred to as "adjusted flows."

Monthly water yields, derived from streamflow data, were related to monthly climatic and land-use data through a set of annual multiple-regression equations to produce estimates of monthly water yields from NHD*Plus* catchments. The time series of annual regression parameter estimates provides a basis for assessing possible changes in responses between individual explanatory variables and water yields, which may be associated with climate change or variability. Monthly water-yield estimates are computed for each catchment on the basis of the annual regression equations and then multiplied by the corresponding drainage areas to estimate monthly flows. Flows are accumulated downstream from catchments to estimate streamflow in all stream segments defined within NHD*Plus*. At stream segments with active streamgages, upstream estimated water yields are adjusted so that resultant flows match measured flows.

In addition to estimation of water yields and flows during periods of streamflow measurement, AFINCH can be used for prediction. Monthly water yields can be predicted by use of predicted climate variables that are specified in the regression equations by assuming that the water-yield response to land use, and land-use characteristics themselves, are invariant with time. This assumption, however, is difficult to substantiate, so the resulting predicted yields and flows may have limited utility as predicted climatic variables diverge from observed climatic conditions.

The methods developed were applied only to a subregion of the Great Lakes Basin because AFINCH requires that the NHD*Plus* datasets accurately route flow through the stream network. A small percentage of the network required editing; however, complete editing of the entire basin was beyond the scope of the project. Application development, rather than implementation, was stressed in this aspect of the Great Lakes Basin Pilot. The hydrologic subregion used in the example application was 0405 (fig. 33), and results from this subregion are used to illustrate use of AFINCH.

The AFINCH computer program includes visualization tools to help the analyst identify anomalies in water yields (for details, see Holtschlag, 2009). In particular, apparent incremental monthly water yields are plotted by year for each month and streamgage in the analysis to help the user identify anomalies that might be related to unspecified water-use or streamflow data error. In figure 34, the atypically low water yields at streamgage 04106400 (West Fork Portage Creek at Kalamazoo, Mich.) in 2000 shown by the solid white color for the months of March through June indicates that the stream is either losing water or not gaining water at nearly the same rate at other parts of the basin. Because streams do not commonly lose water in Michigan from natural causes, and because this gage data pattern does not match the seasonal patterns for the other gages shown in the figure, this anomaly may indicate unspecified water withdrawals in the area gaged by 04106400.

AFINCH provides an interactive environment for specifying explanatory variables in regression equations for estimating adjusted monthly water yields. When the analyst is satisfied with the form of the regression, AFINCH computes constrained and unconstrained estimates of water yields for all catchments and flows in all reach segments defined within NHD*Plus* within the specified period of analysis. The results of these analyses are written to output files, which can be analyzed further within AFINCH or with other applications.

Estimated hydrographs based on monthly median values can be generated for any NHD*Plus* reach segment (fig. 35). For the segment identified by reachcode 04050001000590, low flows are noted in water years 1984, 1988, 1996, and 1999, and high flows noted for water years 1985 and 1986. The length of the hydrograph is determined by the period of analysis specified by the AFINCH user. These hydrographs may be used directly in assessing flow in the selected reach segment, or the time series of monthly data may be further evaluated within AFINCH to examine the statistical characteristics of the hydrograph.

Monthly flow-duration curves show the likelihood that flows of various magnitudes will be equaled or exceeded (fig. 36). Monthly flow-duration curves have a similar shape as daily flow-duration curves, which are commonly used in flow-duration analyses, except near the upper and lower limits of the flow-duration curve. In this case, AFINCH estimates fill in the duration curve for a streamgage that operated during only part of the analysis period of water years 1971–2000.

AFINCH-estimated water yield may be mapped to visualize the distribution of water yields for the area of interest

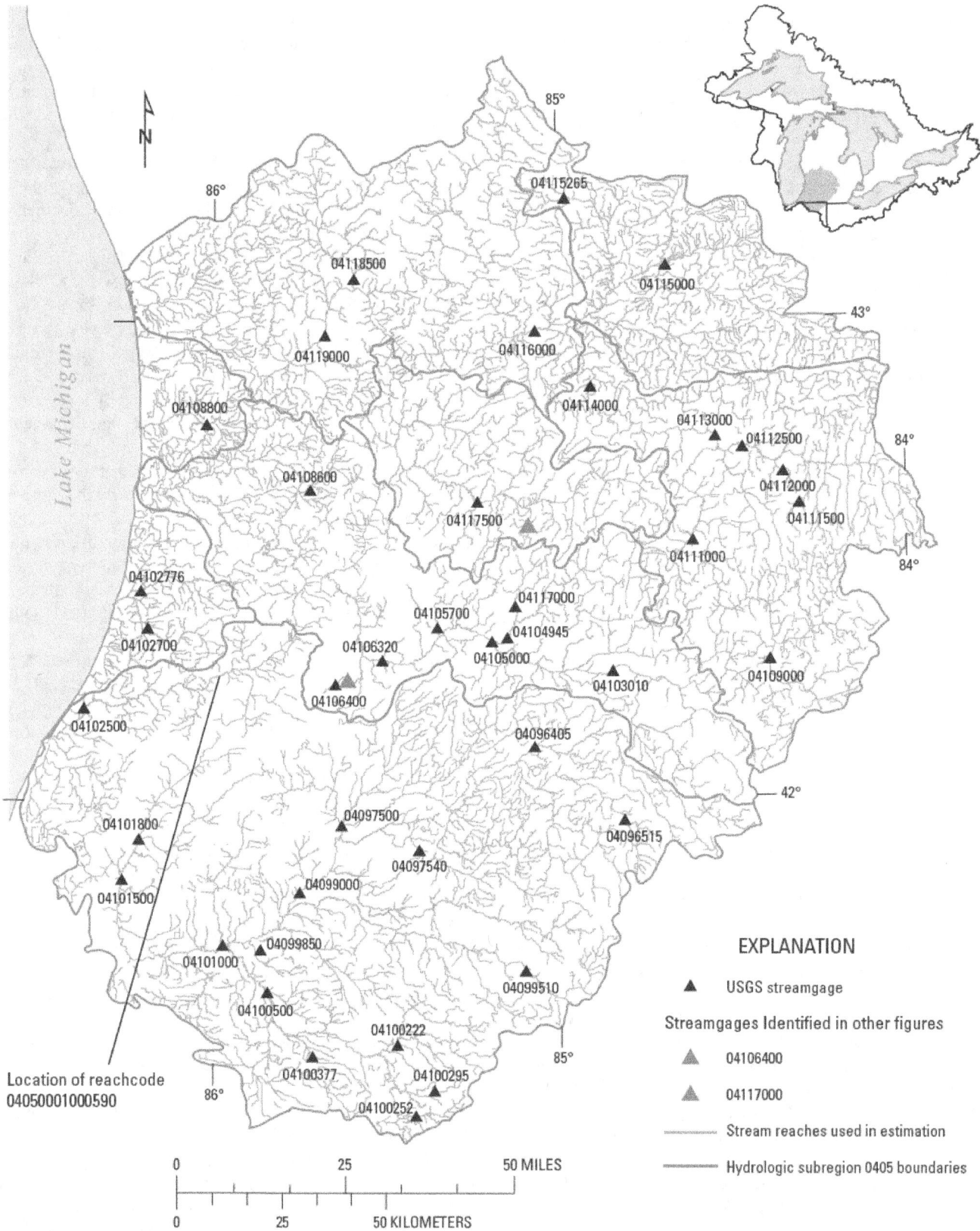

Figure 33. NHDPlus stream reaches and USGS streamgage locations in hydrologic subregion 0405 used in AFINCH estimation. Locations of streamgages and ungaged stream segment referenced in examples are noted.

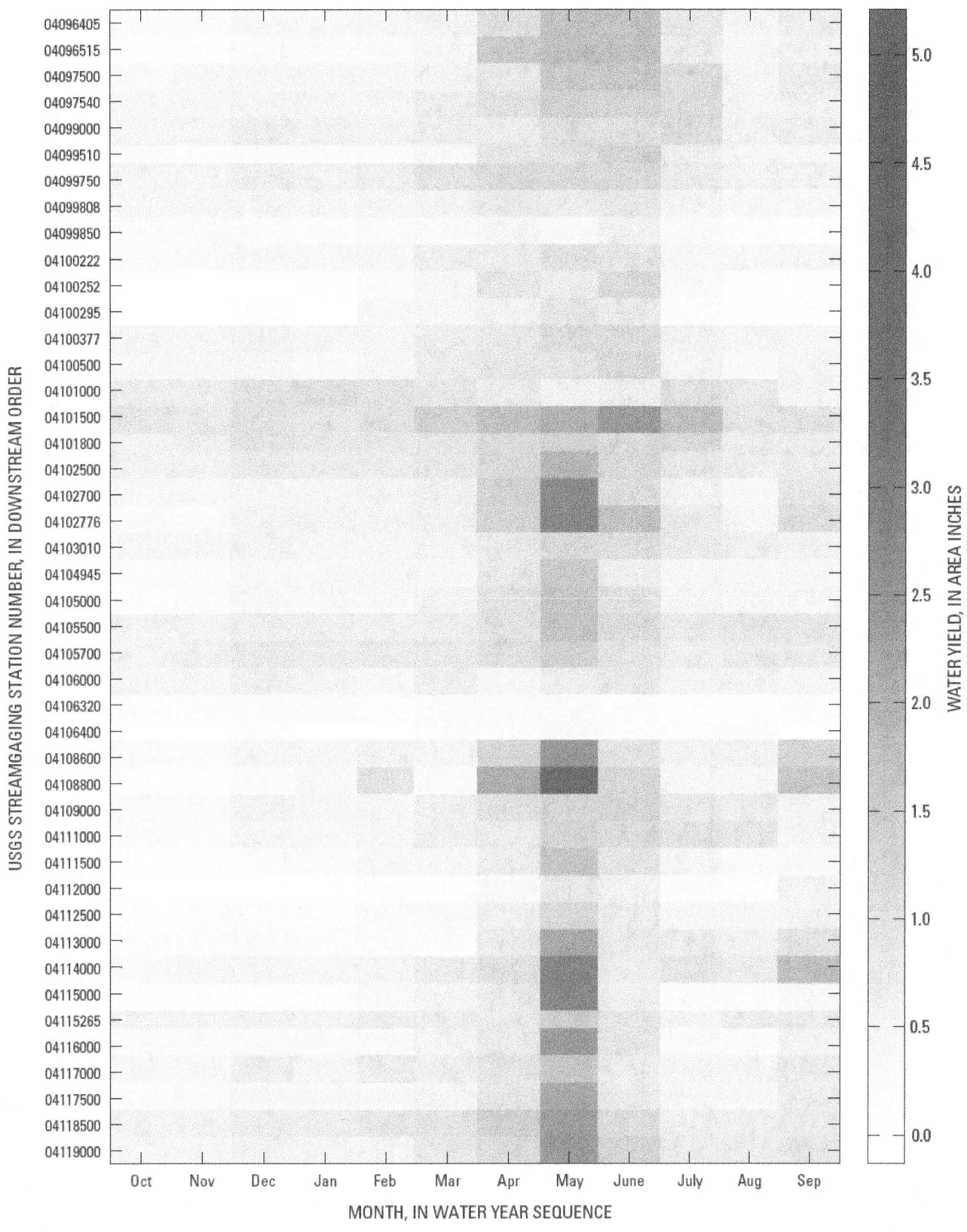

Figure 34. Apparent incremental yield at streamgages within subregion 0405 (graph allows AFINCH user to identify potential anomalies in the regression and focus analysis to discover the reason for the anomalies; from Holtschlag, 2009).

(Holtschlag, 2009). As an example, constrained water yields in May 2000 in southern catchments tend to be lower than yields in the northern part of the hydrologic subregion (fig. 37). This yield map shows where streamflow is generated, so areas of high yield would be expected to have higher streamflows. Higher streamflows may be associated with lower stream temperatures in the summer and warmer stream temperatures in the winter due to the moderating effect of groundwater input on the stream. Water-availability decisions may depend on the impact of water withdrawals on ecological flows; therefore, knowledge of the distribution of flows in a watershed may be important for sound management decisions.

Accumulated monthly flows also may be mapped (Holtschlag, 2009). The accumulated flows for October 2003 (fig. 38), highlight the variation of flow in the hydrologic subregion and the density of the stream network used in the estimation. Headwaters and small streams with flows less than 5 ft³/s are common, and larger river systems, including the St. Joseph River, Grand River, and Kalamazoo River in the western part of the subregion being tested are clearly visible.

The estimated flows for each reach discharging to a Great Lake may be used to compute the monthly surface-water

runoff to the Great Lakes. Surface-water runoff to the Great Lakes is a major component of the regional water budget (fig. 17; tables 3 and 4), and generating more accurate estimates of this part of the water budget will improve lake-level fore-casting and understanding of the system. AFINCH has the potential to greatly improve these estimates because of the mass-balance constraints inherent in the approach and because it produces both estimates and uncertainties. Knowledge of estimated uncertainties in monthly flows can be incorporated in subsequent analysis to understand the overall uncertainty in the monthly mass balance for the Great Lakes. Current work with AFINCH is focused on editing the NHD*Plus* datasets for the Great Lakes Basin to allow for

- application of the modeling tools,

- study of water-use data to define data requirements and availability,

- evaluation of options to incorporate miscellaneous measurements into the set of tools available to the user, and

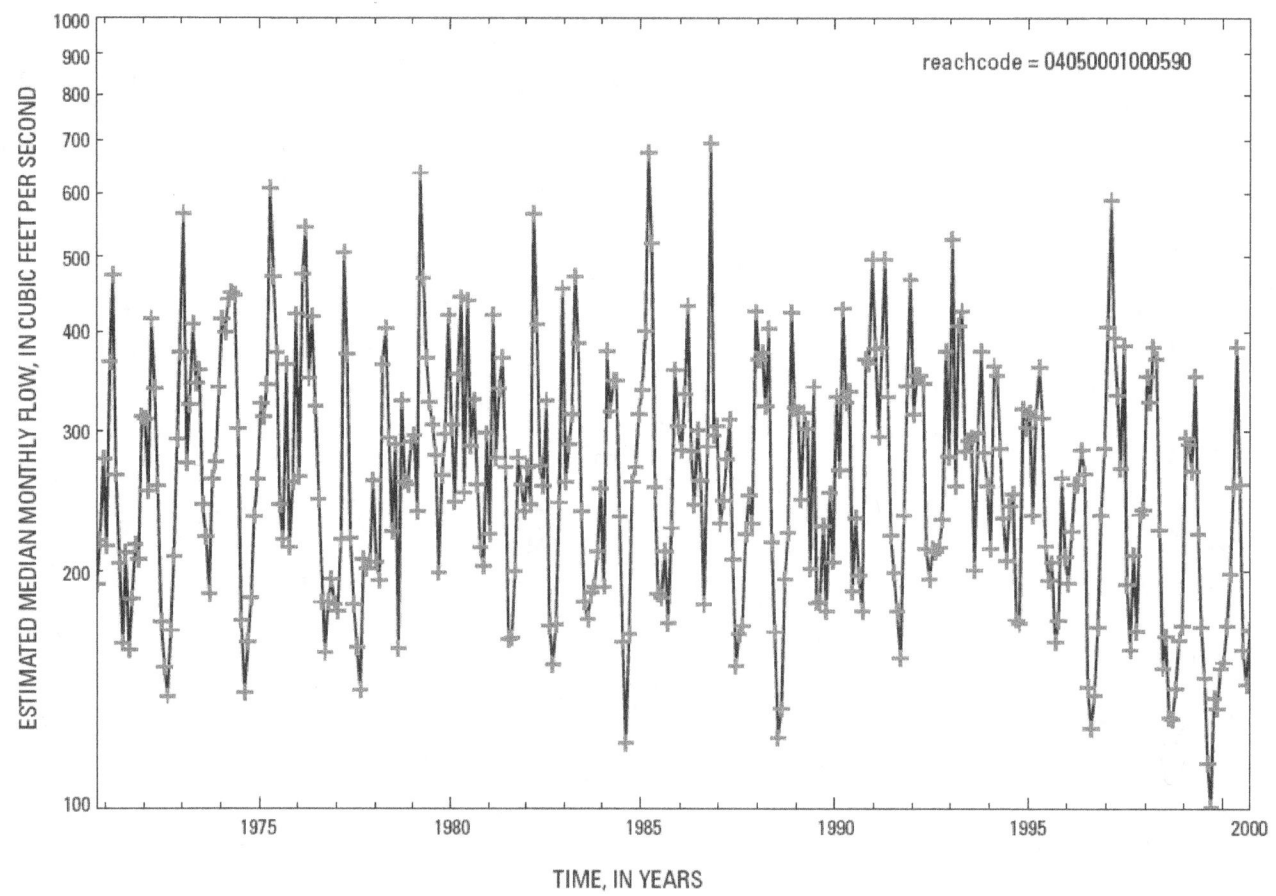

Figure 35. Estimated monthly hydrograph for water years 1970–2000 generated with AFINCH for an ungaged stream in hydrologic subregion 0405; reachcode = 0405001000590, flow in cubic feet per second.

- refinement of temporal aspects of the regression methods to allow the system to consider information gained by gages that are active at times other than the current month of interest.

Water Withdrawals and Water Use

Just as the use of general consumptive-use coefficients for broad sectors may not yield accurate estimates of consumptive water use, the practice of considering only annual average use or water withdrawals may not be adequate to support water-resources management decisions. Data were

available from various sectors for monthly water withdrawals and return flows three states that are partly in the Great Lakes Basin—Ohio, Indiana, and Wisconsin. These data were evaluated to determine the monthly variation in water withdrawal and consumptive use. In addition to monthly variation, the water-withdrawal trends were compared between sectors and between states (Shaffer, 2009).

All water-withdrawal sectors examined by Shaffer (2009) exhibited variations in monthly withdrawals and consumptive use (fig. 39A–F). As expected, the largest percentage change in withdrawal during the year was for irrigation, with most withdrawals occurring in the summer and very little for the rest of the year (fig. 39A–E). The consistency of the trend of

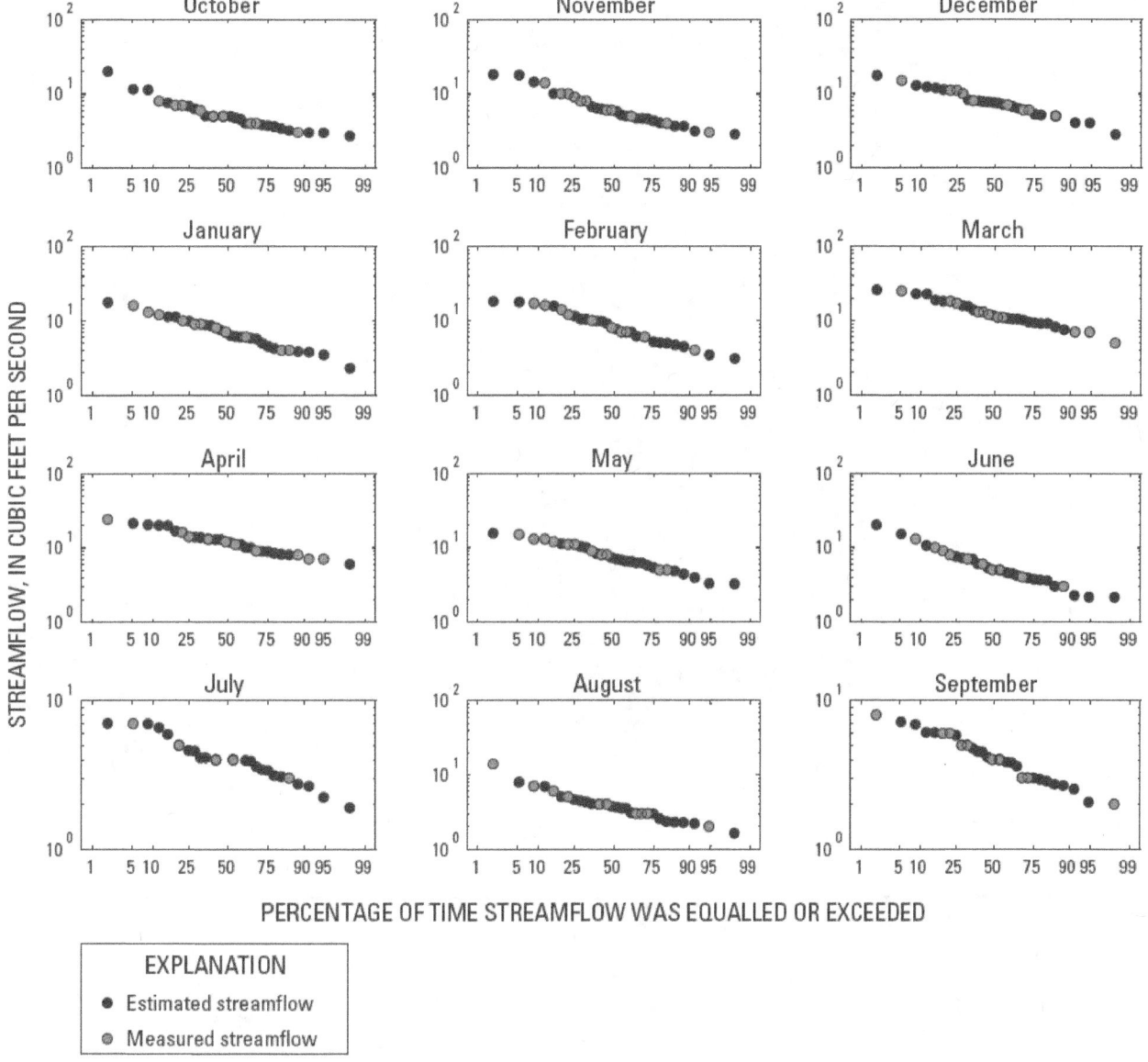

Figure 36.   Monthly flow-duration curves for water years 1971–2000 with measured streamflows for water years 1971–75 and 1995–2000 at USGS streamgage 04117000, Quaker Brook near Nashville, Mich. (from Holtschlag, 2009).

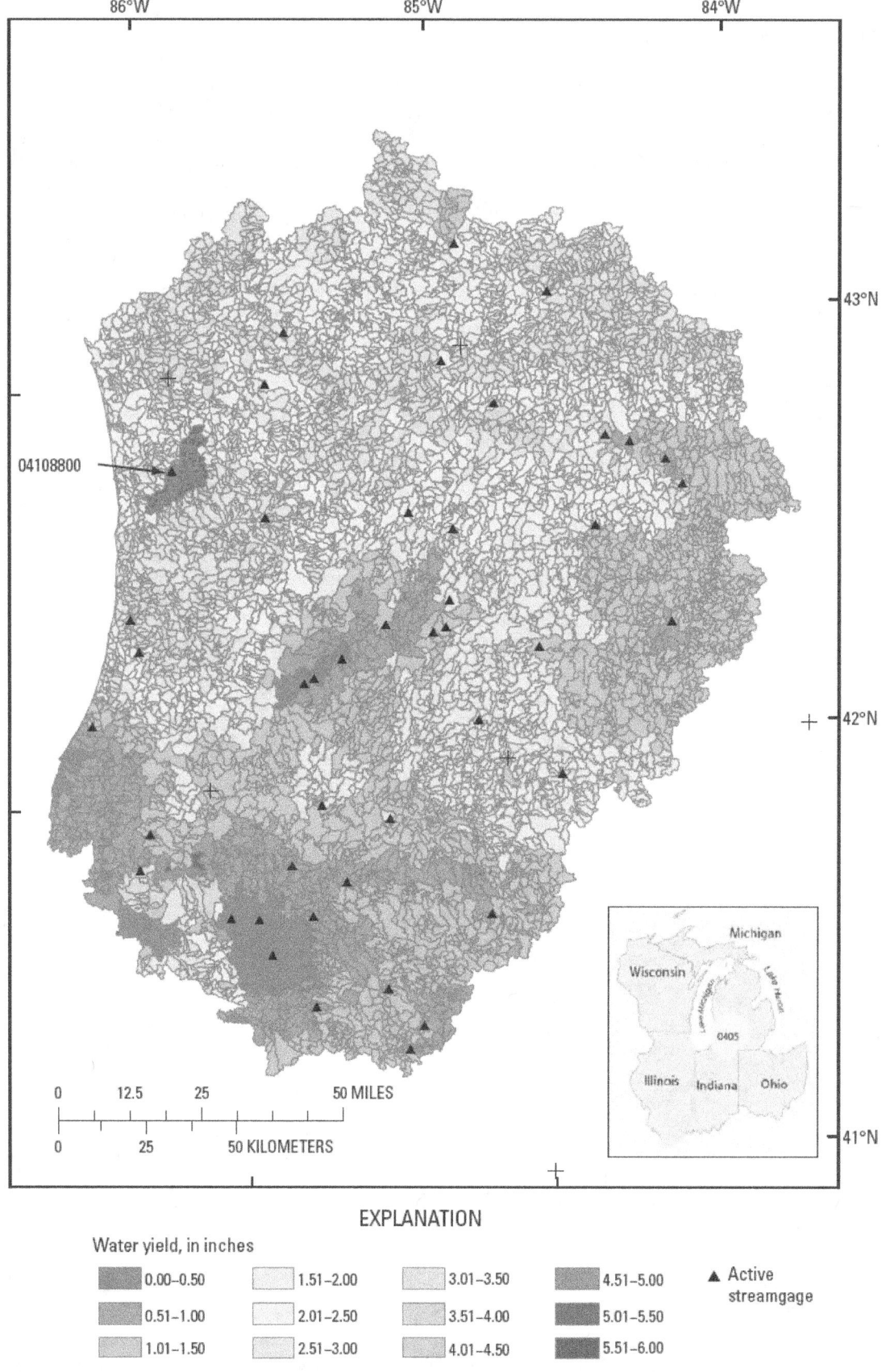

Figure 37. Constrained estimates of water yield for watersheds from the NHDPlus dataset for hydrologic subregion 0405 for May 2000, developed by using AFINCH (from Holtschlag, 2009).

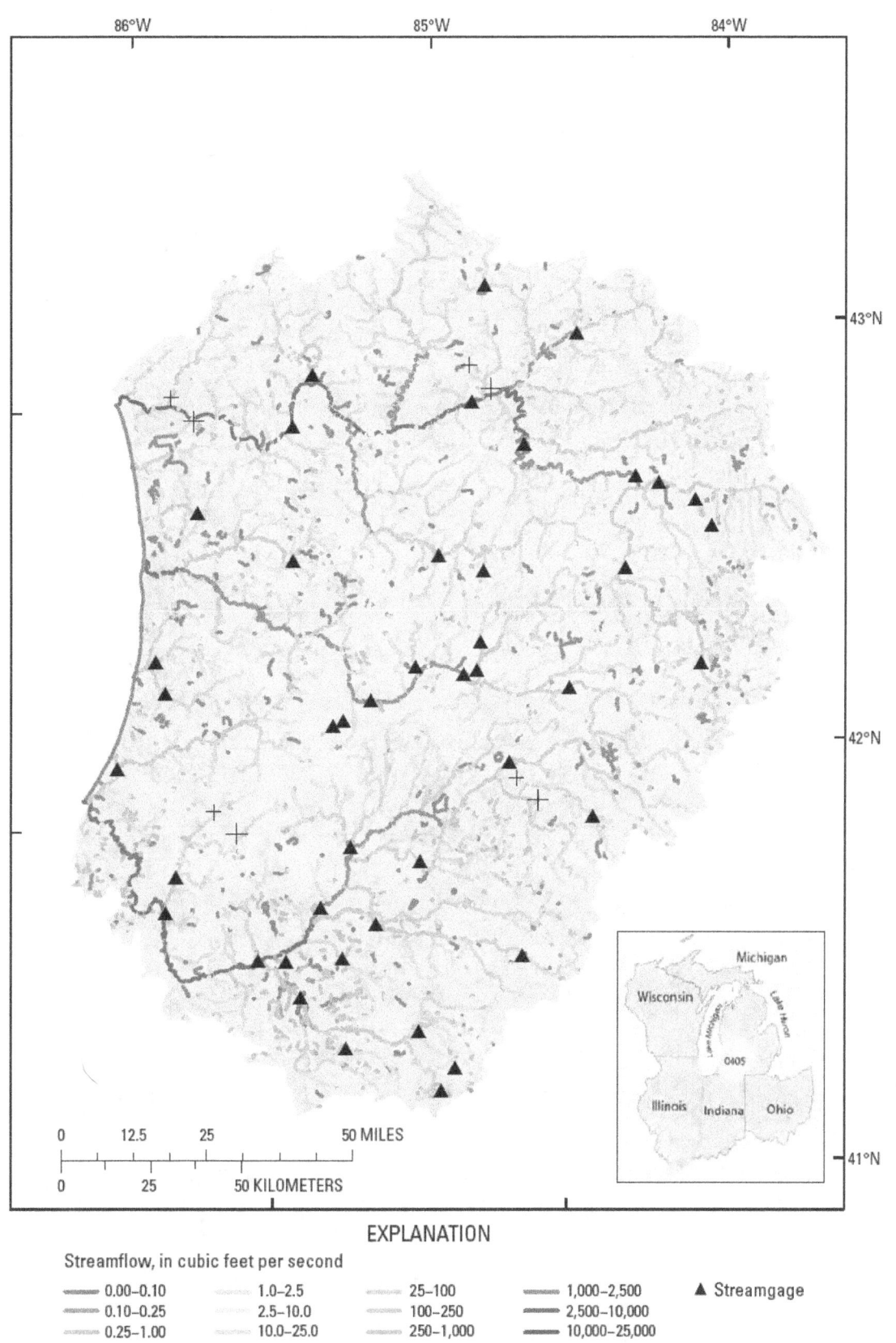

Figure 38.   Constrained estimates of accumulated flows for stream segments in hydrologic subregion 0405 for October 2003, developed by using AFINCH (from Holtschlag, 2009).

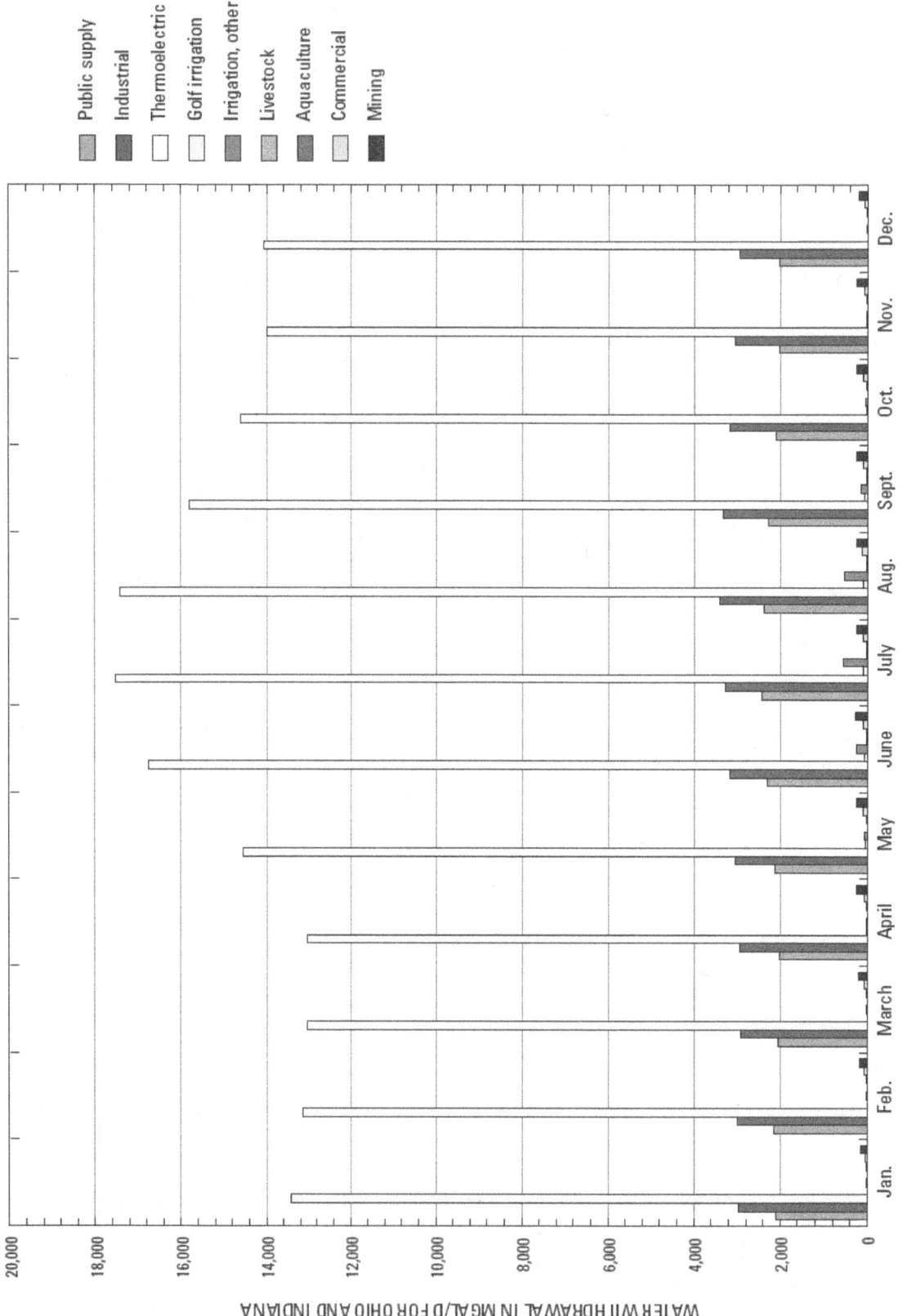

Figure 39.   Average monthly water withdrawals for water-use sectors for Ohio and Indiana, 1999–2005, in million gallons per day. *A,* All sectors.

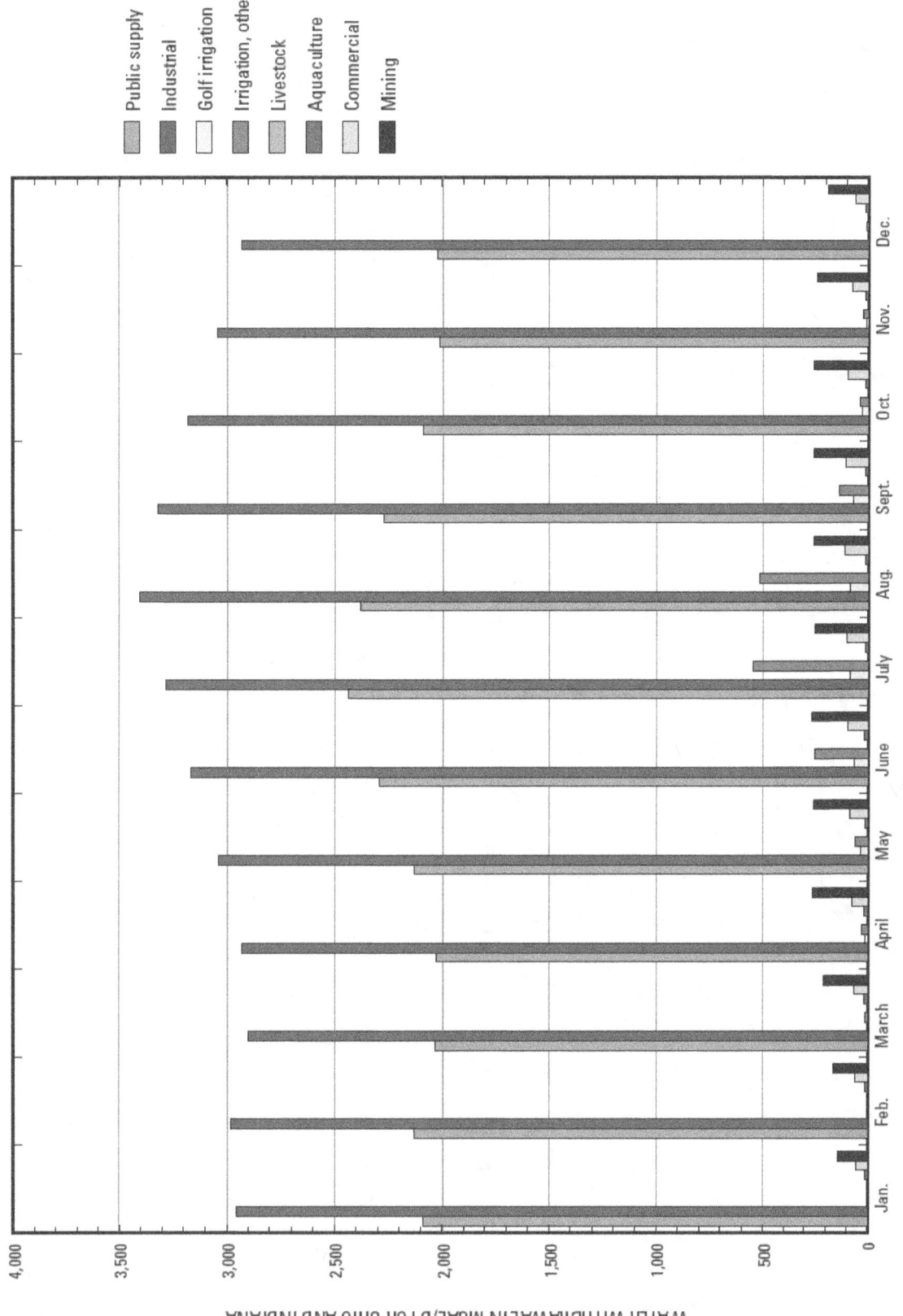

Figure 39. Average monthly water withdrawals for water-use sectors for Ohio and Indiana, 1999–2005, in million gallons per day. *B*, Withdrawals for thermoelectric power generation excluded.

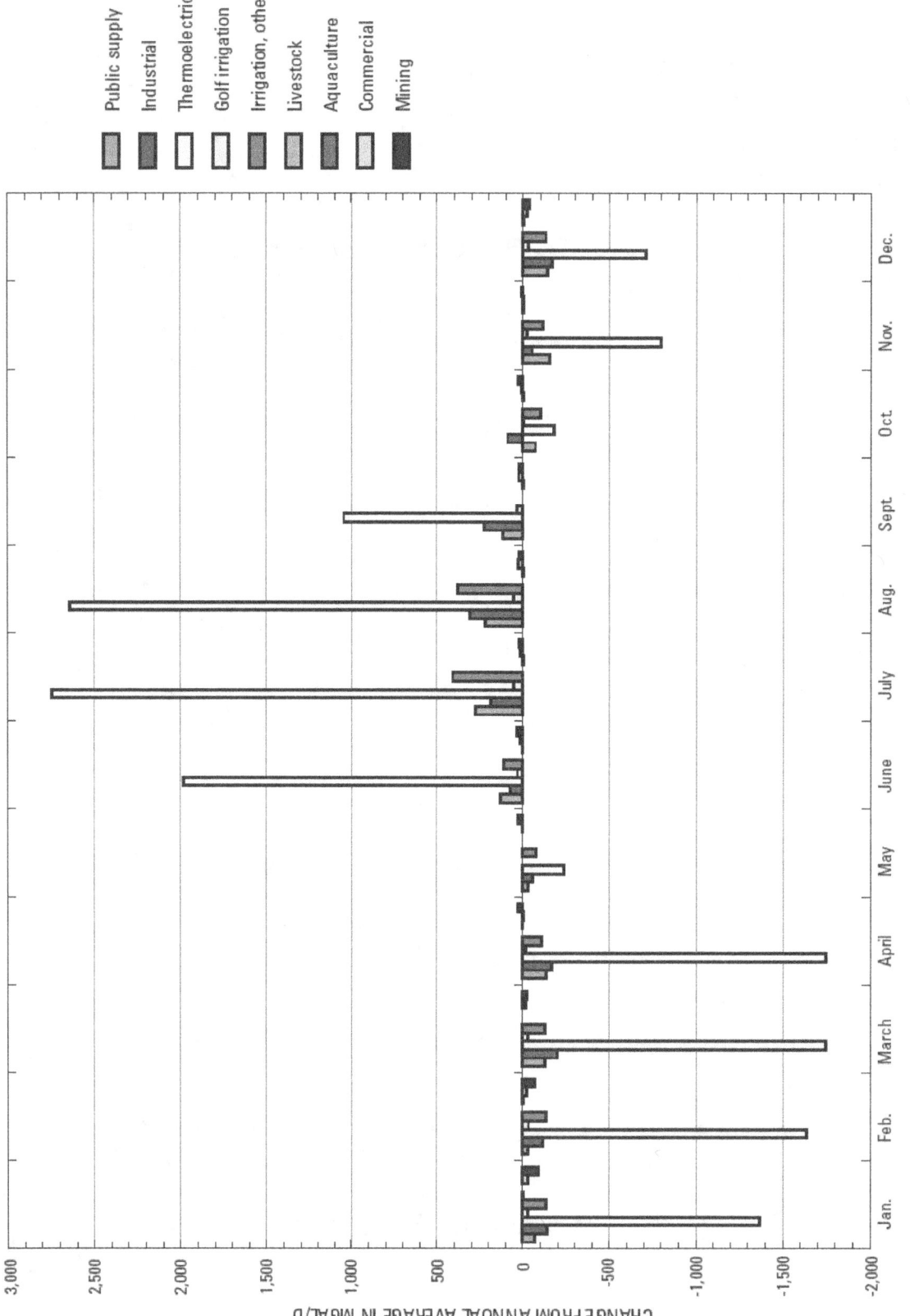

Figure 39. Average monthly water withdrawals for water-use sectors for Ohio and Indiana, 1999–2005, in million gallons per day. *C*, Withdrawal expressed as difference from annual average, in million gallons per day.

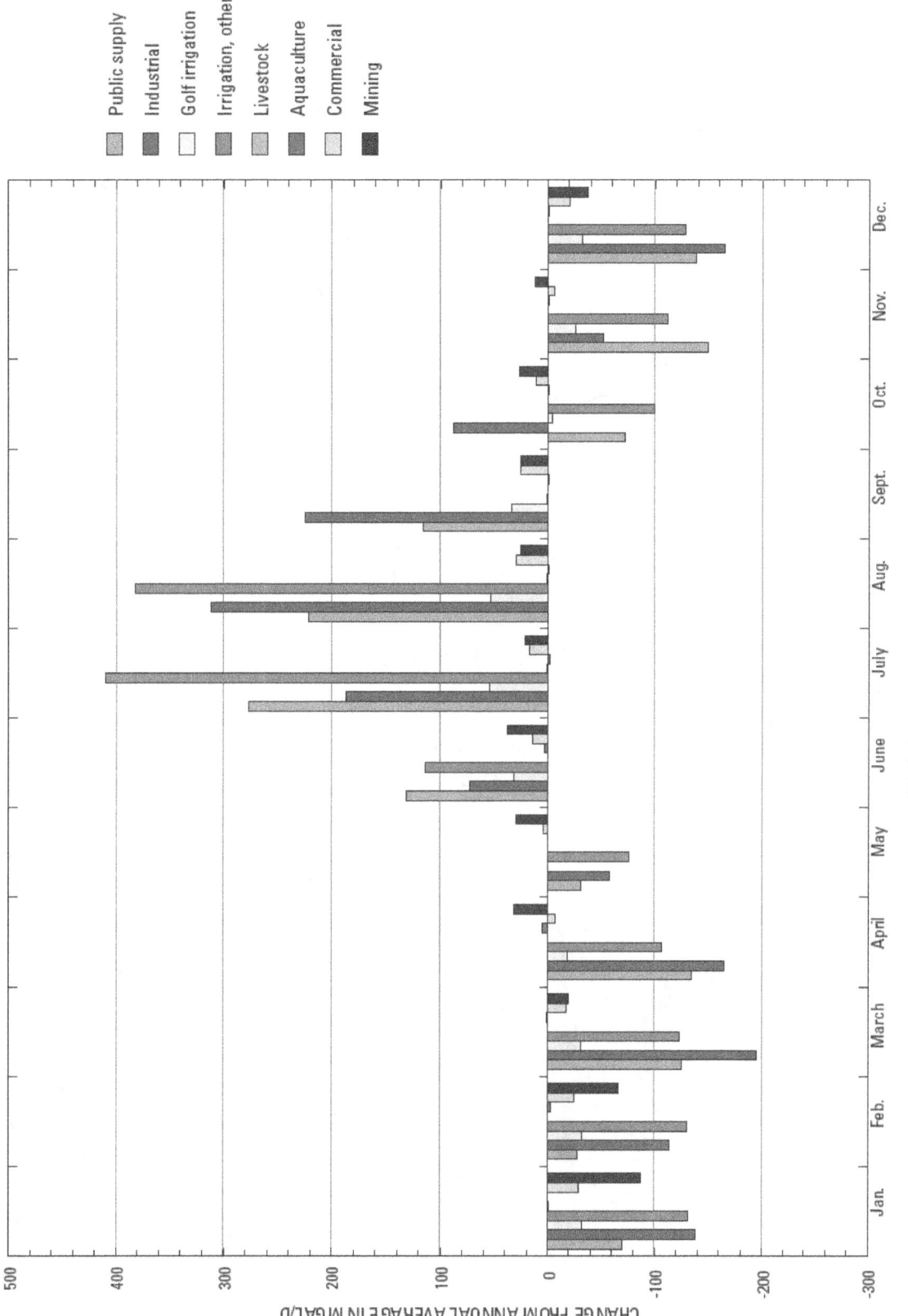

Figure 39. Average monthly water withdrawals for water-use sectors for Ohio and Indiana, 1999–2005, in million gallons per day. *D,* Difference from annual average for each sector, excluding withdrawals for thermoelectric power.

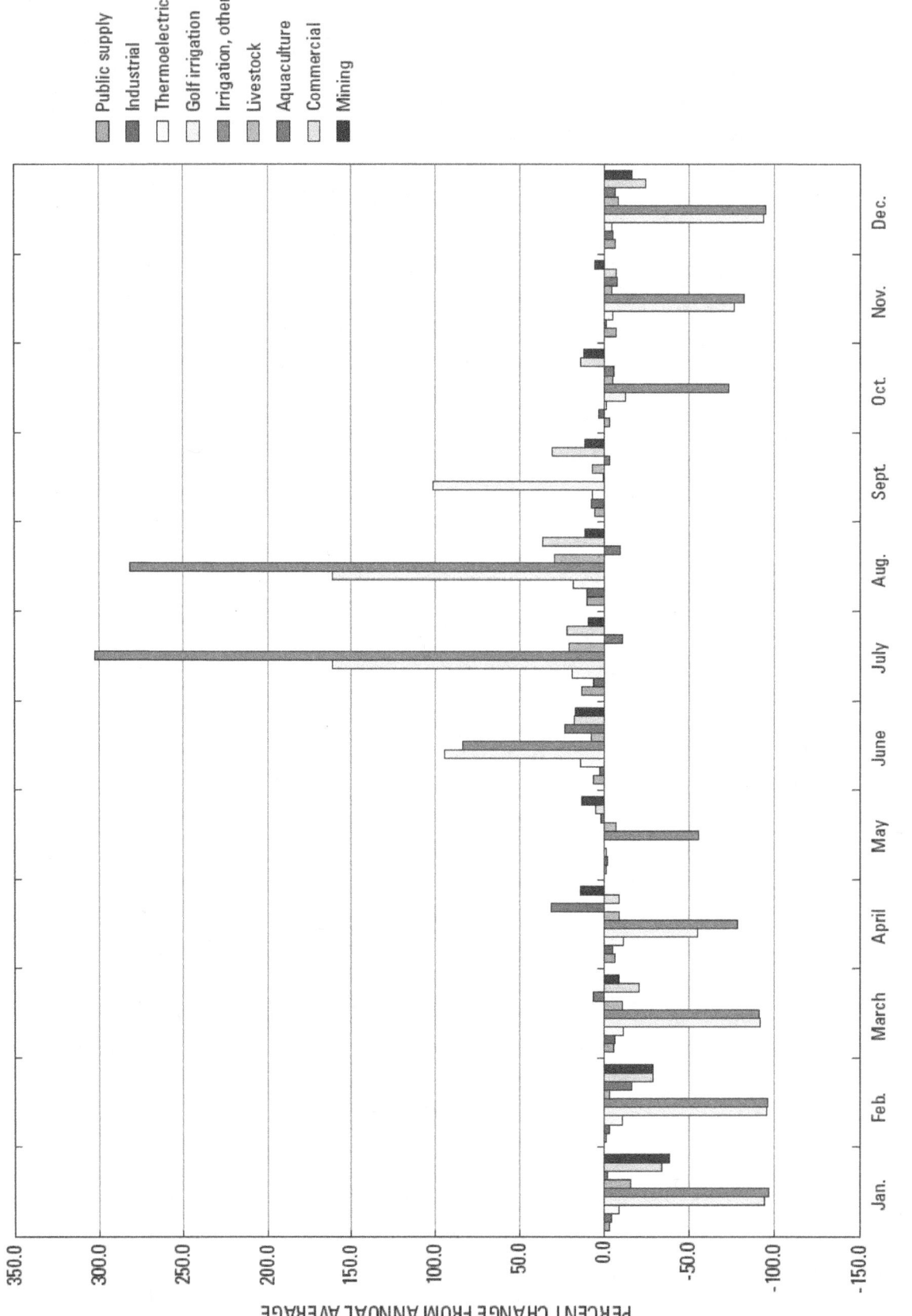

Figure 39. Average monthly water withdrawals for water-use sectors for Ohio and Indiana, 1999–2005, in million gallons per day. *E,* Difference from annual average, expressed as percent of annual average.

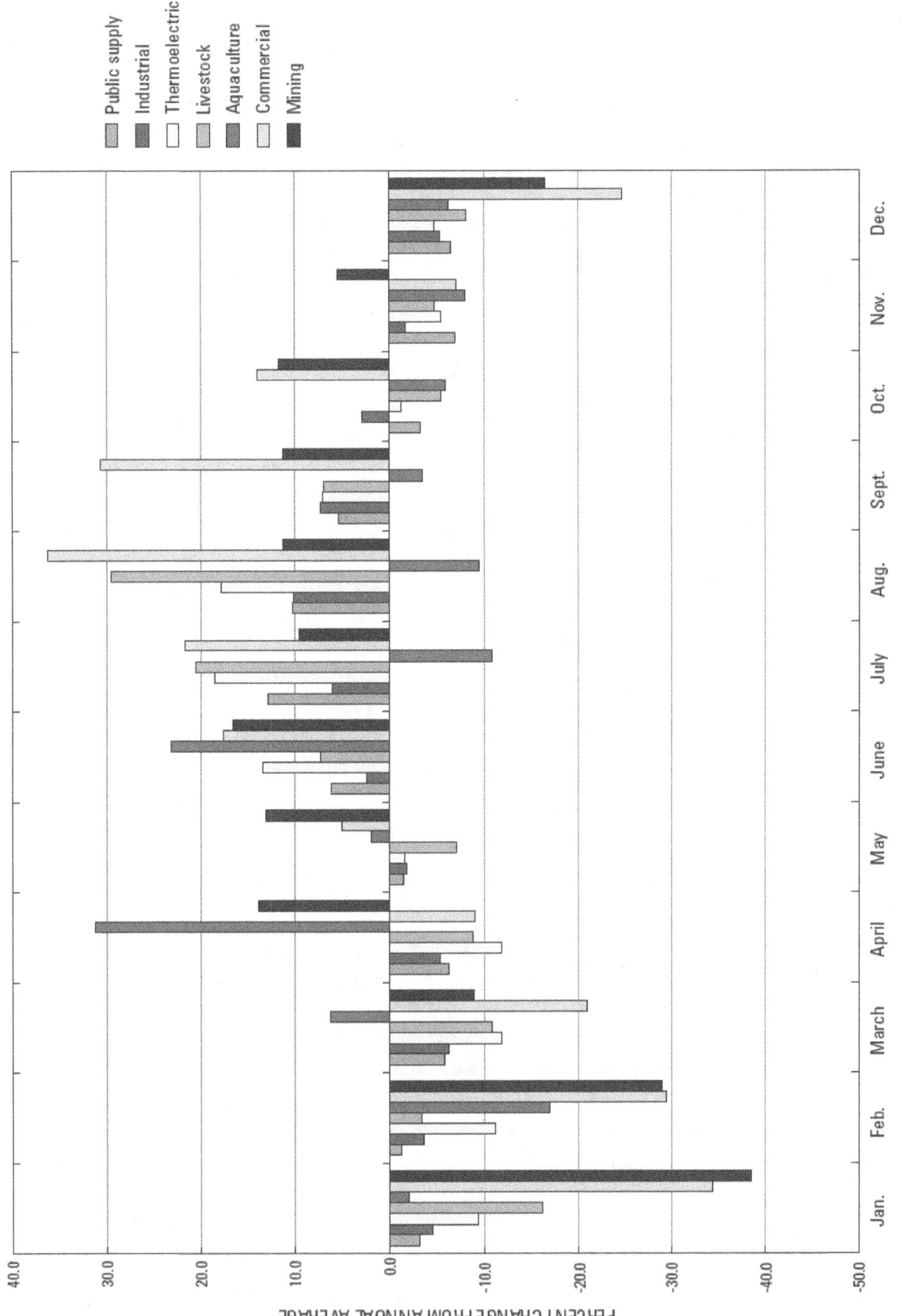

Figure 39. Average monthly water withdrawals for water-use sectors for Ohio and Indiana, 1999–2005, in million gallons per day. *F*, Difference from annual average, expressed as percent of annual average excluding irrigation sectors.

increased withdrawal in summer and decreased withdrawals for the rest of the year, however, is much stronger than expected across all sectors (fig. 39C, D, F). The only sector that does not show this strong yearly variation is aquaculture, which is a small contributor to the total withdrawals (fig. 39B, D). Water withdrawals for thermoelectric power generation increased the most in terms of withdrawal rate among all categories during the summer months, but, because this is the largest water withdrawal, the corresponding percentage increase was less than 20 percent (fig. 39E). In absolute terms, the amount of increase of public-supply and industrial water withdrawals were close to the increase for irrigation

supply (fig. 39B). Because of the large amount of withdrawals, however, the percentage change for these sectors was smaller (fig. 39E, F): public-supply withdrawals increased by 10–12 percent from the annual average during the summer months, and industrial water withdrawals increased by as much as 10 percent of the annual average.

Higher water withdrawals shown in figure 39 typically occur during periods when natural streamflows are below the annual average. This pattern is illustrated by examining monthly municipal water withdrawals for 2004–6 for Lansing, Mich. (Carol Luukkonen, U.S. Geological Survey, written commun., 2010), and the flow measured at the USGS

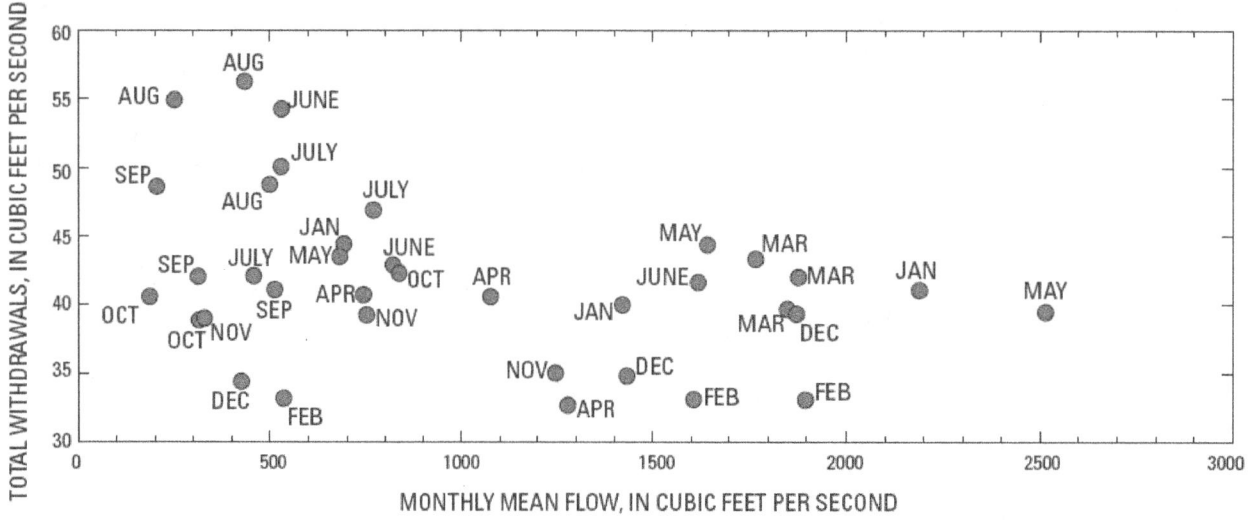

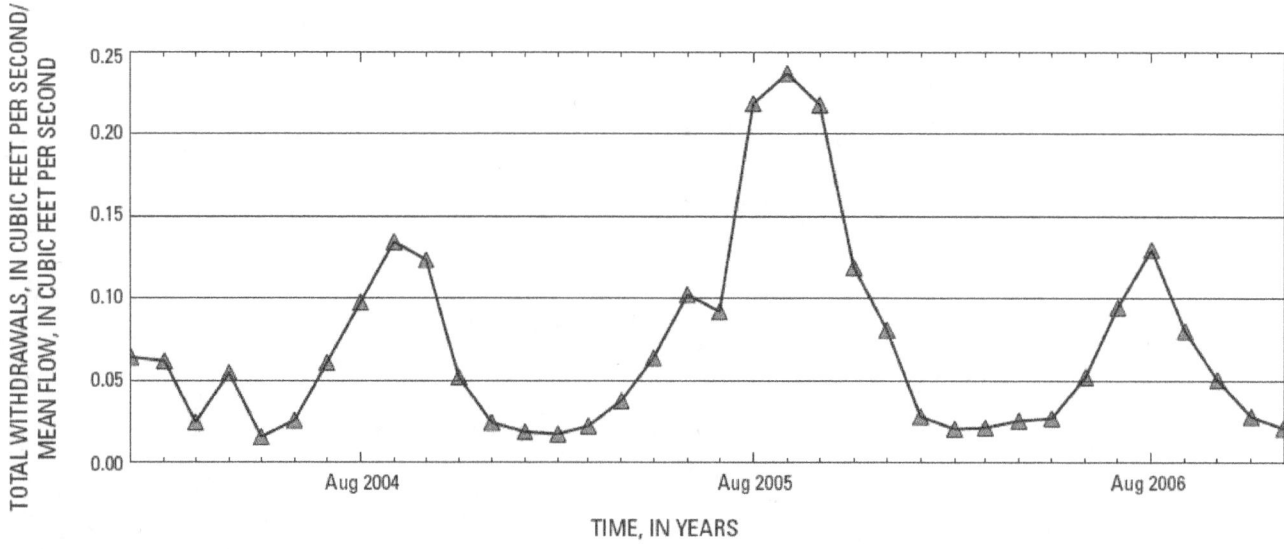

Figure 40.   Monthly municipal water withdrawals for Lansing, Mich., during 2004–6 (expressed as an average rate in cubic feet per second) and monthly mean flow from USGS streamgage 04113000, Grand River at Lansing, Mich. (in cubic feet per second).

streamgage on the Grand River at Lansing (station 04113000) (fig. 40). Monthly withdrawal, expressed as an average rate, varied by less than 30 ft³/s, whereas monthly flow at the Grand River streamgage varied more than 2,000 ft³/s during the 3-year period—an indication that increased withdrawals are not causing the observed decrease in flow. At this streamgage, and for most streamgages in the region, flows tend to be low and withdrawals tend to be high during late summer and early fall. If the impact of withdrawals on streamflow at a particular gage was potentially significant, considering only annual averages in both streamflow and use could greatly underestimate the effect of water withdrawals on streams. Because the effect of withdrawals on streamflow or stream ecosystems may be a water-availability constraint, the dynamics of the system should be well quantified. Ideally, water withdrawal and return information would be incorporated into water-resources analysis with tools such as AFINCH to analyze the human-affected hydrology of the system; that is, the flows through pipes, reservoirs, irrigation-distribution systems, and water and wastewater-treatment plants could be considered in the analysis of the hydrology of an area. These flows could be treated more like parts of the local hydrologic system to achieve a more comprehensive view of the hydrology and the role of humans in the hydrologic system.

Local-Scale Water Availability Analysis Within the U.S. Great Lakes Basin

In this section of the report, aspects of water-availability studies are combined to illustrate a more comprehensive water-availability analysis at the local scale. At this local scale, the potential effect of new groundwater withdrawal on streamflow is analyzed. This analysis combines groundwater and surface-water aspects of the pilot study. Using the same local-scale example, the sensitivity of the water resources to climate change within the Great Lakes Basin is analyzed by use of the models developed in this project and one potential scenario generated by a global climate models (GCM). Techniques for network analysis based on the groundwater-flow and surface-water-characteristics models developed in this project also are presented.

Inset Groundwater-Flow Model Integrating Groundwater and Surface-Water Availability

Regional officials and the public are interested in groundwater/surface-water interaction and the potential interaction between pumping wells and streamflow depletion (Reeves and others, 2009). To illustrate how regional or subregional

groundwater-flow models may be used to help gain insight on this question, a refined, or inset, groundwater-flow model was developed for part of the Lake Michigan Basin groundwater-flow model. This inset model allows for simulation of groundwater flow at much finer spatial and temporal scales. Several factors motivated the development of the inset model: (1) the smallest cell size of the Lake Michigan Basin groundwater-flow model, 5,000 ft on a side, is too large to resolve individual streams that may be affected by groundwater withdrawals, (2) the large cell size of the subregional model also prevents resolution of the position of individual wells, and (3) the cell size is much larger than would be required to accurately model the flow between groundwater and surface-water features (Haitjema and others, 2001; Feinstein and others, 2010).

The appropriate cell size within MODFLOW to accurately simulate flow between groundwater and surface-water systems was investigated by Haitjema and others (2001). The authors developed a "characteristic length" that can be used to relate aquifer and streambed properties and also to serve as a guidance for cell size (Haitjema and others, 2001; Hunt and others, 2003). For accurate representation of the flow between a surface-water body and the aquifer where gradients in head may be large, the cell size for a finite-difference model for groundwater flow should be about one-tenth of the characteristic length; and in areas of less variation, the cell size should be approximately one characteristic length. The characteristic length may be written as

$$\lambda = \sqrt{Tc} \qquad (7)$$

Here,

λ is the characteristic length, L,

T is the transmissivity of the aquifer, L²/T,

c is a characteristic stream resistance, T, given by d/K, where

d is the streambed thickness, L, and

K is the hydraulic conductivity of the streambed materials, L/T.

Evaluating a representative characteristic length for the subregional groundwater-flow model yields values on the order of 1,000 ft, and for accurate representation of streamflow depletion caused by groundwater pumping, the inset model was designed to have cell sizes on the order of 0.1λ. Cells of this size also help resolve geometry issues and allow simulation of wells within hundreds of feet from streams (see Feinstein and others, 2010, appendix 2).

The inset model is located in the Lower Peninsula of Michigan, in a headwater region near the Lake Michigan Basin surface-water divide (fig. 41). The inset model was constructed in two steps. First, an intermediate model approximately 450 mi² was extracted from the Lake Michigan Basin groundwater-flow model. The cell size for the intermediate model is 500 ft by 500 ft, and it was extracted by applying Telescopic Mesh Refinement (Leake and Claar, 1999) to a 23-cell by 22-cell part of the subregional MODFLOW model

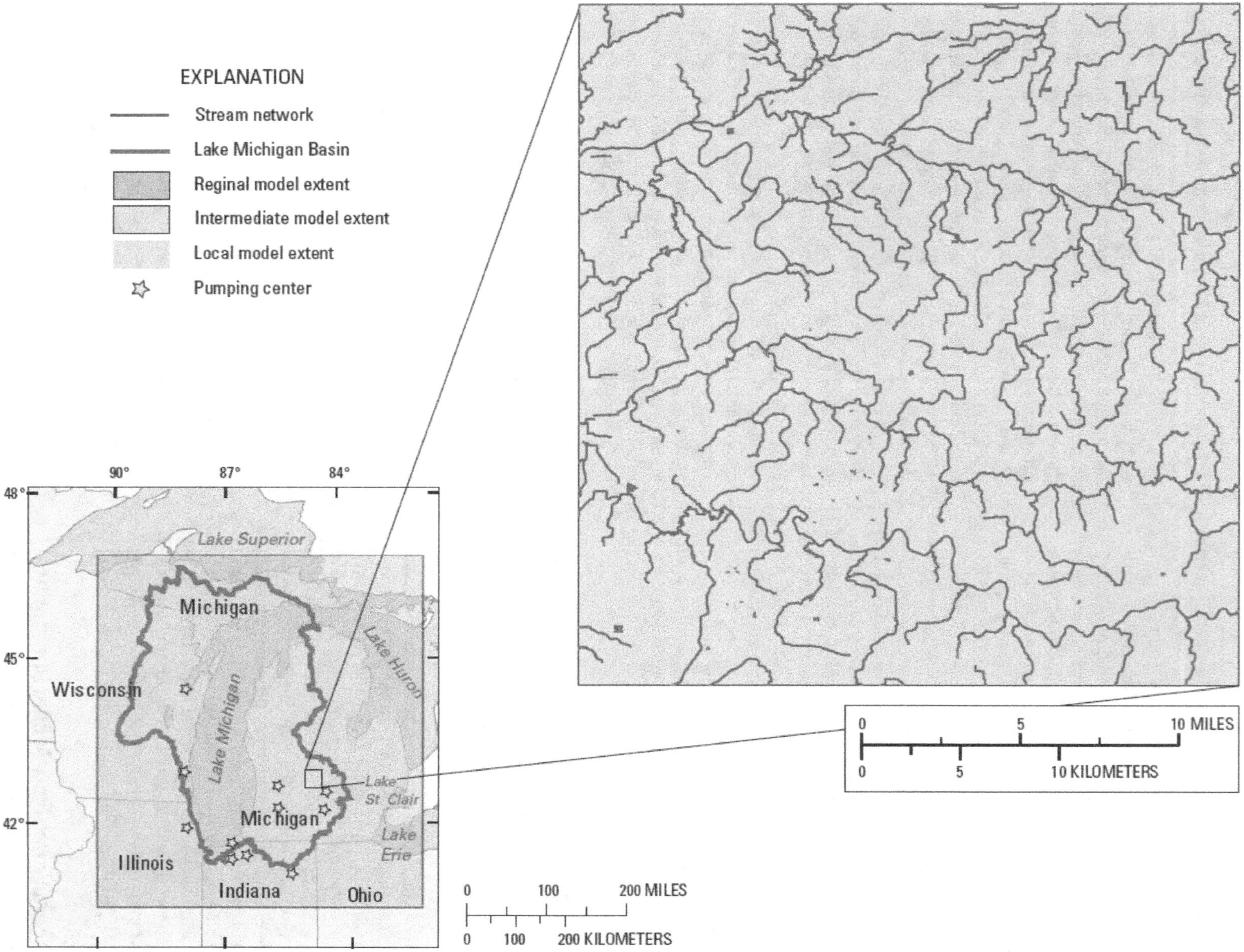

Figure 41.   Inset-model overview showing subregional, intermediate, and local-scale model areas.

discussed previously (Hoard, 2010; Feinstein and others, 2010; Hoard, 2010). In the second step, a local model with an area of approximately 21 mi^2 discretized into 71 ft by 71 ft cells was developed within the intermediate model. Shared-node Local Grid Refinement (LGR) (Mehl and Hill, 2005) on a 50-cell by 50-cell intermediate-model grid, equivalent to 5-cell by 5-cell grid from the original subregional model, was used to construct the local model (Hoard, 2010).

The geometry and characteristics of the surface-water network and topography of the land surface were the major changes in input for the intermediate and local models. Details of how these models were extracted from the subregional model are presented by Hoard (2010). Briefly, for the intermediate model, the top and bottom elevations of the finite-difference cells were smoothed to eliminate blocky transitions at the original cell boundaries within the intermediate model domain. The top elevation of layer 1, which represents the land surface, was recomputed by averaging values from the 30-m digital elevation model (DEM) (U.S. Geological Survey, 2001). The surface elevations and stream topography were checked and smoothed to ensure that the streams stayed in the topographic channels in the 30-m DEM. A similar process was used for cell tops and bottoms, top elevation of layer 1, and stream geometry when the local model was extracted from the intermediate model (except in this case, the cell size was less than the 30-m DEM, and, therefore, the nearest elevation value from the DEM was assigned to each finite-difference cell).

The representation of the stream geometry improves dramatically from the subregional model to the local mode (fig. 42), and this more accurate representation allows for simulation of groundwater/surface-water interaction for a single well and stream. The refinement of the streams also improved the simulation of the shallow groundwater system in the local model compared to the subregional model. In the subregional model, many cells in layer 1 include a surface-water feature. This limits the ability of the subregional model to simulate the shallow groundwater system because groundwater levels in the uppermost active layer will be strongly tied to the boundary conditions imposed by the surface-water features. (For more discussion of this limitation, see Feinstein and others, 2010.) In the subregional model, approximately 64 percent of the cells have surface-water features within the area of the local model; in the intermediate model, for this same area, approximately 14 percent of the cells are surface-water features; and for the local model, only 2.3 percent of the cells represent surface water-features.

In addition to refined geometry, a more detailed algorithm, the Stream-Flow Routing package (SFR1) (Prudic and others, 2004), was used to simulate the streams within the intermediate and local models compared to the algorithm used in the subregional model (River package). The SFR1 package was chosen because it routes flow through the streams and therefore explicitly simulates stream/groundwater interaction. The inputs required to use this package are an ordered

stream network, streambed conductance, streambed elevation, and stream geometry. An ordered stream network provides an accounting of the connections between individual stream segments, which are assigned by the user, so that flow may be routed through the system. Streamflow routing between the intermediate and local models was accomplished with a beta version of LGR (Steffen Mehl, U.S. Geological Survey, written commun., 2008). To implement this version of the LGR, stream segments that cross the boundary between the intermediate and the local model had to be split at the local model boundary. An additional challenge in using the SFR1 package for this application, beyond resolving the topography and stream geometry, was that flow in the stream had to be assigned for any stream flowing into the intermediate model from the subregional model.

To determine the flow in the streams crossing into the intermediate model, the AFINCH application discussed previously was used. The flow for gaged and ungaged streams in the network was computed by using AFINCH, and monthly flows for each simulation were assigned as inflows for the crossing streams to the intermediate model. Because the same base datasets were used to develop the constrained regression within AFINCH and the input to the intermediate and local models, the estimated flows from AFINCH did not have to be extensively processed to be used for the SFR1 input. The procedure for generating the SFR1 package for the local model was the same as that for the intermediate model except that starting flows were not assigned to streams that originate outside the local model boundary because that flow was being routed from the intermediate model to the local model through LGR (Hoard, 2010).

Monthly simulation periods or "stress periods," as defined previously, were used for the inset-model simulations to better illustrate temporal dynamics of the system compared to stress periods in the subregional model on the order of 5 years or more. The Soil-Water-Balance (SWB) (Westenbroek and others, 2010) approach used to estimate recharge for the subregional model was applied to the intermediate and local grids, and the daily values from the SWB were averaged to produce average monthly recharge values that are held constant for each stress period. To ensure consistency between streamflow and groundwater recharge, the same monthly precipitation values used in the SWB computation of recharge were used in the estimate of streamflow with the AFINCH program. Details on estimates of recharge to the intermediate and local models are given by Hoard (2010).

The local and intermediate models were used to illustrate three capabilities: assessment of groundwater/surface-water interaction, assessment of changes to the local groundwater system in response to climate variability, and use of local models to guide data collection in order to reduce uncertainty in model predictions (network analysis). The network analysis is discussed in the next section, after an examination of groundwater/surface-water interaction and climate change results.

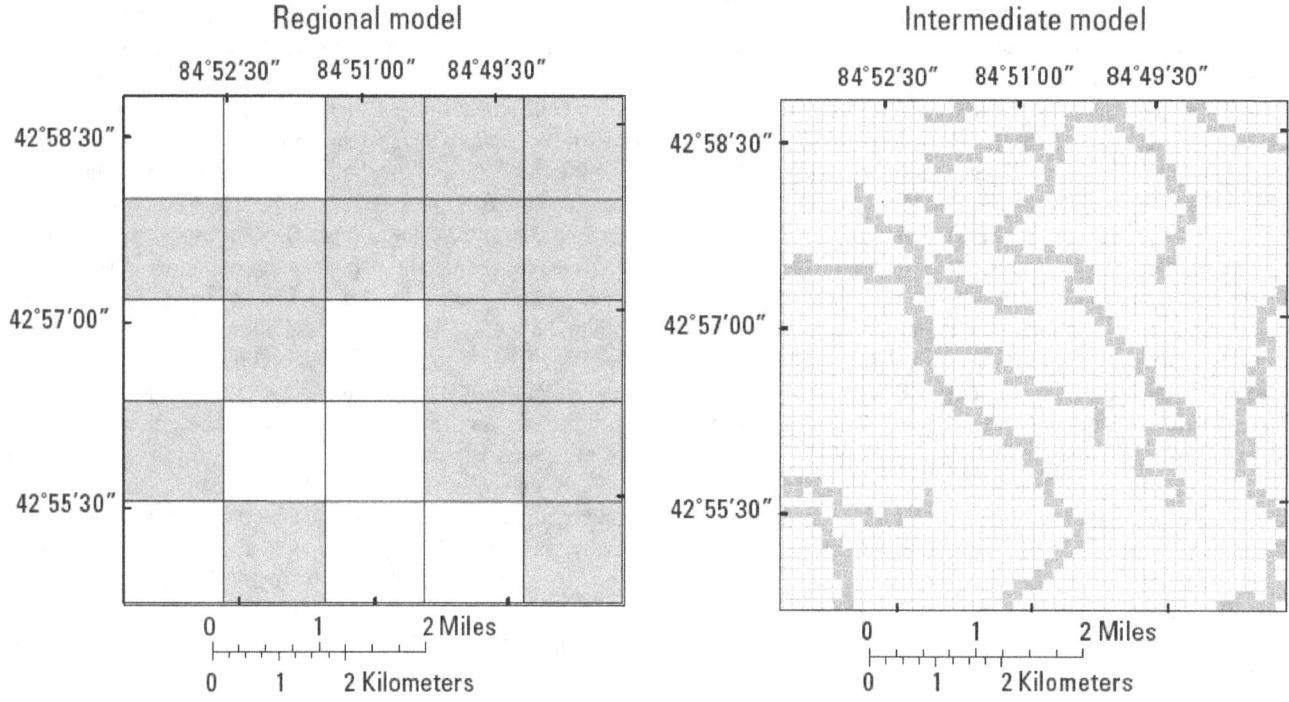

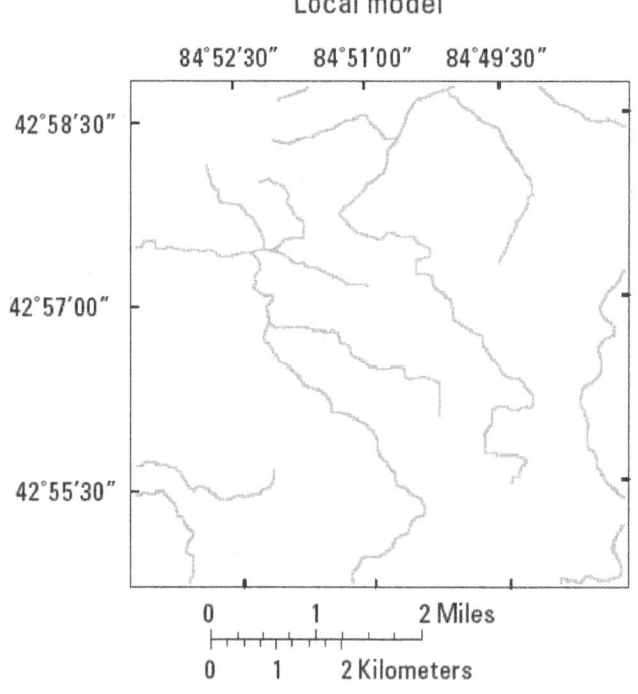

Figure 42.   Surface-water network for subregional, intermediate, and local groundwater-flow models.

Groundwater/Surface-Water Interaction

The local model was used to evaluate streamflow depletion by a high-capacity pumping well. To illustrate this interaction, the effect of the well on a test stream and local watershed to this stream is reported. The well is hypothetical, and the local model was not recalibrated to site-specific data after extraction from the subregional model. In practice, site-specific calibration of the local model is important in order to obtain reliable simulation results. Four test cases were simulated: (1) a control (or base) case where no new well is added, (2) placement of a high-capacity well in the glacial deposits simulated in layer 1 of the model, (3) placement of a high-capacity well in the glacial deposits simulated in layer 2 of the model, and (4) placement of a high-capacity well in the bedrock aquifer simulated as layer 5 in the model. In each case, the well was placed 430 ft from the stream, the pumping rate assigned to the well was 71.4 gal/min, and the Gage package (documented in Prudic and others, 2004) was used to record the flow in the stream near the well (fig. 43). The simulation period was 1991–99, with monthly stress periods as noted above. The pumping in cases 2–4 started in 1991 and was held constant for the entire simulation; the only changes from one stress period to the next were the imposed recharge to the system and the inflows to the SFR1 streams as computed by using SWB and AFINCH.

The effect of this rather modest amount of pumping on streamflow is illustrated in hydrographs of base flow. Withdrawing water from layers 1, 2, or 5 lowers the estimated base flow, especially during low-flow period, in all cases (fig. 44). By subtracting the base-case computed from the other cases, the difference caused by the introduced well in cases 2–4 is produced (figs. 44–45). The well typically removes between 10 and 100 percent of the base flow depending on the recharge conditions imposed during each stress period. In this case, well depth did not strongly change the capture of streamflow by the well. This type of simulation result could be used to evaluate effects on environmental flows by comparing them to the ecological requirements of the stream, including changes in these requirements through the year to estimated base flow (Richter, 2009). Further coupling with rainfall-runoff models (for example, Markstrom and others, 2008) could be used to estimate total streamflow through the year.

Streamflow depletion by the introduced pumping well is the important feature of the analysis, and this depletion also may be evaluated by examining the source of water to the pumping well in a similar fashion as done for the subregional model. Water budgets echo the results evident in the hydrographs: the well placed in either layer 1, 2, or 5 affects local streamflow (fig. 45). As the well is placed deeper in the system, the effect of the well is spread to neighboring watershed slightly because capture of water that would have entered the nearby stream is reduced as capture of water from lateral sources is increased. Water from lateral sources is water crossing the boundary of the local watershed shaded in figure 43; this water is primarily captured from surface-water features in nearby watersheds.

To illustrate the importance of local site conditions on streamflow capture by a pumping well, the series of simulations were repeated with a layer of low hydraulic conductivity introduced to the system. For this second set of simulations, the hydraulic conductivity of layer 4 was reduced approximately 4 orders of magnitude to 2.8×10^{-5} ft/d. The effects of this low-hydraulic-conductivity layer are to increase the proportion of water captured from the stream when the well is placed in the shallow system (layers 1 and 2) and to decrease the proportion of the water captured from the stream when the well is placed in layer 5 (fig. 46). The low-conductivity layer was added to reduce the hydraulic connection between the bedrock aquifer (layer 5) and the shallow aquifer system and headwater stream. At the scale of the subregional model, such a thin low-conductivity layer would be hard to identify, calibrate, or justify; but, on the local scale, this low layer is important to the assessment of the potential impact of the water withdrawal on ecological flows in this headwater stream. The subregional model serves as a good platform to build the local-scale models, but, these results indicate that the local-scale models require site-specific calibration and may require refinement of local aquifer properties. This observation is revisited in the results of the network analysis.

Response to Climate Change

Similar to the climate-change analysis at the subregional scale, temperature and precipitation data from an atmosphere-ocean coupled general circulation model (AOGCM) (Maurer and others, 2002; Hayhoe and others, 2008) were used to generate a climate-change scenario to illustrate the use of the inset model to study the potential effects of climate change on the shallow groundwater system. As before, this particular AOGCM provided daily temperature and precipitation realizations from 1960 to 2099 and reflected an assumed scenario of high global greenhouse gas emissions (A1fi scenario) (Hayhoe and others, 2008).

Use of the climatic data derived from the AOGCM as the input to the SWB model provided a means to estimate future recharge and the effects global climate change may have on recharge (see Hoard, 2010). The SWB results were again averaged to produce monthly estimates of recharge for the local model (fig. 47). These recharge values exhibit a great deal of interannual variability, resulting in wide ranges of values for each month. Typically, there is no recharge to the system in the summer months in any of the three periods: 1991–2000, 2013–22, or 2035–44. As noted in figure 47, the annual average recharge value increased slightly from 1991 to 2016 and then decreased gradually. From 2024 to 2044, the average annual recharge computed by the SWB program with temperature and precipitation from the AOGCM was less than the annual average recharge for the set of scenarios from 1991 through 1999.

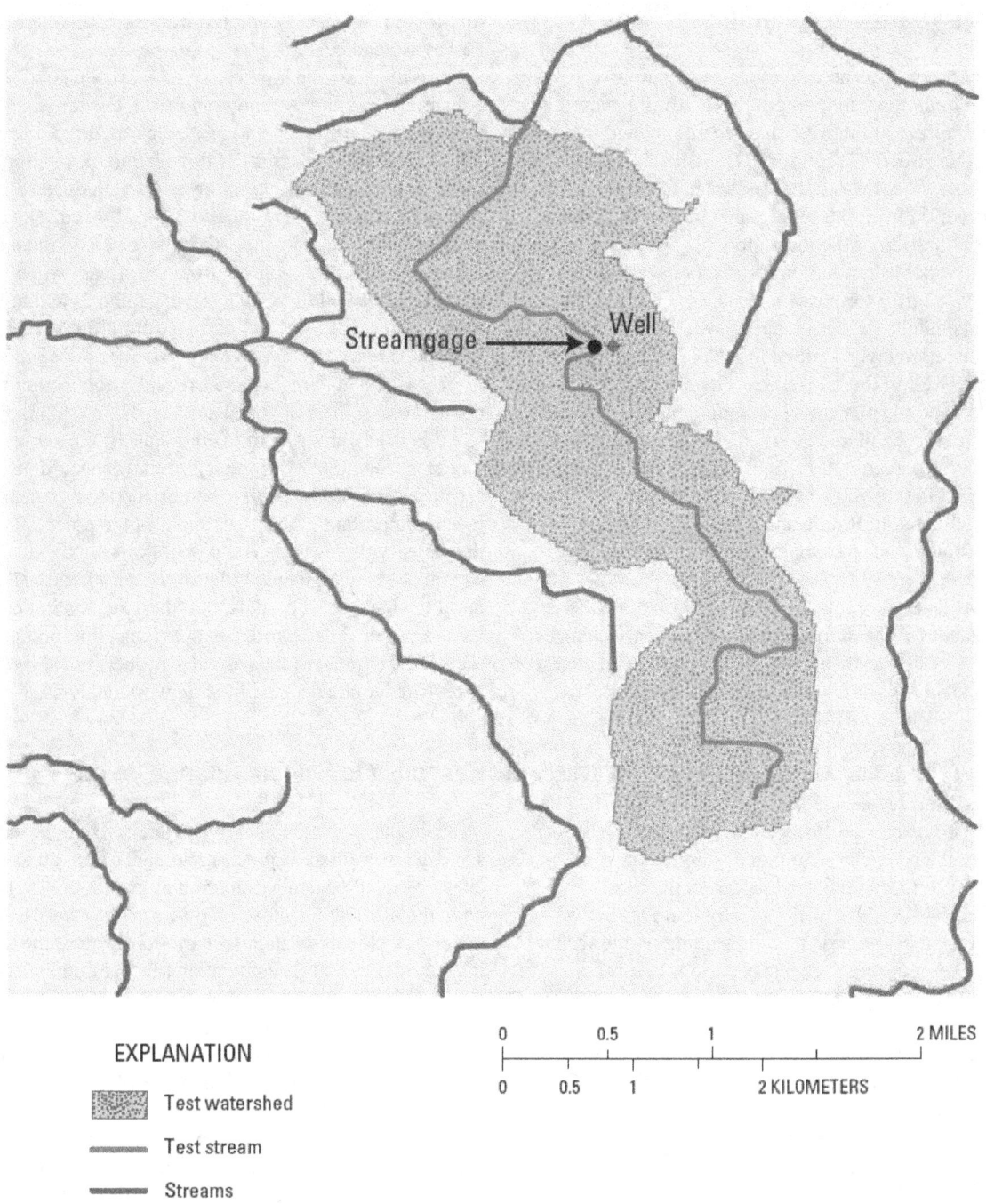

Figure 43.   Streams in local inset model with model gage, hypothetical well, and test watershed and stream indicated (from Hoard, 2010).

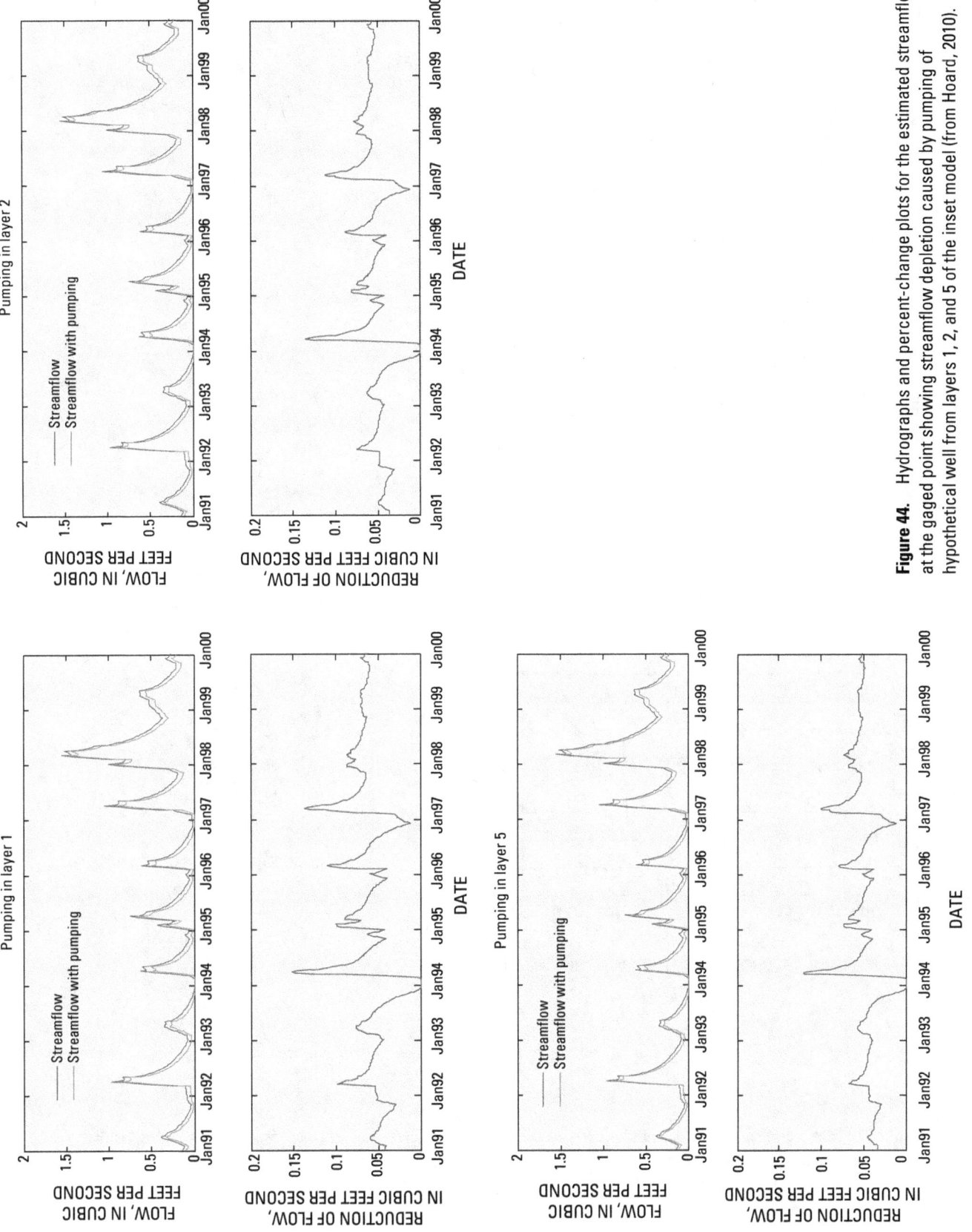

Figure 44. Hydrographs and percent-change plots for the estimated streamflow at the gaged point showing streamflow depletion caused by pumping of hypothetical well from layers 1, 2, and 5 of the inset model (from Hoard, 2010).

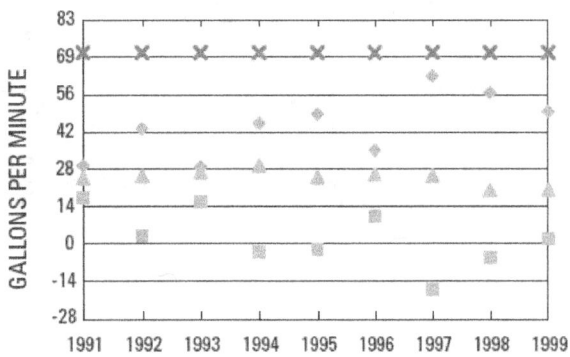

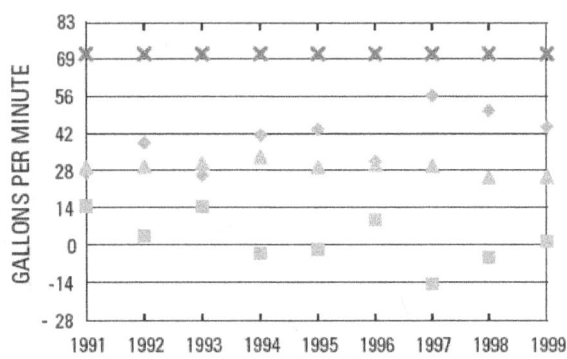

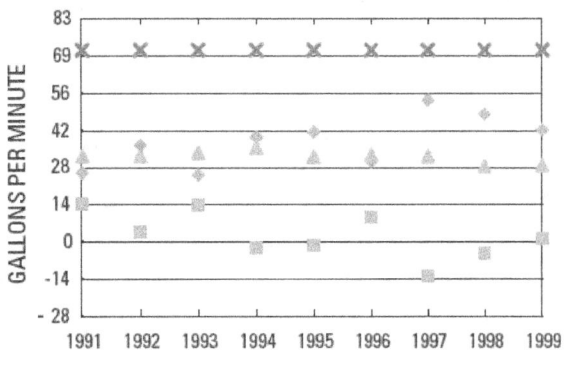

ANNUAL SOURCE OF WATER TO WELL 1991–99

Well pumps 71.4 gallons per minute from layer 1

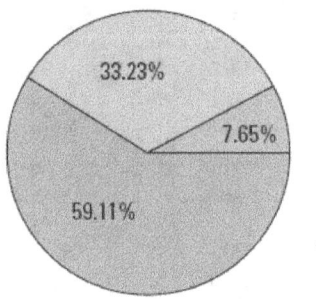

Well pumps 71.4 gallons per minute from layer 2

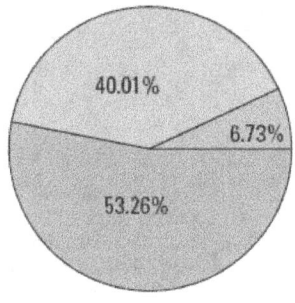

Well pumps 71.4 gallons per minute from layer 5

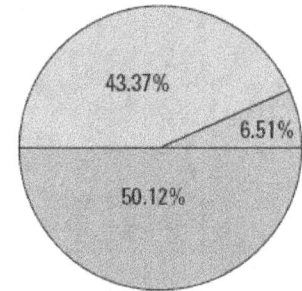

NET SOURCE OF WATER TO WELL 1991–99

EXPLANATION

◆ Stream source

▨ Storage source

▲ Lateral-flow source

✕ Sum sources

Figure 45.   Source of water to the hypothetical well in layers 1, 2, and 5 of the local inset model (from Hoard, 2010; Mgal/d, million gallons per day).

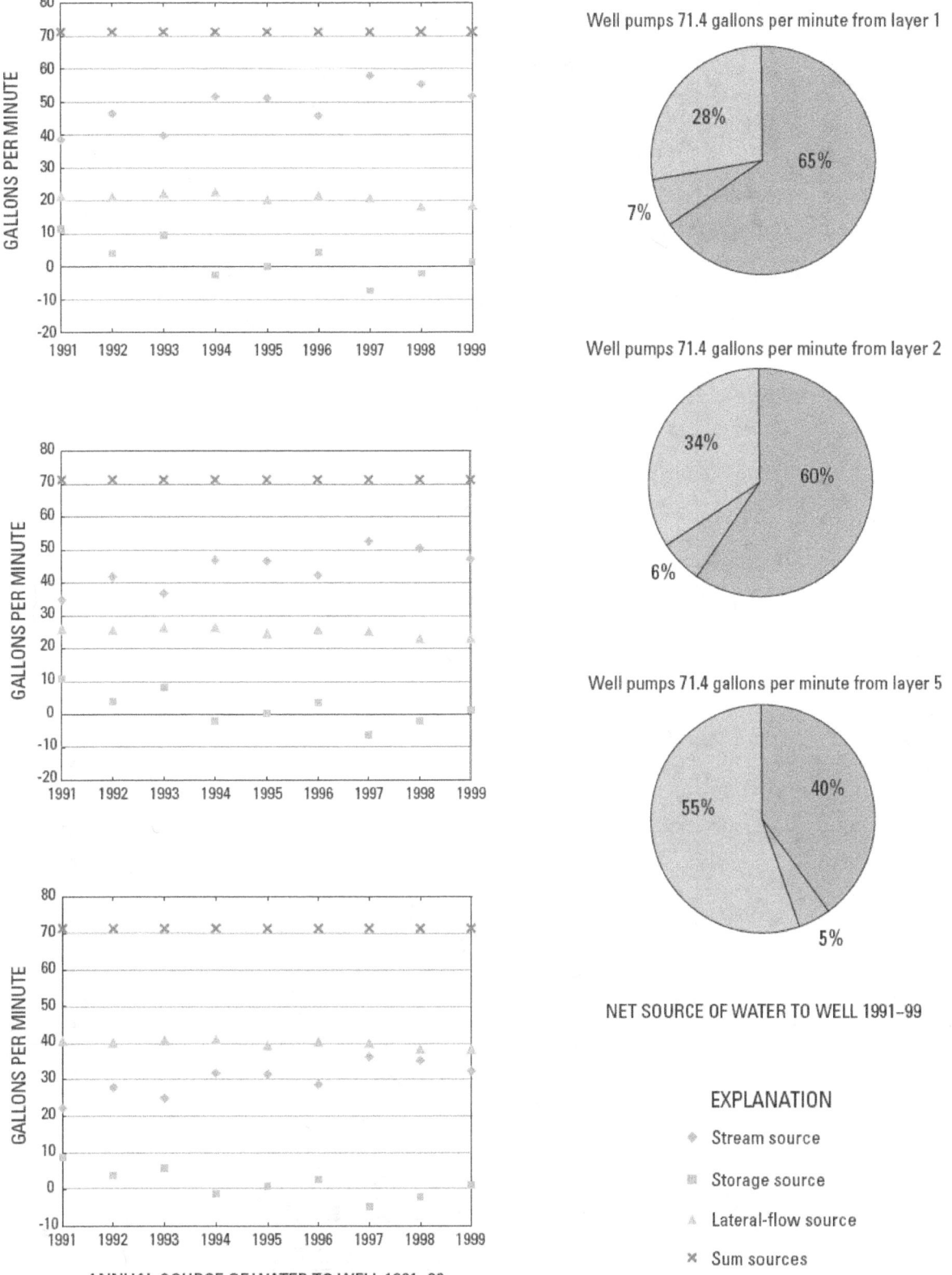

Figure 46. Source of water to hypothetical well in layers 1, 2, or 5 of local inset model, with low-hydraulic-conductivity layer added to the model (Mgal/d, million gallons per day).

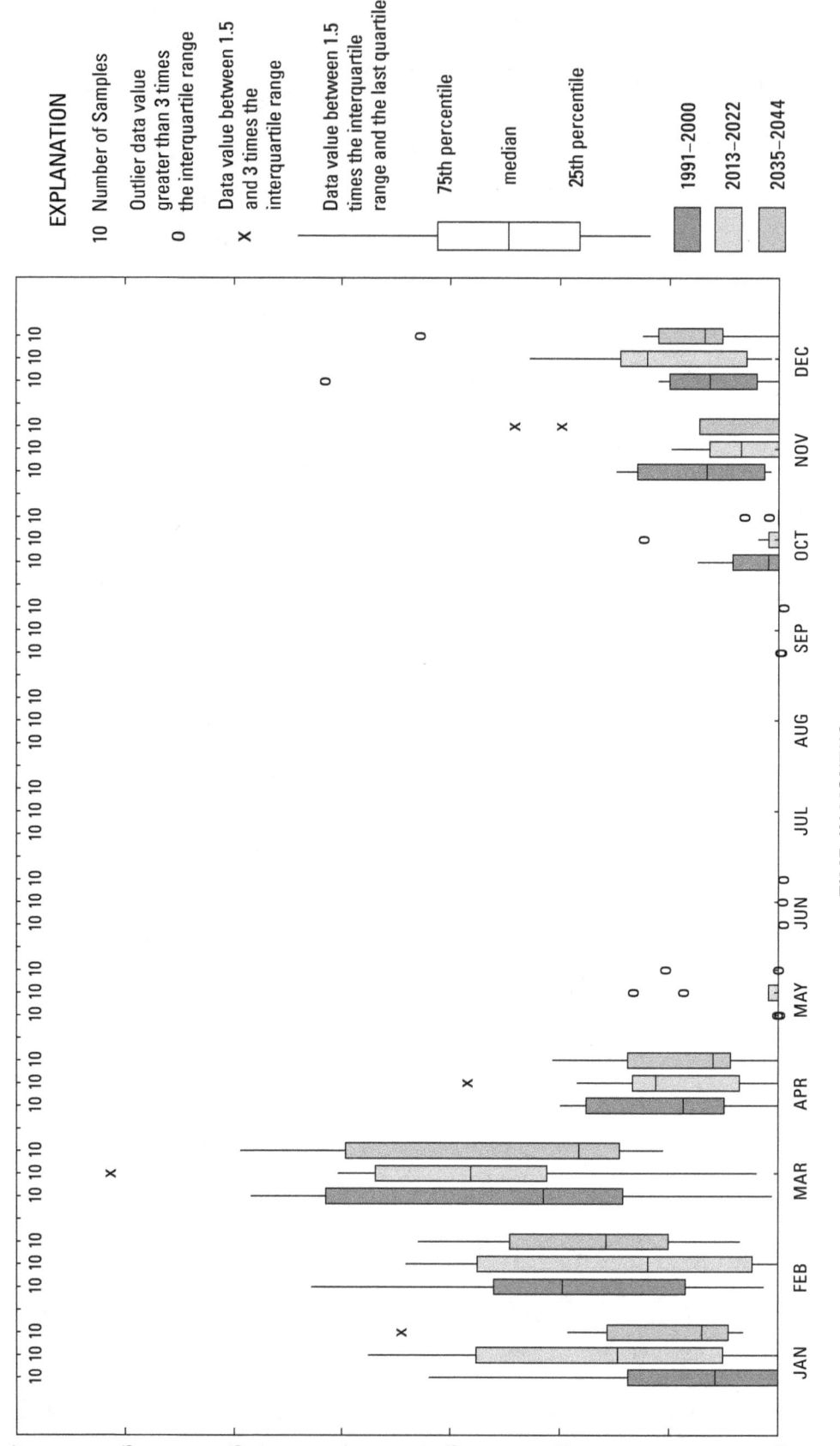

Figure 47. Seasonal distribution of recharge values from the atmosphere-ocean coupled general circulation model (AOGCM) used for the inset-model climate-change scenario, by decade.

Monthly base-flow values computed by the inset model at the gage (fig. 43) mirrored the variability noted in the estimated recharge values, although base flow tends to vary less and have a smoother distribution across the year (fig. 48). The predicted increase in recharge during 2013–22 produces more base flow to the stream. The base flow for March approximately doubles from the 1991–99 period to the 2013–22 period, and peak streamflow for all three time periods tends to occur in April. For the third time period, 2035–44, the base flow is much less than for either of the other two time periods, and, on average, the stream is dry for much of the year. These simulations driven by the AOGCM illustrate the sensitivity of the headwater stream to rather small changes in recharge. In periods when the long-term average recharge is higher, simulations show that base flow is maintained during dry seasons by release of groundwater from storage. As the long-term average recharge decreases, groundwater storage is depleted, and the aquifer cannot maintain the same base-flow levels during dry seasons.

Full analysis of the effects of climate change would require simulation of a suite of potential climate-change scenarios and consideration of potential land- and water-use changes. Land use and water use, however, are held constant for this example simulation. Potential feedback or other non-linear effects within the system also should be considered. For example, under conditions of higher atmospheric CO_2, plants may use water more efficiently and have lower water demand (Kamps and others, 2008; Kruijt and others, 2008). This secondary effect would have to be included in the SWB algorithms used to estimate recharge to the system. Longer growing seasons may allow different crops or different crop schedules. Changes in agricultural practice in response to changes in climate could change the timing and amount of irrigation demands on the groundwater system. The purpose of the simulation shown in this section was to illustrate the ability of the inset model to respond to small changes in recharge amounts and timing that would allow for more thorough analysis.

Monitoring and Network Analysis

Water-availability analysis is not possible without basic data on flows, storage, and processes within the system. Long-term monitoring supported every part of every aspect of the Great Lakes Basin Pilot: groundwater monitoring was required to calibrate the Lake Michigan Basin groundwater-flow model (Feinstein and others, 2010), surface-water monitoring was crucial to the development and application of AFINCH (Holtschlag, 2009) and the analysis of regional trends (Hodgkins and others, 2007), and water-use data were used in the analysis of monthly and seasonal variation (Shaffer, 2009) and form the basis for both actual and estimated withdrawals from 1865 to 2005 used in the groundwater-flow model (Buchwald and others, 2010). The importance of long-term data is discussed by, for example, Taylor and Alley (2001) and Feinstein and others (2004). Water-use data collection and water-use

estimation techniques are discussed by the National Research Council (2002).

Given the importance of long-term monitoring, how should monitoring networks be planned and evaluated? "Network analysis" is used to evaluate monitoring networks, but this generic term may refer to many different activities. Most importantly, specific networks must be designed to answer specific questions. Likewise, specific network analyses must be designed to answer specific questions. For example, monitoring designed to measure flows in headwater streams and effects of development on these flows might require many streamgages in headwater systems, but monitoring to improve the estimate of water flux and contaminant loading to the Great Lakes might require streamgages at the river mouths where major streams enter the Great Lakes. When the network is analyzed, the purpose will have to be specified: development effects on headwaters or loading to the Great Lakes. Groundwater monitoring designed to observe the effects of climate would be quite different from groundwater monitoring designed to document the effects of a large pumping center. For more background on network-design issues—specifically, network design for the USGS National Streamflow Information Program, including an overview of methods and evaluation of different factors influencing network design—see the detailed discussion by the National Research Council (2004).

The surface-water-characteristics model and groundwater-flow models may be used to help evaluate monitoring networks, quantify prediction uncertainty, and target areas where additional data should be collected to improve model estimates. Two techniques are discussed in the following paragraphs: a resampling bootstrap analysis using AFINCH to explore the design of a surface-water monitoring network (Koltun and Holtschlag, 2010) and a prediction-uncertainty based approach using the local-scale groundwater-flow model in which the uncertainty of model estimates are evaluated and the value of new observations or additional information regarding model parameters is assessed (Fienen and others, 2010).

Example Bootstrap Analysis for Surface-Water Monitoring Network

Bootstrap analysis is a type of resampling technique in which the same dataset used to estimate a characteristic of a system also is used to estimate its uncertainty. The uncertainty analysis involves repeated computations of the characteristic with subsets of the original data. The major advantage of this technique is that additional datasets are not required; moreover, the existing model used for the original estimate can be used for the bootstrap analysis without major modification. The bootstrap approach is especially good at identifying important components of uncertainty in the existing system. Its major disadvantage is that causes of uncertainty other than due to sample size and composition are not explored.

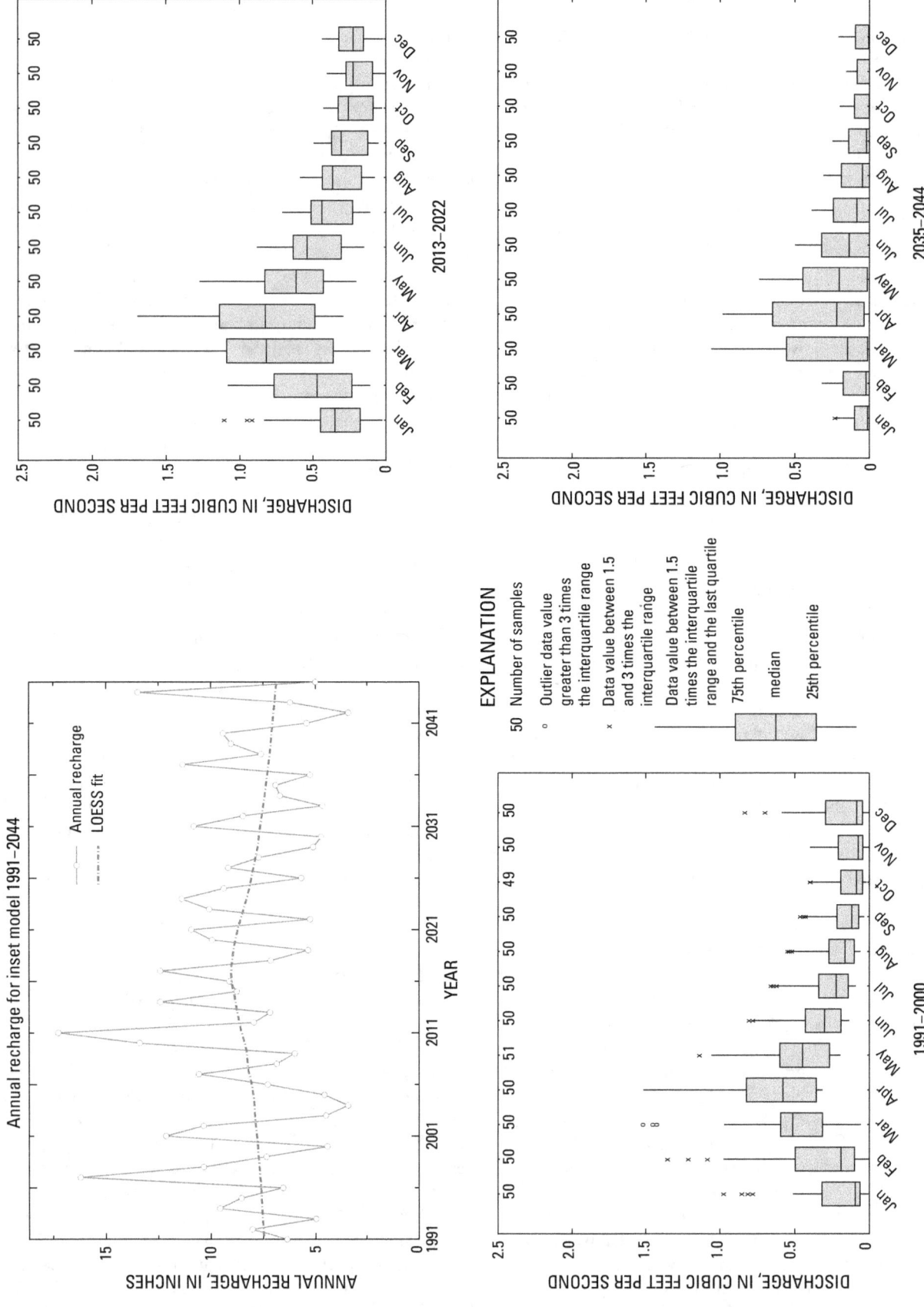

Figure 48. Annual recharge for the inset-model climate-change scenario and base flow, by month, computed by the model for 1991–2000, 2013–22, and 2035–44 (from Hoard, 2010).

A bootstrap analysis was applied to streamflow estimates developed for hydrologic subregion 0405 (Southeast Lake Michigan) by use of the AFINCH model (Koltun and Holtschlag, 2010). In the analysis, AFINCH was first run to compute monthly flow estimates for water years 1971–2003 with the full set of 75 streamgages that were active for one or more years during this time period. To examine the effects of sample size and composition on estimate uncertainty, subsets of the gages were created by randomly censoring (removing) approximately 10, 20, 30, 40, 50, and 75 percent of the gages from the full 75-gage data set. Thirty subsets were created for each of the 6 censoring levels and each of those subsets was used to estimate monthly flows. The resulting estimates were used to evaluate estimate precision and accuracy as a function of the size and composition of the gage network operated in the subregion.

Streamflow estimates for each of six flow lines (representations of stream reaches) were aggregated by censoring level, and results were analyzed to assess (a) how the size and composition of the streamflow-gaging network affected the average apparent errors and variability of the estimated flows and (b) whether results for certain months were more variable than for others. The six flow lines were categorized into one of three types depending upon their network topology and position relative to operating streamflow-gaging stations.

Statistical analysis of the model results indicates that (1) less precise (that is, more variable) estimates resulted from smaller streamflow-gaging networks as compared to larger streamflow-gaging networks, (2) precision of AFINCH flow estimates at an ungaged flow line is improved by operation of one or more streamflow gages upstream and (or) downstream in the enclosing basin, (3) no consistent seasonal trend in estimate variability was evident, and (4) flow lines from ungaged basins appeared to exhibit the smallest absolute apparent percent errors (APEs) and smallest changes in average APE as a function of increasing censoring level. Koltun and Holtschlag (2010) attributed the counterintuitive results described in item (4) to using the estimate from the full-gage network as the base for comparisons and also to an insensitivity in the average model-derived estimates to changes in the streamflow-gaging-network size and composition. Another analysis demonstrated that errors for flow lines in ungaged basins have the potential to be much larger than indicated by their APEs if measured relative to their true (but unknown) flows.

"Missing gage" analyses, based on examination of censoring subset results where the streamflow gage of interest was omitted from the calibration data set, were done to better understand the true error characteristics for ungaged flow lines as a function of network size. Figure 49 shows results examined for 2 water years, indicating that the probability of computing a monthly streamflow estimate within 10 percent of the true value with AFINCH decreased from greater than 0.9 at about a 10-percent network-censoring level to less than 0.6 as the censoring level approached 75 percent. In addition, estimates for typically dry months tended to be characterized by larger percent errors than typically wetter months.

Example Model-Uncertainty Analysis Using the Local Groundwater-Flow Model

Estimates of uncertainty in model-prediction results are derived by using first-order second-moment techniques that combine model sensitivity and input uncertainty. (For discussion of underlying mathematics of these techniques, see Fienen and others, 2010.) Three approaches can be used for uncertainty analysis of a calibrated model: (1) observations can be added to the calibration dataset, (2) observations can be excluded from the calibration dataset, or (3) better information on model parameters can be obtained. In an analysis of the local-scale (inset) model (Hoard, 2010), Fienen and others (2010) focused on approaches 1 and 3 to examine uncertainty in predictions of groundwater levels and base flow to a stream. Base-flow prediction is especially relevant because of the interest in streamflow depletion by wells; further, uncertainty analysis can indicate where in the modeled area additional observations should be made or what parameters should be measured to reduce prediction uncertainty.

Two suites of software were examined in this study: OPR/PPR (Tonkin and others, 2007; 2008), which is typically used in conjunction with UCODE (Poeter and others, 2005), and PREDUNC/PREDVAR, which are part of the suite of PEST tools (Doherty, 2010a,b). Although different philosophical and numerical approaches characterize the two software suites, both can be used to estimate prediction uncertainty as a function of model sensitivity, sensitivity of the prediction to changes in the parameters and sensitivity of each observation to each parameter, and some measure of uncertainty of parameters and observations.

The PEST tools were designed to facilitate inverse analysis if the number of parameters is larger—and often much larger—than the number of observations; such situations are sometimes referred to as "underdetermined problems." Regularization is imposed for the underdetermined problems to allow for solution. Conversely, UCODE is designed for "overdetermined problems," where the number of parameters is kept small, typically less than the number of observations. Fienen and others (2010) show that PREDUNC and OPR/PPR are equivalent under certain assumptions and that numerical efficiency may indicate the use of one or the other, depending upon the number of parameters and the number of observations. For either suite of tools, the analyst must specify the prediction of interest. For OPR or PREDUNC, potential locations for additional observations must be specified if analysis of the addition of observations is desired.

The subregional Lake Michigan Basin groundwater-flow model was developed with PEST tools but with a combination of approaches (Feinstein and others, 2010). Parameters were minimized and large zones were used for most of the model (overdetermined approach); however, pilot points and regularization were adopted for one geologic unit (underdetermined approach) (Feinstein and others, 2010).

PREDUNC and PREDVAR were applied to three different parameterizations of the local inset groundwater-flow

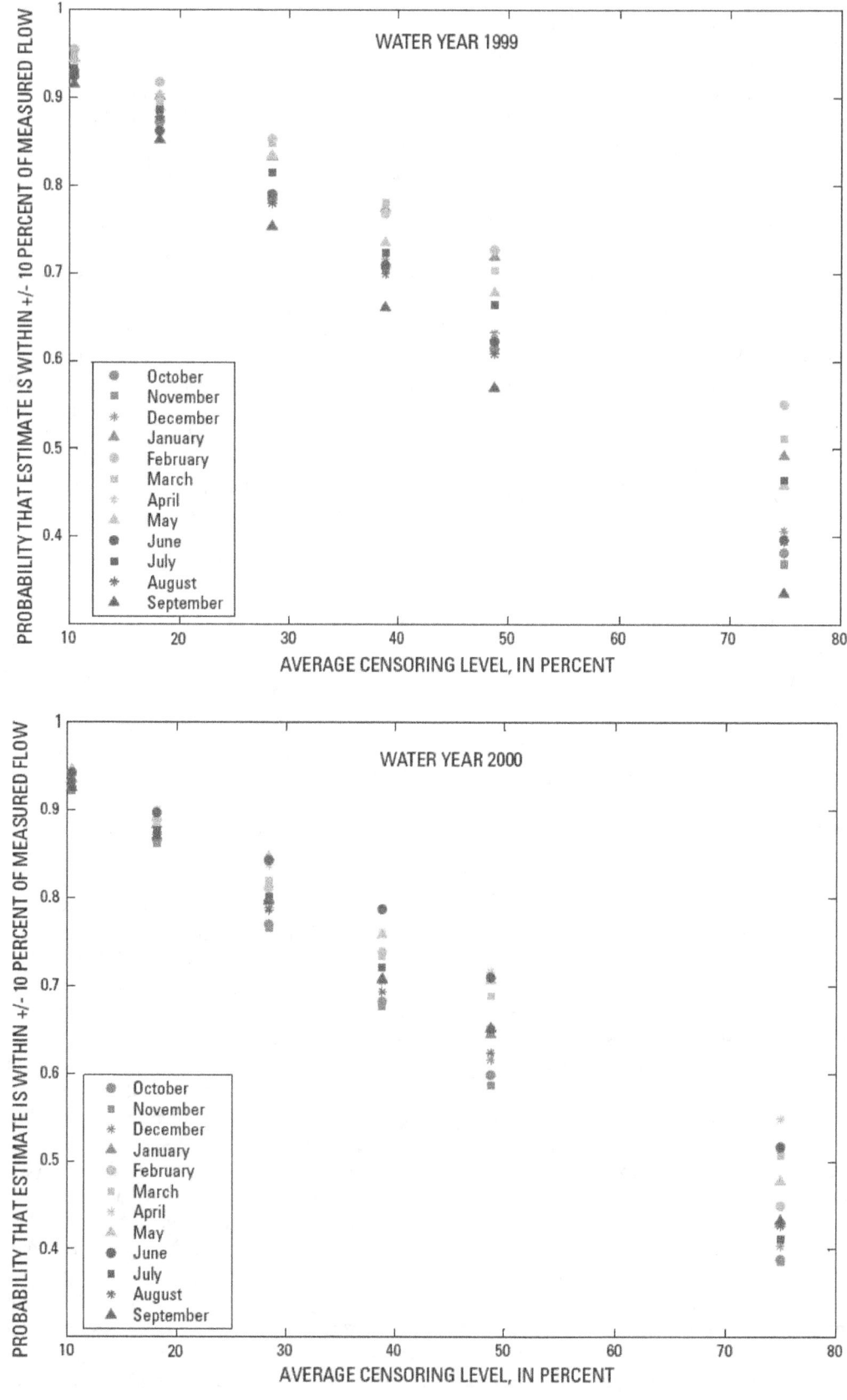

Figure 49. Relation between censoring level and probability of estimating monthly flow within 10 percent of measured value, from bootstrap analysis of AFINCH-generated streamflows for hydrologic subregion 0405 (from Koltun and Holtschlag, 2010).

model to illustrate use of these utilities for network analysis and to investigate the influence of the underlying subregional model structure on analysis of the local model:

1. The simplest parameterization of the local model was to adopt the inset-model structure and apply simple multipliers to eight inset-model parameters: horizontal hydraulic conductivities of layers 1, 2, and 3; vertical hydraulic conductivities of layers 1, 2, and 3; recharge array; and streambed leakance for all streams. These multipliers acted on values for the entire inset model.

2. In the second parameterization, the 25 underlying cells from the subregional model were treated as zones. The hydraulic conductivities within each zone were uniform, but a multiplier was assigned to each zone so that each could, potentially, be calibrated. The zones also individually contributed to prediction uncertainty, and more resolution of contribution to prediction uncertainty from the individual hydraulic-conductivity values was expected. The second approach resulted in 300 hydraulic-conductivity parameters—25 horizontal and 25 vertical hydraulic conductivities for each of the 6 layers in the inset model. Stream leakance and recharge were treated with single multipliers in the same way as for the first parameterization.

3. The final parameterization used 400 pilot points regularized by kriging for both horizontal and vertical hydraulic conductivity in each of the 6 layers of the inset model. Recharge and streambed leakage also were parameterized by using pilot points in the third case.

The local inset model was used to generate the test case. A well was placed in the second layer of the model, the extraction rate was set to 500 gal/min, and uncertainty was analyzed for two predictions: head in layer 1 near the well and flow at a streamgage on a nearby headwater stream (H115_259 and gage 17 in fig. 50). The contribution of the parameters to prediction uncertainty was analyzed for the first parameterization, and the location of additional head observations to reduce either head or flow prediction uncertainty was explored for all three parameterizations.

Assessing the parameter contributions to prediction uncertainty allows the analyst to identify the most important parameters in terms of the specified prediction. Measurement of these parameters should reduce both parameter uncertainty and prediction uncertainty. In the simplest parameterization, multipliers on the eight parameters were considered. The relative pattern for each parameter remained the same, but the multiplier could be used to uniformly vary the parameter values. For the two predictions of interest, recharge and streambed leakance contributed the most to the prediction uncertainty (fig. 51). In the case of the uncertainty in the head prediction, recharge is the most important parameter. Estimated uncertainty depends on the uncertainty of the input parameters. In

this case, the estimate of input-parameter uncertainty indicates a 90-percent confidence that the input value is within one order of magnitude. This is quantified by specifying a standard deviation of the log-transform value of the parameter to 0.25. If the uncertainty in the estimate of input recharge is reduced (perhaps through measurement) such that the standard deviation for this parameter becomes 0.0625, then the vertical hydraulic conductivity of layer 1 and the horizontal hydraulic conductivity of layer 2 become the most important parameters (fig. 51, right panel). These results are consistent with expectations, because the pumping well is placed in layer 2 and the observation of interest is in layer 1. In the case of uncertainty in the flow estimate at the streamgage, streambed leakance is the most important parameter contributing to the uncertainty of the flow estimate. Reduction of uncertainty in recharge does little to affect this observation.

An alternative to measuring a parameter, which may be expensive or difficult, is collection of additional head observations. Those head observations that would decrease prediction uncertainty the most can be identified by mapping the contribution of each potential observation to the prediction uncertainty (Fienen and others, 2010). For the inset-model analysis, candidate locations for such head observations were sought by using PREDUNC in combination with two grids of points: a coarse, 10 × 10 grid of points was used to test the entire local inset-model area, and a refined, 35 × 28 grid surrounding the pumping well and predictions of interest was used to focus analysis where the most benefit from head observations was expected (fig. 52). The effect of adding a new observation in either layer 1 or layer 2 was analyzed. The spacing of the refined grid of points could not be used across the entire local inset-model domain because the computations became intractable.

The decrease in head and flow prediction uncertainty at the specified locations was computed for each candidate location, and the resulting values were mapped for the three parameterizations and for potential observations from layer 1 or 2 (figs. 53 and 54). The most important finding of this analysis is the profound effect of the chosen parameterization scheme on the results obtained. For head predictions, the pilot-point parameterization depicted in the rightmost panel of figure 53 is the only one that obviously matches the expected outcome. The figure shows clear structure in the potential reduction in uncertainty, with the greatest reduction near the point of interest although biased slightly away from the stream. The bias away from the stream is more evident for observations in layer 2. The potential observation point with the highest value would be selected as a monitoring location to decrease the prediction uncertainty as observations were collected and incorporated through recalibration of the numerical model. The same method used with the simple-multiplier ("KLM") parameterization does not clearly identify a point or points for additional observation: when normalized by the reduction in uncertainty from the pilot-point test, the reduction in uncertainty in the KLM test is small, and the locations are not very well isolated. The lack of spatial coherence arises

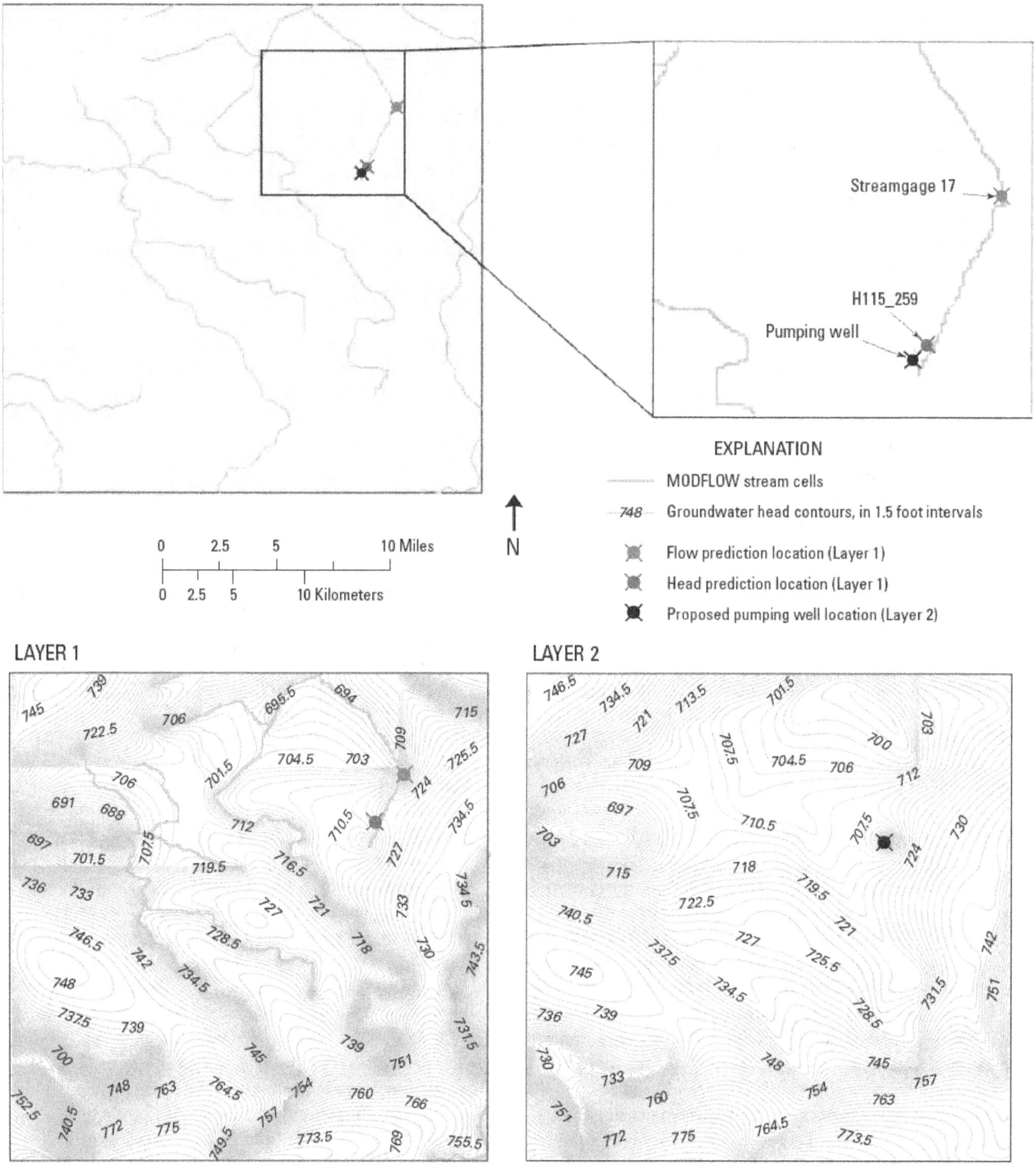

Figure 50.   Head contours in layer 1 (left panel) and layer 2 (right panel) from the local inset model. The contour interval is 1.5 feet, and the locations of the pumping well (black symbol), uncertainty in head prediction (blue symbol, H115_259), and uncertainty in flow prediction (red symbol, Gage 17) are indicated. The pumping well is in layer 2, and the uncertainty locations are evaluated for layer 1 (from Fienen and others, 2010).

from the use of a single multiplier for hydraulic conductivity for the whole layer. Observations anywhere will potentially influence the estimates of hydraulic conductivity. The parameterization involving the 300 hydraulic-conductivity parameters ("300K") is more challenging to evaluate. Unlike the KLM approach, the 300K parameterization allows for hydraulic conductivity across the domain to vary independently for the 25 zones. Yet, the normalized plots show that the predicted decrease in head uncertainty in the 300K test is, again, very small compared to the pilot-point test. More testing would be required to determine the spatial-parameterization "tipping

point" required to yield coherent results; but on the basis of these results, it lies somewhere between the 25-zone density of the 300K case and the 400-point density of the pilot-point case.

Reduction in the flow-prediction uncertainty resulting from additional observation at the candidate locations is similar to that for head-prediction uncertainty (fig. 54). The pilot-point parameterization shows clear structure in the potential reduction and greatest reduction near the point of interest but, again, biased slightly away from the stream. The potential observation point with the highest value would be selected as

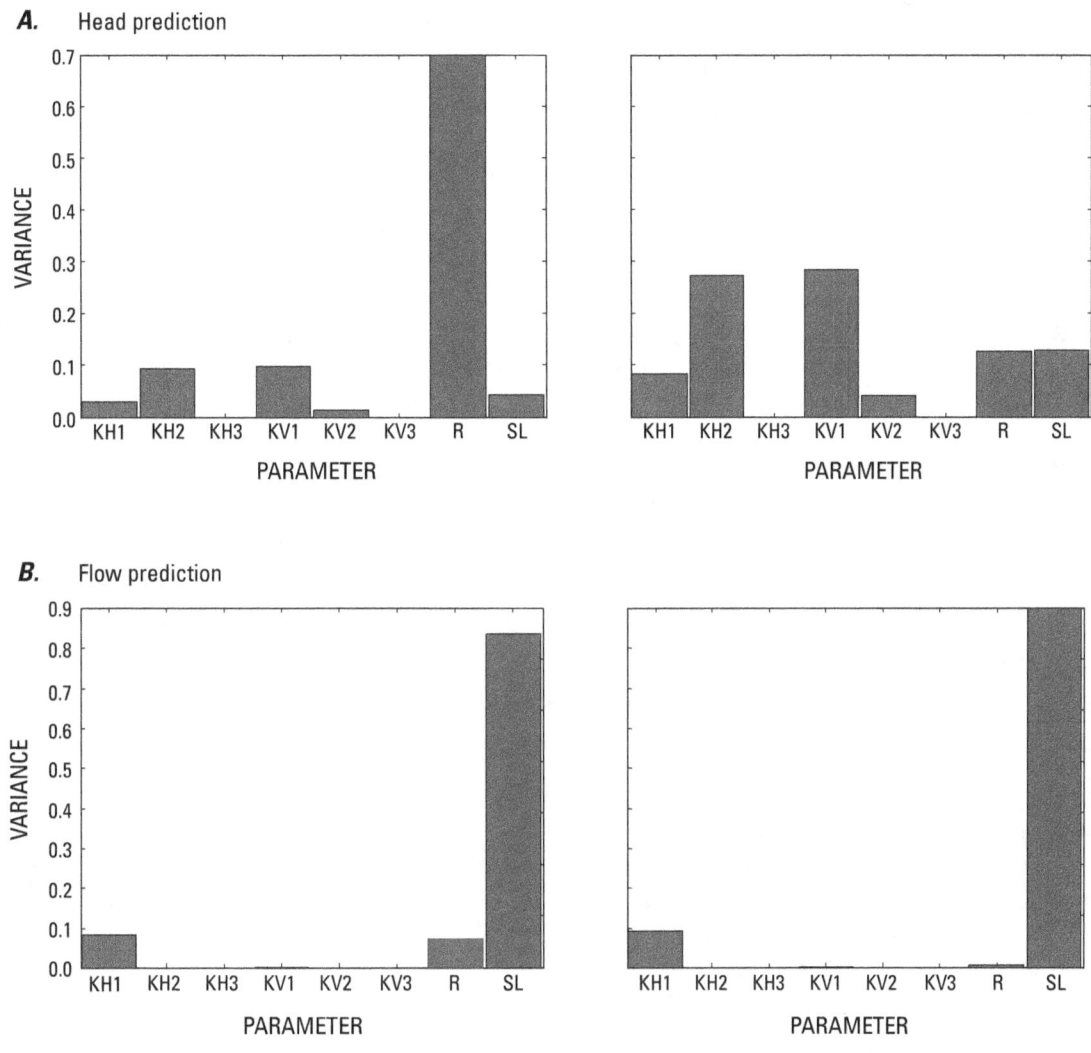

Figure 51.   Relative contribution to prediction uncertainty from each parameter for A, head prediction and B, flow prediction within the local inset model at the locations specified in figure 50. The left-hand panels were computed with initial uncertainty set to 0.25 for each parameter, and the right-hand panels were computed with uncertainty set to 0.25 for all parameters except recharge. A reduced uncertainty for recharge of 0.0625 was used in the right-hand panels (from Fienen and others, 2010).

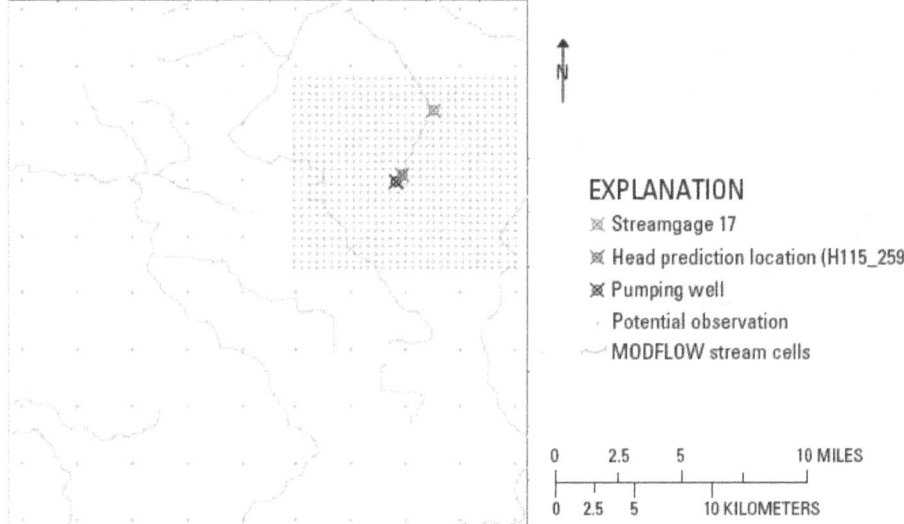

Figure 52.   Grid of candidate locations for additional head observations in prediction uncertainty analysis based on local inset model (from Fienen and others, 2010).

a monitoring location to decrease the flow-prediction uncertainty as observations were collected and incorporated through recalibration of the numerical model. The KLM and 300K parameterizations show the same behavior as seen previously for reduction of head-prediction uncertainty. And, as with the head-prediction analysis, more testing would be required to find the spatial-parameterization tipping point yielding coherent results for reduction in flow-prediction uncertainty.

Summary of Pilot Study

Beginning in 2005, water availability and use were assessed for the U.S. part of the Great Lakes Basin through the Great Lakes Basin Pilot of a USGS national assessment of water availability and use. The focus of this study was on defining the storage and dynamics of water resources and the human demands on water in the Great Lakes region. The study focused on several spatial and temporal scales, and highlighting the importance of scale is a key outcome of the project. To illustrate both the abundant regional availability of water and the potential for local shortages of water, the U.S. Geological Survey provided scientific information, data, and analysis to help define water resources in the region and quantify demands on the resources. The multiscale nature of the study challenges water-resource managers and the public to think about regional water resources in an integrated way and to understand how future changes to the system driven by water withdrawals and returns, climate variability, or

land-use change may be accommodated by informed water-resources management. Major features of the study include the following:

- The regional water budget, compiled from many sources, was summarized and discussed to highlight the overall abundance of water in the Great Lakes region. Subregional and local studies within the pilot demonstrated, however, that water-availability limitations may arise in the region because of variations in water supply and demand in both space and time.

- Results from a groundwater-flow model of the Lake Michigan Basin (Feinstein and others, 2010) show that groundwater budgets west of Lake Michigan are quite different from those east of Lake Michigan. Pumping of the deep bedrock aquifer west of Lake Michigan has resulted in a large drawdown in water levels, has induced flow from outside the predevelopment groundwater basin into the Great Lakes Basin, and has captured groundwater that would have naturally discharged to Lake Michigan. The groundwater-flow system east of Lake Michigan is dominated by pumping wells capturing water that would have been discharged to inland surface water or, in places, by pumping wells inducing flow from inland surface water. Water levels have declined in areas of pumping east of Lake Michigan, but these declines are much less than those west of the lake.

- Local-scale analysis combining groundwater and surface-water modeling shows that a single pumping well can affect a nearby stream, even to the point of drying the stream during some of the year (Hoard, 2010). Regional approaches cannot represent this level of detail, and use of streamflow estimates alone to quantify water availability neglects the dynamics of the groundwater system and its response to new pumping stresses. A combined approach quantifying both groundwater and surface-water resources, coupled with detailed information regarding the dynamics of existing water withdrawals and returns, would yield the most information for water-availability decisions at the local scale.

- Temporal trends in Great Lakes water levels (Wilcox and others, 2007) and streamflow and precipitation in the basin (Hodgkins and others, 2007) were quantified, revealing the dynamic nature of the regional water budget and the need to understand temporal changes

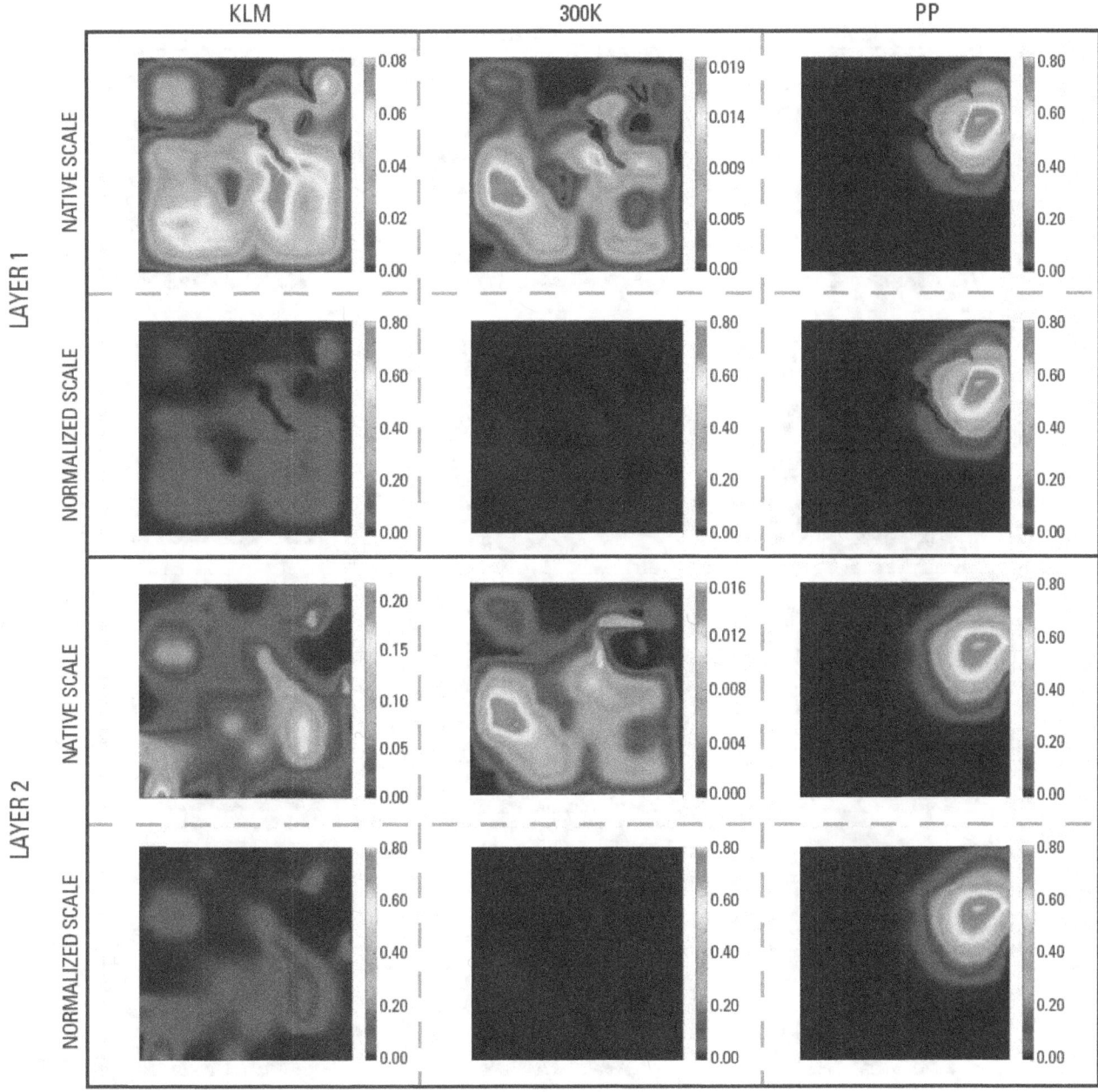

Figure 53. Observation uncertainty contribution for the head prediction at H115_259 for layers 1 and 2 and three different parameterizations of the test area, based on the local inset model (from Fienen and others, 2010).

for water-availability analysis. Variations in water withdrawals and flows during the year and over many years show that water-management decisions may have to be based on more than long-term annual average flows or withdrawals. Large withdrawals during times of naturally low flows may be constrained by a lack of water to supply the demand or by societal decisions to maintain flows at target values to protect the ecological function of a stream.

- Water withdrawals for 2005 were compiled by watershed (Mills and Sharpe, 2010) and, for much of the area, major groundwater withdrawals were compiled and estimated from 1865 through 2005 (Buchwald and others, 2010) for input to a groundwater-flow model of the Lake Michigan Basin (Feinstein and others, 2010). In response to questions regarding estimation of consumptive water use in the region, consumptive-use coefficients and monthly variation in consumptive use were explored and quantified

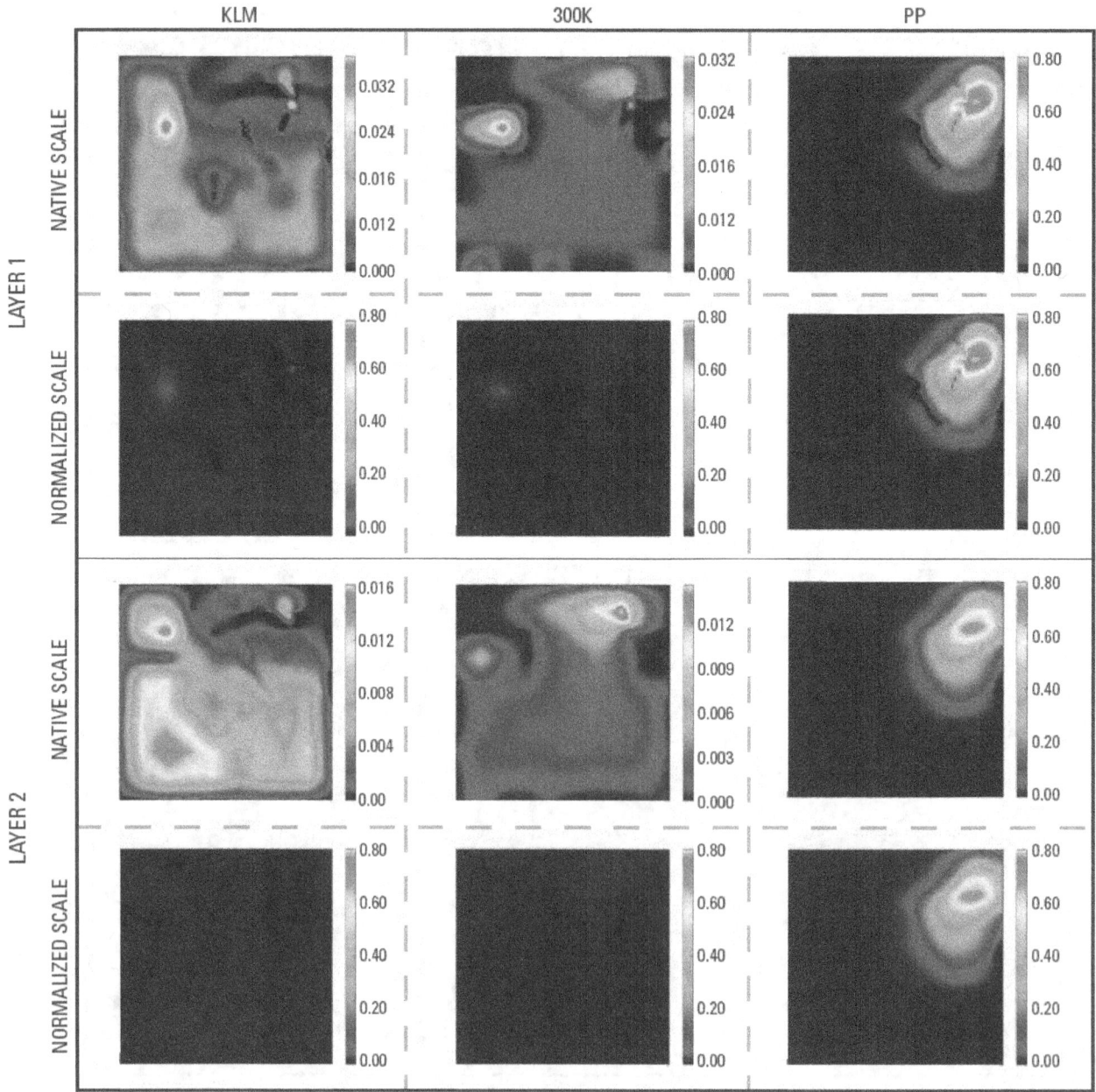

Figure 54. Observation uncertainty contribution for the flow prediction at the hypothetical streamgage for layers 1 and 2 and three different parameterizations of the test area, based on the local inset model (from Fienen and others, 2010).

(Shaffer and Runkle, 2007; Shaffer, 2008; 2009). Water withdrawals from all water-use sectors were shown to vary seasonally, the greatest withdrawals occurring in summer.

- Groundwater is a major source for water in the region (Mills and Sharpe, 2010). Groundwater provides hundreds of cubic miles of regional storage (Coon and Sheets, 2006; Sheets and Simonson, 2006), and the groundwater system plays an important role in routing water from precipitation to streams as base flow (Neff and others, 2006). The groundwater contribution to water availability is best quantified through use of a groundwater-flow model because of the interplay between the hydrogeology of the system, natural boundaries, and imposed withdrawals. The groundwater-flow model that was developed for the Lake Michigan Basin was used to illustrate the response of the groundwater budget to development in the region from predevelopment to present (Feinstein and others, 2010). This model also serves to integrate and synthesize information regarding the hydrogeology and groundwater use in the region (Arihood, 2009; Lampe, 2009; Buchwald and others, 2010). From a methodological perspective, several alternative models were tested and presented, and this use of alternative models may serve as a example for future groundwater-availability studies (Feinstein and others, 2010).

- Summary indicators were introduced in this report to condense the water-budget information produced by the groundwater-flow model. These indicators revealed the contrast in groundwater dynamics and response to development between the eastern and western sides of the Lake Michigan Basin.

- Methods development and application were important in the Great Lakes Basin Pilot.

  - The AFINCH modeling system was developed to produce estimates of streamflow characteristics for ungaged basins; these estimates are constrained to match observations at streamgages if such observations are available (Holtschlag, 2009). The system also is useful for water-use accounting. AFINCH could be used to develop, for example, time series of flows for ungaged basins that could be related to stream ecology and used to define ecological flows.

  - The Lake Michigan Basin groundwater-flow model relied on methods development and application to account for glacial hydrogeology (Arihood, 2009) and for calibration of the extensive model with many parameters and observations (detailed in Feinstein and others, 2010).

- Recently developed methods to use the regional model to address local groundwater issues were applied and their use demonstrated (Hoard, 2010).

- Finally, surface-water and groundwater models were applied to demonstrate analysis of data worth and ways to estimate where additional observations should be collected to decrease prediction uncertainty in the models (Fienen and others, 2010; Koltun and Holtschlag, 2010).

Challenges for Future Water-Availability Studies

The Great Lakes Basin Pilot was a true pilot project, designed to identify opportunities and challenges for a potential nationwide program. In addition, several new methods to estimate aspects of water availability were developed, applied, or tested. The focus of this study was on the storage of water in the system, flux of water through the system, and water use relating to human activity. Understanding these features of the water budgets of the region is paramount to developing estimates of water availability given constraints that are recognized today or that may be imposed in the future.

Studies summarizing consumptive water use and seasonal variations in water use highlight inconsistencies in water-use data collection and reporting across the region. Much of the reported water use in some sectors relies heavily on estimates, and the estimation procedures have been inconsistent among states in the region and, for some categories of use, inconsistent over time. Further, classification of specific water uses into broad sectors has not consistent between states or between state and Federal agencies. Resolving these inconsistencies and developing methods to improve estimates for the broad sectors and different categories within those sectors remains a challenge.

Estimation of surface-water characteristics across the basin with the AFINCH modeling system developed in the pilot was hampered by the requirement that all streams in the geographic dataset used to develop and report the analysis be routed through the stream network. Existing datasets are closely representative of actual physical conditions, but a small percentage of streams in the system during the pilot project were found to be disconnected or improperly routed. Correcting these problems is labor intensive and time consuming.

The AFINCH system for analysis of streamflows offers capabilities to account for water use and, in this way, it may be used as a streamflow-accounting tool. Site-specific water-withdrawal information, however, is often not available throughout the Great Lakes Basin, and accounting for more diffuse withdrawals such as domestic use or agricultural irrigation to examine their effects on streamflow is difficult. One advantage of using AFINCH for estimation of streamflow characteristics is that anomalous results will be produced if major water uses are not included in the analysis, signaling the analyst of the potential missing information.

The tension between developing a regional groundwater-flow model capable of representing regional hydrologic-system behavior and the desire to address problems of local interest is a challenge for regional groundwater-availability studies. Regional models often cannot represent local behavior well enough to address local questions. Therefore, the pilot project tested methods to allow regional models to be extended and used as a base for additional analysis addressing local questions (such as the illustrative inset model discussed in this report). These methods were indeed found to clarify the potential local response in water levels and base flow to groundwater withdrawals. For site-specific questions, more refinement of the hydrogeologic characteristics of the inset model would be needed to produce a more reliable model. One other issue that remains a challenge to both the subregional and local-scale groundwater-flow models is that traditional models treat recharge as separate from the imposed pumping on the system. This separate treatment may be valid on the subregional scale; but as questions become more site specific, the potential for pumping to modify recharge to the local aquifer should be included in the simulation. For situations where recharge can be influenced by pumping, coupled groundwater/surface-water models that generate recharge to the groundwater system as part of the simulation would be desired. (See, for example, Markstrom and others, 2008.)

Indicators that combine various components of the water budget with water withdrawals (and potentially return flows) help condense these data, but such combined indicators may be difficult to explain and understand. Simple indicators including groundwater levels or streamflows are straightforward and easily understood. These simple indicators, however, vary across the region and may not properly serve as an integrated metric capable of summarizing a mass of diverse information. Combined indictors summarize data more appropriately, but they may be more difficult to understand. Comparison of several combined indicators to values from the literature underscores the nature of water resources in the Great Lakes Basin and the dominance of flow in the system over human uses. The combined indicators also help highlight differences in groundwater budgets between different areas of the Lake Michigan Basin. This same information, however, may be communicated without the combined indicators. The effectiveness of different indicators for making informed water-resources decisions should be evaluated when selecting a set of indicators to summarize water availability on a national scale.

References

Alley, W.M., Reilly, T.E., and Franke, O.L., 1999, Sustainability of ground-water resources: U.S. Geological Survey Circular 1186, 79 p. (Also available at *http://pubs.usgs.gov/circ/circ1186/.*)

Anderson, M.T., and Woosley, L.H., Jr., 2005, Water availability for the western United States—Key scientific challenges: U.S. Geological Survey Circular 1261, 85 p. (Also available at *http://pubs.usgs.gov/circ/2005/circ1261/.*)

Arihood, L.D., 2009, Processing, analysis, and general evaluation of well-driller logs for estimating hydrogeologic parameters of the glacial sediments in a ground-water flow model of the Lake Michigan Basin: U.S. Geological Survey Scientific Investigations Report 2008–5184, 26 p. (Also available at *http://pubs.usgs.gov/sir/2008/5184/.*)

Arnold, T.L., Warner, K.L., Groschen, G.E., Caldwell, J.P., and Kalkhoff, S.J., 2008, Hydrochemical regions of the glacial aquifer system, northern United States, and their environmental and water-quality characteristics: U.S. Geological Survey Scientific Investigations Report 2008–5015, 83 p., with appendixes. (Also available at *http://pubs.usgs.gov/sir/2008/5015/.*)

Arthington, A.H., Bunn, S.E., Poff, N.L., and Naiman, R.J., 2006, The challenge of providing environmental flow rules to sustain river ecosystems: Ecological Applications, v. 16, no. 4, p. 1311–1318.

Assel, R.A., Quinn, F.H., and Sellinger, C.E., 2004, Hydroclimatic factors of the recent record drop in Laurentian Great Lakes water levels: Bulletin of the American Meteorological Society, v. 85, no. 8, p. 1143–1151, accessed March 1, 2010, at *http://dx.doi.org/10.1175%2FBAMS-85-8-1143.*

Ayotte, J.D., Flanagan, S.M., and Morrow, W.S., 2007, Occurrence of uranium and ^{222}radon in glacial and bedrock aquifers in the northern United States, 1993–2003: U.S. Geological Survey Scientific Investigations Report 2007–5037, 84 p. (Also available at *http://pubs.usgs.gov/sir/2007/5037/.*)

Baldwin, J.L., 1973, Climates of the United States: Washington, D.C., U.S. Department of Commerce, National Oceanic and Atmospheric Administration, 113 p.

Bondelid, Tim; Johnston, Craig; McKay, Cindy; Moore, Rich; and Rea, Alan, 2006, NHD*Plus* user guide: Prepared for U.S. Environmental Protection Agency and U.S. Geological Survey, 114 p. (Also available at *http://www.horizon-systems.com/NHDPlus/data/NHDPLUS_UserGuide.pdf.*)

Bredehoeft, John, 1997, Safe yield and the water budget myth (editorial): Ground Water, v. 35, no. 6, p. 929.

Bredehoeft, J.D., 2002, The water budget myth revisited— Why hydrogeologists model: Ground Water, v. 40, no. 4, p. 340–345.

Bredehoeft, J.D., Papadopulos, S.S., and Cooper, H.H., Jr., 1982, Groundwater—The water-budget myth, *in* Scientific basis of water resources management: Washington, D.C., National Academy Press, Studies in Geophysics, p. 51–57.

Buchwald, C.A., Luukkonen, C.L., and Rachol, C.M., 2010, Estimation of ground-water use for a ground-water flow model of the Lake Michigan Basin and adjacent areas, 1864–2005: U.S. Geological Survey Scientific Investigations Report 2010–5068, 120 p. (Also available at *http://pubs.usgs.gov/sir/2010/5068/.*)

Buschbach, T.C., 1964, Cambrian and Ordovician strata of northeastern Illinois: Illinois State Geological Survey Report of Investigation 218, 90 p.

Catacosinos, P.A., Westjohn, D.B., Harrison III, W.B., Wollensak, M.S., and Reynolds, R.F., 2001, Stratigraphic lexicon for Michigan: Michigan Department of Environmental Quality, Geological Survey Division Bulletin 8, 56 p.

Cherkauer, D.S., 2009, Groundwater budget indices and their use in assessing water supply plans for southeastern Wisconsin (draft): Southeastern Wisconsin Regional Planning Commission Technical Report 46, 56 p.

Cherkauer, Doug; Frank, Nancy; Grundl, Tim; and Kl, Val, 2006, Sort hydrological myths from facts before setting water precedents: Milwaukee, [Wis.,] Journal Sentinel, accessed March 17, 2010, at *http://www.jsonline.com/news/opinion/29200004.html.*

Commission for Environmental Cooperation, 1997, Ecological regions of North America—Toward a common perspective: Montréal, Communications and Public Outreach Department of the Commission for Environmental Cooperation Secretariat, 71 p. (Also available at *http://www.cec.org/pubs_docs/documents/index.cfm?varlan=english&id=344.*)

Coon, W.F., and Sheets, R.A., 2006, Estimate of ground water in storage in the Great Lakes Basin, United States, 2006: U.S. Geological Survey Scientific Investigations Report 2006–5180, 19 p. (Also available at *http://pubs.usgs.gov/sir/2006/5180/.*)

Council of Great Lakes Governors, 2001, The Great Lakes Charter Annex—A supplementary agreement to the Great Lakes Charter: Chicago, 8 p. (Also available at *http://www.cglg.org/projects/water/docs/GreatLakesCharterAnnex.pdf.*)

Council of Great Lakes Governors, 2005a, Great Lakes-St. Lawrence River Basin sustainable water resources agreement: 29 p. (Also available at *http://www.cglg.org/projects/water/docs/12-13-05/Great_Lakes-St_Lawrence_River_Basin_Sustainable_Water_Resources_Agreement.pdf.*)

Council of Great Lakes Governors, 2005b, Great Lakes-St. Lawrence River Basin water resources compact: 27 p. (Also available at *http://www.cglg.org/projects/water/docs/12-13-05/Great_Lakes-St_Lawrence_River_Basin_Water_Resources_Compact.pdf.*)

Council of Great Lakes Governors, 2008, February 28 letter to U.S. Congress members: Chicago, 7 p. (Also available at *http://www.cglg.org/projects/priorities/docs/FY09LettertoCongress22508.pdf.*)

Council of Great Lakes Governors, 2009, State/provincial reporting protocols to regional database: Great Lakes Water Use Information Initiative, 5 p. (Also available at *http://www.cglg.org/projects/water/WaterUseInformationInitiative.asp.*)

Croley, T.E., II, 2003, Great Lakes climate change hydrologic impact assessment—I.J.C. Lake Ontario-St. Lawrence River regulation study: National Oceanic and Atmospheric Administration, Great Lakes Environmental Research Laboratory, NOAA Technical Memorandum GLERL–126, 77 p. (Also available at *http://www.glerl.noaa.gov/pubs/techrept.html.*)

Cunnane, C., 1978, Unbiased plotting positions—A review: Journal of Hydrology, v. 37, no. 3–4, p. 205–222.

Daly, Christopher; Gibson, W.P.; Taylor, G.H.; Johnson, G.L.; and Pasteris, Phillip, 2002, A knowledge-based approach to the statistical mapping of climate: Climate Research, v. 22, no. 2, p. 99–113.

Delin, G.N., and Risser, D.W., 2007, Ground-water recharge in humid areas of the United States—A summary of ground-water resources program studies, 2003–06: U.S. Geological Survey Fact Sheet FS–2007–3007, 4 p. (Also available at *http://pubs.usgs.gov/fs/2007/3007/.*)

Dickinson, J.E.; Land, Michael; Faunt, C.C.; Leake, S.A.; Reichard, E.G.; Fleming, J.B.; and Pool, D.R., 2006, Hydrogeologic framework refinement, ground-water flow and storage, water-chemistry analyses, and water-budget components of the Yuma area, southwestern Arizona and southeastern California: U.S. Geological Survey Scientific Investigations Report 2006–5135, 88 p. (Also available at *http://pubs.usgs.gov/sir/2006/5135/pdf/sir20065135.pdf.*)

Dietz, Thomas; Dolšak, Nives; Ostrom, Elinor; and Stern, P.C., 2002, The drama of the commons, *in* Ostrom, Elinor; Dietz, Thomas; Dolšak, Nives; Stern, P.C.; Stonich, Susan; and Weber, E.U., eds., The drama of the commons: Washington, D.C., National Academy Press, p. 3–35.

Dietz, Thomas; Ostrom, Elinor; and Stern, P.C., 2003, The struggle to govern the commons: Science, v. 302, no. 5652, p. 1907–1912.

Doherty, John, 2010a, PEST, Model-independent parameter estimation—User manual (5th ed., with slight additions): Brisbane, Australia, Watermark Numerical Computing. (Also available at *http://www.pesthomepage.org/Downloads.php.*)

Doherty, John, 2010b, Addendum to the PEST manual: Brisbane, Australia, Watermark Numerical Computing. (Also available at *http://www.pesthomepage.org/Downloads.php.*)

Dorr, J.A., Jr. , and Eshman, D.F., 1970, Geology of Michigan: Ann Arbor, Mich., University of Michigan Press, 476 p.

Faunt, C.C., ed., 2009, Groundwater availability of the Central Valley aquifer, California: U.S. Geological Survey Professional Paper 1766, 225 p. (Also available at *http://pubs.usgs.gov/pp/1766/.*)

Faunt, C.C.; Hanson, R.T.; Belitz, Kenneth; and Rogers, Laurel, 2009, California's Central Valley groundwater study—A powerful new tool to assess water resources in California's Central Valley: U.S. Geological Survey Fact Sheet 2009–3057, 4 p.

Feinstein, D.T., Eaton, T.T., Hart, D.J., Krohelski, J.T., and Bradbury, K.R., 2005, Regional aquifer model for southeastern Wisconsin; Report 1—Data collection, conceptual model development, numerical model construction, and model calibration: Southeastern Wisconsin Regional Planning Commission Technical Report 41, 81 p. (Also available at *http://www.sewrpc.org/publications/techrep/tr-041_aquifer_simulation_model.pdf.*)

Feinstein, D.T., Hart, D.J., and Krohelski, J.T., 2004, The value of long-term monitoring in the development of ground-water-flow models: U.S. Geological Survey Fact Sheet 11603, 4 p. (Also available at *http://pubs.usgs.gov/fs/fs-116-03/.*)

Feinstein, D.T., Hunt, R.J., and Reeves, H.W., 2010, Regional groundwater-flow model of the Lake Michigan Basin in support of Great Lakes Basin water availability and use studies: U.S. Geological Survey Scientific Investigations Report 2010–5109, 248 p. with appendixes.

Fienen, M.N., Doherty, J.E., Hunt, R.J., and Reeves, H.W., 2010, Using prediction uncertainty analysis to design hydrologic monitoring networks—Example applications from the Great Lakes water availability pilot project: U.S. Geological Survey Scientific Investigations Report 2010–5159, 44 p. (Also available at *http://pubs.usgs.gov/sir/2010/5159/.*)

Fitzpatrick, F.A., Knox, J.C., and Whitman, H.E., 1999, Effects of historical land-cover changes on flooding and sedimentation, North Fish Creek, Wisconsin: U.S. Geological Survey Water-Resources Investigations Report 99–4083, 12 p. (Also available at *http://wi.water.usgs.gov/pubs/WRIR-99-4083/.*)

Freeze, R.A., and Cherry, J.A., 1979, Groundwater: Englewood Cliffs, N.J., Prentice-Hall, 604 p.

Gebert, W.A., and Krug, W.R., 1996, Streamflow trends in Wisconsin's driftless area: Water Resources Bulletin, v. 32, no. 4, p. 733–744.

Gilbertson, Michael, 2001, The precautionary principle and early warnings of chemical contamination of the Great Lakes, *in* Harremoës, Poul; Gee, David; MacGarvin, Malcolm; Stirling, Andy; Keys, Jane; Wynne, Brian; and Guedes Vaz, Sofia, eds., Late lessons from early warnings—The precautionary principle 1896–2000: Copenhagen, European Environment Agency, Environmental Issue Report 22 (Luxembourg, Office for Offical Publications of the European Communitites), p. 126–134. (Also available at *http://www.eea.europa.eu/publications/environmental_issue_report_2001_22.*)

Government of Canada and U.S. Environmental Protection Agency, 1995, The Great Lakes—An environmental atlas and resource book (3d ed.): U.S. Environmental Protection Agency EPA–905–B–95–001 and Environment Canada EN40–349/1995E, 46 p., map scales differ. (Also available at *http://www.epa.gov/glnpo/atlas/.*)

Granholm, J.M., 2005, Temporary moratorium on bottled water permits and approvals: State of Michigan Executive Directive No. 2005–5. (Also available at *http://www.michigan.gov/gov/0,1607,7-168-36898_36899-118987--,00.html.*)

Grannemann, N.G., and Reeves, H.W., 2005, Great Lakes Basin water availability and use—A study of the National Assessment of Water Availability and Use Program: U.S. Geological Survey Fact Sheet 2005–3113, 4 p. (Also available at *http://pubs.usgs.gov/fs/2005/3113/pdf/FS2005_3113.pdf.*)

Gray, H.H., Droste, J.B., Patton, J.B., Rexroad, C.B., Shaver, R.H., 1985, Correlation chart showing Paleozoic supplement stratigraphic units of Indiana: Indiana Geological Survey Miscellaneous Map 48.

Great Lakes Commission, 1976, Great Lakes Basin framework study: Ann Arbor, Mich., 105 p., with appendixes in 23 separate volumes.

Great Lakes Commission, 2002, Annual report of the Great Lakes regional water use database repository, representing 1998 water use data in gallons [variously paginated]. (Also available at *http://www.glc.org/wateruse/database/pdf/1-beginning-gallons-98.pdf.*)

Great Lakes Commission, 2003, Toward a water resources management decision support system for the Great Lakes-St. Lawrence River Basin—Status of data and information on water resources, water use, and related ecological impacts: 142 p., with appendixes. (Also available at *http://www.glc.org/wateruse/wrmdss/finalreport.html.*)

Great Lakes Commission, 2006, Annual report of the Great Lakes regional water use database repository, representing 2004 water use in gallons: 105 p. (Also available at *http://www.glc.org/wateruse/database/pdf/2004-gallons.pdf.*)

Great Lakes Commission, 2008, Investing in a national treasure—Great Lakes Commission legislative priorities, FY2009: 4 p.

Great Lakes Information Network, 2006, People in the Great Lakes region, accessed April 22, 2008 at *http://www.greatlakes.net/envt/flora-fauna/people.html.*

Great Lakes Regional Collaboration, 2005, The Great Lakes Regional Collaboration strategy, accessed April 14, 2008, at *http://www.glrc.us/strategy.html.*

Groschen, G.E., Arnold, T.L., Harris, M.A., Dupré, D.H., Fitzpatrick, F.A., Scudder, B.C., Morrow, W.S., Jr., Terrio, P.J., Warner, K.L., and Murphy, E.A., 2004, Water quality in the upper Illinois River Basin, Illinois, Indiana, and Wisconsin, 1999–2001: U.S. Geological Survey Circular 1230, 32 p. (Also available at *http://pubs.usgs.gov/circ/2004/1230/.*)

Haitjema, Henk; Kelson, Vic; and de Lange, Wim, 2001, Selecting MODFLOW cell sizes for accurate flow fields: Ground Water, v. 39, no. 6, p. 931–938.

Hanson, R.T.; Martin, Peter; and Koczot, K.M., 2003, Simulation of ground-water/surface-water flow in the Santa Clara-Calleguas ground-water basin, Ventura County, California: U.S. Geological Survey Water-Resources Investigations Report 02–4136, 214 p. (Also available at *http://pubs.usgs.gov/wri/wri024136/wrir024136.pdf and http://pubs.usgs.gov/wri/wri024136/app.book.pdf.*)

Harbaugh, A.W., Banta, E.R., Hill, M.C., and McDonald, M.G., 2000, MODFLOW-2000, the U.S. Geological Survey modular ground-water model—User guide to modularization concepts and the ground-water flow process: U.S. Geological Survey Open-File Report 00–92, 121 p. (Also available at *http://water.usgs.gov/nrp/gwsoftware/modflow2000/modflow2000.html.*)

Hayhoe, Katherine; Wake, Cameron; Anderson, Bruce; Liang, X.-Z.; Maurer, Edwin; Zhu, Jinhong; Bradbury, James; Degaetano, Art; Stoner, A.M.; and Wuebbles, Donald, 2008, Regional climate change projections for the northeast USA: Mitigation and Adaptation Strategies for Global Change, v. 13, no. 5–6, p. 425–436.

Healy, R.W., Winter, T.C., LaBaugh, J.W., and Franke, O.L., 2007, Water budgets—Foundations for effective water-resources and environmental management: U.S. Geological Survey Circular 1308, 90 p. (Also available at *http://pubs.usgs.gov/circ/2007/1308/.*)

Helsel, D.R., and Hirsch, R.M., 2002, Statistical methods in water resources: U.S. Geological Survey Techniques of Water-Resources Investigations, book 4, chap. A3, 510 p. (Also available at *http://pubs.usgs.gov/twri/twri4a3/html/pdf_new.html.*)

Hirsch, R.M., Hamilton, P.A., Miller, T.L., and Myers, D.N., 2008, Water availability—The connection between water use and quality: U.S. Geological Survey Fact Sheet 2008–3015, 4 p. (Also available at *http://pubs.usgs.gov/fs/2008/3015/.*)

Hoard, C.J., 2010, Implementation of local grid refinement in MODFLOW from the Lake Michigan Basin regional groundwater flow model: U.S. Geological Survey Scientific Investigations Report 2010–5117, 25 p.

Hodgkins, G.A., Dudley, R.W., and Aichele, S.S., 2007, Historical changes in precipitation and streamflow in the U.S. Great Lakes Basin, 1915–2004: U.S. Geological Survey Scientific Investigations Report 2007–5118, 31 p. (Also available at *http://pubs.usgs.gov/sir/2007/5118/.*)

Holtschlag, D.J., 2009, Application guide for AFINCH—Analysis of flows in networks of channels described by NHD*Plus*: U.S. Geological Survey Scientific Investigations Report 2009–5188, 106 p. (Also available at *http://pubs.usgs.gov/sir/2009/5188/*.)

Holtschlag, D.J., and Nicholas, J.R., 1998, Indirect ground-water discharge to the Great Lakes: U.S. Geological Survey Open-File Report 98–579, 25 p. (Also available at *http://mi.water.usgs.gov/pdf/glpf.pdf*.)

Horn, M.A.; Moore, R.B.; Hayes, Laura; and Flanagan, S.M., 2008, Methods for and estimates of 2003 and projected water use in the seacoast region, southeastern New Hampshire: U.S. Geological Survey Scientific Investigations Report 2007–5157, 87 p., plus 2 appendixes on CD–ROM.

Hough, J.L., 1958, Geology of the Great Lakes: Urbana, Ill., University of Illinois Press, 313 p.

Hull, D.N., 1990 (compiler), revised by Larson, G.E., 2000, and Slucher, E.R., 2004, Generalized column of bedrock units in Ohio: Ohio Department of Natural Resources, Division of Geological Survey, accessed April 24, 2008, at *http://www.dnr.state.oh.us/Portals/10/pdf/stratcol.pdf*.

Hunt, Randy, 2003, A water science primer, *in* Meine, Curt, ed., Wisconsin's waters—A confluence of perspectives: Transactions of the Wisconsin Academy of Sciences, Arts, and Letters, v. 90, p. 11–21.

Hunt, R.J., Haitjema, H.M., Krohelski, J.T., and Feinstein, D.T., 2003, Simulating ground water-lake interactions—Approaches and insights: Ground Water, v. 41, no. 2, p. 227–237.

Hutson, S.S., Barber, N.L., Kenny, J.F., Linsey, K.S., Lumia, D.S., and Maupin, M.A., 2004, Estimated use of water in the United States in 2000: U.S. Geological Survey Circular 1268, 46 p. (Also available at *http://pubs.usgs.gov/circ/2004/circ1268/*.)

International Joint Commission, 1985, Great Lakes diversions and consumptive uses—A report to the governments of the United States and Canada under the 1977 reference: 82 p. (Also available at *http://www.ijc.org/php/publications/pdf/ID586.pdf*.)

International Joint Commission, 2006, Advice to governments on their review of the Great Lakes Water Quality Agreement—A special report to the governments of Canada and the United States: 34 p. (Also available at *http://www.ijc.org/rel/pdf/advicefinalwc.pdf*.)

International Joint Commission, 2008, Treaty between the United States and Great Britain relating to boundary waters, and questions arising between the United States and Canada, signed 1909, accessed April 28, 2008 at *http://www.ijc.org/rel/agree/water.html*.

International Upper Great Lakes Study, 2009, Impacts on upper Great Lakes water levels—St. Clair River: International Upper Great Lakes Study Board, Draft Report, v. 1, 216 p. (Also available at *http://www.iugls.org/en/home_accueil.htm*.)

Juckem, P.F., Hunt, R.J., Anderson, M.P., and Robertson, D.M., 2008, Effects of climate and land management change on streamflow in the driftless area of Wisconsin: Journal of Hydrology, v. 355, no. 1–4, p. 123–130.

Kammerer, J.C., 1987, Largest rivers in the United States (water fact sheet): U.S. Geological Survey Open-File Report 87–242, 2 p.

Kamps, Pierre; Nienhuis, Philip; and Witte, Flip, 2008, Effects of climate change on the water table in the coastal dunes of the Amsterdam water supply, *in* Poeter, Eileen; Hill, Mary; and Zheng, Chunmiao, eds., MODFLOW and More 2008—Ground Water and Public Policy: Golden, Colo., International Groundwater Modeling Center, p. 125–129.

Kay, R.T., 1999, Radium in ground water from public-water supplies in northern Illinois: U.S. Geological Survey Fact Sheet 137–99, 4 p. (Also available at *http://il.water.usgs.gov/pubs/fs137_99.pdf*.)

Kenny, J.F., ed., 2004, Guidelines for preparation of state water-use estimates for 2000: U.S. Geological Survey Techniques and Methods 4–A4, 49 p. (Also available at *http://pubs.usgs.gov/tm/2005/tm4A4/pdf/TM4-A4.pdf*.)

Kleweno, D.D., 2009, NASS—Michigan 2008–2009 highlights: National Agricultural Statistics Service, Michigan Field Office NR–09–77, 4 p. (Also available at *http://www.nass.usda.gov/Statistics_by_State/Michigan/Publications/MichiganFactSheets/STHILGTS.pdf*.)

Kolata, D.R., 1990, Overview of sequences. *in* Leighton, M.W., Kolata, D.R., Oltz, D.F., and Eidel, J.J., eds., Interior cratonic basins: Tulsa, Okla., American Association of Petroleum Geologists Memoir 51, p. 59–73.

Kolata, D.R., and Graese, A.M., 1983, Lithostratigraphy and depositional environments of the Maquoketa Group (Ordovician) in northern Illinois: Illinois State Geological Survey Circular 528, 49 p.

Koltun, G.F., and Holtschlag, D.J., 2010, Application of AFINCH as a tool for evaluating the effects of streamflow-gaging-network size and composition on the accuracy and precision of streamflow estimates at ungaged locations in the Southeast Lake Michigan Hydrologic Subregion: U.S. Geological Survey Scientific Investigations Report 2010–5020, 14 p. (Also available at *http://pubs.usgs.gov/sir/2010/5020/.*)

Kruijt, Bart; Witte, J.-P.M.; Jacobs, C.M.J.; and Kroon, Timo, 2008, Effects of rising atmospheric CO_2 on evapotranspiration and soil moisture—A practical approach for the Netherlands: Journal of Hydrology, v. 349, no. 3–4, p. 257–267.

Lake Michigan Technical Committee, 2006, Lake Michigan lakewide management plan (LaMP) 2006: U.S. Environmental Protection Agency [variously paginated]. (Also available at *http://www.epa.gov/glnpo/michigan.html.*)

Lampe, D.C., 2009, Hydrogeologic framework of bedrock units and salinity distributions for a simulation of groundwater flow for the Lake Michigan Basin: U.S. Geological Survey Scientific Investigations Report 2009–5060, 49 p. (Also available at *http://pubs.usgs.gov/sir/2009/5060/.*)

Langevin, C.D., Shoemaker, W.B., and Guo, Weizing, 2003, MODFLOW-2000, the U.S. Geological Survey modular ground-water model—Documentation of the SEAWAT-2000 version with the variable-density flow process (VDF) and the integrated MT3DMS transport process (IMT): U.S. Geological Survey Open-File Report 03–426, 43 p. (Also available at *http://fl.water.usgs.gov/Abstracts/ofr03_426_langevin.html.*)

Leake, S.A., and Claar, D.V., 1999, Procedures and computer programs for telescopic mesh refinement using MODFLOW: U.S. Geological Survey Open-File Report 99–238, 53 p. (Also available at *http://az.water.usgs.gov/MODTMR/tmr.html.*)

Lorenz, D.L., Robertson, D.M., Hall, D.W., and Saad, D.A., 2009, Trends in streamflow and nutrient and suspended-sediment concentrations and loads in the Upper Mississippi, Ohio, Red, and Great Lakes River Basins, 1975–2004: U.S. Geological Survey Scientific Investigations Report 2008–5213, 81 p. (Also available at *http://pubs.usgs.gov/sir/2008/5213/.*)

Lydersen, Kari, 2008, Bottled water at issue in Great Lakes—Conservation and commerce clash: Washington Post, p. A07, accessed February 4, 2009, at *http://www.washingtonpost.com/wp-dyn/content/article/2008/09/28/AR2008092802997.html.*

Mandle, R.J., and Kontis, A.L., 1992, Simulation of regional ground-water flow in the Cambrian-Ordovician aquifer system in the northern Midwest, United States: U.S. Geological Survey Professional Paper 1405–C, 97 p.

Markstrom, S.L., Niswonger, R.G., Regan, R.S., Prudic, D.E., and Barlow, P.M., 2008, GSFLOW—Coupled ground-water and surface-water flow model based on the integration of the Precipitation-Runoff Modeling System (PRMS) and the Modular Ground-Water Flow Model (MODFLOW-2005): U.S. Geological Survey Techniques and Methods 6–D1, 240 p. (Also available at *http://water.usgs.gov/nrp/gwsoftware/gsflow/gsflow.html.*)

Maurer, E.P., Wood, A.W., Adam, J.C., Lettenmaier, D.P., and Nijssen, Bart, 2002, A long-term hydrologically based dataset of land surface fluxes and states for the conterminous United States: Journal of Climate, v. 15, no. 22, p. 3237–3251.

Mehl, S.W., and Hill, M.C., 2005, MODFLOW-2005, the U.S. Geological Survey modular ground-water model—Documentation of shared node local grid refinement (LGR) and the boundary flow and head (BFH) package: U.S. Geological Survey Techniques and Methods 6–A12, 68 p. (Also available at *http://water.usgs.gov/nrp/gwsoftware/modflow2005_lgr/mflgr.html.*)

Meyer, S.C., Roadcap, G.S., Lin, Y.-F., and Walker, D.D., 2009, Kane County water resources investigations—Simulation of groundwater flow in Kane County and northeastern Illinois: Illinois State Water Survey ISWS CR 2009–07, 425 p. (Also available at *http://www.isws.illinois.edu/pubs/pubdetail.asp?CallNumber=ISWS+CR+2009%2D07.*)

Mikulic, D.R., Sargent, M.L., Norby, R.D., and Kolata, D.R., 1985, Silurian geology of the Des Plaines River valley, northeastern Illinois: Illinois State Geological Survey Guidebook 17, 56 p.

Miller, J.A., ed., 2000, Ground water atlas of the United States: U.S. Geological Survey Hydrologic Investigations Atlas HA–730 [variously paginated (Also available at *http://pubs.usgs.gov/ha/ha730/gwa.html.*)

Mills, P.C., and Sharpe, J.B., 2010, Estimated withdrawals and other elements of water use in the Great Lakes Basin of the United States in 2005: U.S. Geological Survey Scientific Investigations Report 2010–5031, 95 p. (Also available at *http://pubs.usgs.gov/sir/2010/5031/.*)

Milly, P.C.D.; Betancourt, Julio; Falkenmark, Malin; Hirsch, R.M.; Kundzewicz, Z.W.; Lettenmaier, D.P.; and Stouffer, R.J., 2008, Stationarity is dead—Whither water management?: Science, v. 319, no. 5863, p. 573–574.

Myers, D.N., Thomas, M.A., Frey, J.W., Rheaume, S.J., and Button, D.T., 2000, Water quality in the Lake Erie-Lake Saint Clair drainages, Michigan, Ohio, Indiana, New York, and Pennsylvania, 1996–98: U.S. Geological Survey Circular 1203, 35 p. (Also available at *http://pubs.water.usgs.gov/circ1203/.*)

National Research Council, 2002, Estimating water use in the United States—A new paradigm for the national water-use information program: Washington, D.C., National Academy Press, 176 p.

National Research Council, 2004, Assessing the national streamflow information program: Washington, D.C., National Academies Press, 164 p.

National Science and Technology Council, 2004, Science and technology to support fresh water availability in the United States: Report of the National Science and Technology Council, Committee on Environment and Natural Resources, Subcommittee on Water Availability and Quality, 32 p., accessed March 26, 2008 at *http://www.ostp.gov/galleries/NSTC%20Reports/ScienceWaterAvailability2005.pdf.*

Neff, B.P., Day, S.M., Piggott, A.R., and Fuller, L.M., 2005, Base flow in the Great Lakes Basin: U.S. Geological Survey Scientific Investigations Report 2005–5217, 23 p., with data appendix on 4 CD-ROMs (Also available at *http://pubs.usgs.gov/sir/2005/5217/.*)

Neff, B.P., and Killian, J.R., 2003, The Great Lakes water balance—Data availability and annotated bibliography of selected references: U.S. Geological Survey Water-Resources Investigations Report 02–4296, 37 p.

Neff, B.P., and Nicholas, J.R., 2005, Uncertainty in the Great Lakes water balance: U.S. Geological Survey Scientific Investigations Report 2004–5100, 42 p.

Neff, B.P., Piggott, A.R., and Sheets, R.A., 2006, Estimation of shallow ground-water recharge in the Great Lakes Basin: U.S. Geological Survey Scientific Investigations Report 2005–5284, 20 p. (Also available at *http://pubs.usgs.gov/sir/2005/5284/.*)

Peters, C.A., Robertson, D.M., Saad, D.A., Sullivan, D.J., Scudder, B.C., Fitzpatrick, F.A., Richards, K.D., Stewart, J.S., Fitzgerald, S.A., and Lenz, B.N., 1998, Water quality in the western Lake Michigan drainages, Wisconsin and Michigan, 1992–95: U.S. Geological Survey Circular 1156, 40 p. (Also available at *http://pubs.usgs.gov/circ/circ1156/.*)

Poeter, E.P.; Hill, M.C.; Banta, E.R.; Mehl, Steffen; and Christensen, Steen, 2005, UCODE_2005 and six other computer codes for universal sensitivity analysis, calibration, and uncertainty evaluation: U.S. Geological Survey Techniques and Methods 6–A11, 283 p. (Also available at *http://pubs.usgs.gov/tm/2006/tm6a11/.*)

Poff, N.L., Allan, J.D., Bain, M.B., Karr, J.R., Prestegaard, K.L., Richter, B.D., Sparks, R.E., and Stromberg, J.C., 1997, The natural flow regime—A paradigm for river conservation and restoration: BioScience, v. 47, no. 11, p. 769–784.

Postel, S.L., Daily, G.C., and Ehrlich, P.R., 1996, Human appropriation of renewable fresh water: Science, v. 271, no. 5250, p. 785–788.

Prudic, D.E., Konikow, L.F., and Banta, E.R., 2004, A new stream-flow routing (SFR1) package to simulate stream-aquifer interaction with MODFLOW-2000: U.S. Geological Survey Open-File Report 2004–1042, 95 p. (Also available at *http://pubs.usgs.gov/of/2004/1042/ofr2004-1042.pdf.*)

Reeves, H.W., Hamilton, D.A., Seelbach, P.W., and Asher, A.J., 2009, Ground-water-withdrawal component of the Michigan water-withdrawal screening tool: U.S. Geological Survey Scientific Investigations Report 2009–5003, 36 p. (Also available at *http://pubs.usgs.gov/sir/2009/5003/.*)

Reilly, T.E., Dennehy, K.F., Alley, W.M., and Cunningham, W.L., 2008, Ground-water availability in the United States: U.S. Geological Survey Circular 1323, 70 p. (Also available at *http://pubs.usgs.gov/circ/1323/.*)

Richter, B.D., 2009, Re-thinking environmental flows—From allocations and reserves to sustainability boundaries: River Research and Applications, 12 p., doi:10.1002/rra.1320.

Riveria, A., 2005, How well do we understand groundwater in Canada?: Natural Resources Canada ESS Contribution 2005030, 41 p. (Also available at *http://ess.nrcan.gc.ca/gm-ces/reports/pdf/how_well_understand_gw_canada_e.pdf.*)

Seaber, P.R., Kapinos, F.P., and Knapp, G.L., 1987, Hydrologic unit maps: U.S. Geological Survey Water-Supply Paper 2294, 63 p., 1 pl. in pocket.

Shaffer, K.H., 2008, Consumptive water use in the Great Lakes Basin: U.S. Geological Survey Fact Sheet 2008–3032, 6 p. (Also available at *http://pubs.usgs.gov/fs/2008/3032/pdf/fs2008-3032.pdf.*)

Shaffer, K.H., 2009, Variations in withdrawal, return flow, and consumptive use for Ohio and Indiana with selected data from Wisconsin, 1999–2004: U.S. Geological Survey Scientific Investigations Report 2009–5096, 93 p. (Also available at *http://pubs.usgs.gov/sir/2009/5096/.*)

Shaffer, K.H., and Runkle, D.L., 2007, Consumptive water-use coefficients for the Great Lakes Basin and climatically similar areas: U.S. Geological Survey Scientific Investigations Report 2007–5197, 191 p. (Also available at *http://pubs.usgs.gov/sir/2007/5197/.*)

Sheets, R.A., and Simonson, L.A., 2006, Compilation of regional ground-water divides for principal aquifers corresponding to the Great Lakes Basin: U.S. Geological Survey Scientific Investigations Report 2006–5102, 23 p. (Also available at *http://pubs.usgs.gov/sir/2006/5102/.*)

Solley, W.B., Merk, C.F., and Pierce, R.R., 1988, Estimated use of water in the United States in 1985: U.S. Geological Survey Circular 1004, 82 p. (Also available at *http://pubs.er.usgs.gov/usgspubs/cir/cir1004.*)

Sun, R.J., Weeks, J.B., and Grubb, H.F., 1997, Bibliography of regional aquifer-system analysis program of the U.S. Geological Survey, 1978–96: U.S. Geological Survey Water-Resources Investigations Report 97–4074, 63 p. (Also available at *http://water.usgs.gov/ogw/rasa/html/introduction.html.*)

Taylor, C.J., and Alley, W.M., 2001, Ground-water-level monitoring and the importance of long-term water-level data: U.S. Geological Survey Circular 1217, 68 p. (Also available at *http://pubs.usgs.gov/circ/circ1217/.*)

The Nature Conservancy, 2008, Ecological Limits of Hydrologic Alteration [ELOHA]—Environmental flows for regional water management: 4 p. (Also available at *http://www.nature.org/initiatives/freshwater/files/eloha_final_single_page_low_res.pdf.*)

Thomas, M.A., 2007, The association of arsenic with redox conditions, depth, and ground-water age in the glacial aquifer system of the northern United States: U.S. Geological Survey Scientific Investigations Report 2007–5036, 26 p. (Also available at *http://pubs.usgs.gov/sir/2007/5036/.*)

Tonkin, M.J., Tiedeman, C.R., Ely, D.M., and Hill, M.C., 2007, OPR–PPR, a computer program for assessing data importance to model predictions using linear statistics: U.S. Geological Survey Techniques and Methods 6–E2, 115 p., plus errata sheet. (Also available at *http://pubs.usgs.gov/tm/2007/tm6e2/.*)

U.S. Congress, 2008, Great Lakes-St. Lawrence River Basin water resources compact: U.S. Congress, 110th, Public Law 110–342, 122 STAT. 3739, [26] p., accessed February 2, 2009, at *http://frwebgate.access.gpo.gov/cgi-bin/getdoc.cgi?dbname=110_cong_public_laws&docid=f:publ342.110.pdf.*

U.S. Environmental Protection Agency, 2002, Primary distinguishing characteristics of level III ecoregions of the continental United States: U.S. Environmental Protection Agency draft report, (18) p. (Also available at *http://www.epa.gov/wed/pages/ecoregions/level_iii.htm.*)

U.S. Environmental Protection Agency, 2006, References for Great Lakes statistics: U.S. Environmental Protection Agency online report, accessed March 26, 2008 at *http://epa.gov/greatlakes/statsrefs.html#Great%20Lakes%20Water%20Volume.*

U.S. Environmental Protection Agency, 2007, Ecoregion maps and GIS resources: U.S. Environmental Protection Agency online report, accessed April 10, 2008 at *http://www.epa.gov/wed/pages/ecoregions.htm.*

U.S. Environmental Protection Agency, 2008, Great Lakes basic information: U.S. Environmental Protection Agency, Great Lakes Program Office online report, accessed February 10, 2009 at *http://epa.gov/greatlakes/basicinfo.html.*

U.S. Geological Survey, 2001, National elevation dataset (NED) 30-meter digitial elevation models (DEM): U.S. Geological Survey National Mapping Division, scale 1:24,000, accessed May 3, 2010 at *http://gisdata.usgs.net/NED.*

U.S. Geological Survey, 2002, Concepts for national assessment of water availability and use: U.S. Geological Survey Circular 1223, 34 p. (Also available at *http://pubs.usgs.gov/circ/circ1223/.*)

U.S. Geological Survey, 2003, Principal aquifers *in* National Atlas of the United States, 1 sheet, accessed February 10, 2009, at *http://www.nationalatlas.gov/mld/aquifrp.html.*

U.S. Geological Survey, 2009, Water use in the United States, accessed June 23, 2009, at *http://water.usgs.gov/watuse/.*

Vogelmann, J.E.; Howard, S.M.; Yang, Limin; Larson, C.R.; Wylie, B.K.; and Van Driel, Nick, 2001, Completion of the 1990's National Land Cover Data Set for the conterminous United States from landsat thematic mapper data and ancillary data sources: Photogrammetric Engineering & Remote Sensing, v. 67, no. 6, p. 650–662, accessed March 31, 2009, at *http://www.asprs.org/publications/pers/scans/2001journal/jun/2001_jun_highlight.pdf.*

Vörösmarty, C.J., Douglas, E.M., Green, P.A., and Revenga, C., 2005, Geospatial indicators of emerging water stress—An application to Africa: Ambio, v. 34, no. 3, p. 230–236.

Vörösmarty, C.J., Green, P., Salisbury, J., and Lammers, R.B., 2000, Global water resources— Vulnerability from climate change and population growth: Science, v. 289, no. 5477, p. 284–288.

W.F. Baird Associates, Coastal Engineers Ltd., 2005, Regime change (man made intervention) and ongoing erosion in the St. Clair River and impacts on Lake Michigan-Huron lake levels: Technical report prepared for GBA Foundation [variously paginated]. (Also available at *http://www.georgianbay.ca/pdf/water_levels/10814%20 St%5B1%5D.%20Clair%20River%20Report_V5_w%20 A%20&%20B.pdf.*)

Wang, Jia; Bai, Xeuzhi; Leshkevich, George; Colton, Marie; Clites, Anne; and Lofgren, Brent, 2010, Severe ice cover on the Great Lakes during winter 2008–2009: EOS, Transactions, American Geophysical Union, v. 91, no. 5, p. 41–50.

Weiskel, P.K., Vogel, R.M., Steeves, P.A., Zarriello, P.J., DeSimone, L.A., and Reis, K.G., III, 2007, Water use regimes—Characterizing direct human interaction with hydrologic systems: Water Resources Research, v. 43, no. 4, W04402, 11 p., doi:10.1029/2006WR005062.

Weist, W.G., Jr., 1978, Summary appraisals of the nations's ground-water resources—Great Lakes Region: U.S. Geological Survey Professional Paper 813–J, 30 p.

Westenbroek, S.M., Kelson, V.A., Dripps, W.R., Hunt, R.J., and Bradbury, K.R., 2010, SWB—A modified Thornthwaite-Mather soil water balance code for estimating ground-water recharge: U.S. Geological Survey Techniques and Methods 6–A31, 65 p. (Also available at *http://pubs. usgs.gov/tm/tm6-a31/.*)

Wilcox, D.A., Thompson, T.A., Booth, R.K., and Nicholas, J.R., 2007, Lake-level variability and water availability in the Great Lakes: U.S. Geological Survey Circular 1311, 25 p. (Also available at *http://pubs.usgs.gov/ circ/2007/1311/.*)

Williamson, C.E., Saros, J.E., and Schindler, D.W., 2009, Climate change—Sentinels of change: Science, v. 323, no. 5916, p. 887–888.

Willman, H.B., Atherton, E., Buschbach, T.C., Collinson, C., Frye, J.C., Hopkins, M.E., Lineback, J.A., and Simon, J.A., 1975, Handbook of Illinois stratigraphy: Illinois State Geological Survey Bulletin 95, 261 p.

Wisconsin Geological and Natural History Survey, 2006, Bedrock stratigraphic units in Wisconsin: Wisconsin Geological and Natural History Survey Open-File Report 2006–06, 1 p.

Young, H.L., Mackenzie, A.J., and Mandle, R.J., 1989, Simulation of ground-water flow in the Cambrian-Ordovician aquifer system in the Chicago-Milwaukee area of the northern midwest, *in* Swain, L.A., and Johnson, A.I., eds., Regional aquifer systems of the United States, aquifers of the midwestern area: American Water Resources Association Monograph Series, no. 13, p. 39–72.

Young, H.L. and Siegel, D.I., 1992. Hydrogeology of the Cambrian-Ordovician aquifer system in the northern Midwest, United States: U.S. Geological Survey Professional Paper 1405–B, 99 p.

Acknowledgments

This project required the efforts of many USGS scientists, support staff, and administrative staff. USGS Enterprise Publishing Network staff provided expert assistance with editing, formatting, posting of online publications, and publishing the entire series of reports produced by the project. The scientists who worked on this project included the following:

USGS Illinois Water Science Center, 1201 West University Avenue, Suite 100, Urbana, IL, 61801

Patrick C. Mills, Hydrologist
  Task Leader for report on water use by Hydrologic Unit Code

Jennifer B. Sharpe, Geographer
  Water-use team

USGS Indiana Water Science Center, 5957 Lakeside Boulevard, Indianapolis, IN, 46278

Leslie D. Arihood, Hydrologist
  Lake Michigan Basin groundwater-flow-model team

Donald V. Arvin, Hydrologist
  Water-use team

Randall Bayless, Research Hydrologist
  Lake Michigan Basin groundwater-flow-model team

David C. Lampe, Hydrologist
  Lake Michigan Basin groundwater-flow-model team

USGS Maine Water Science Center, 196 Whitten Road, Augusta, ME 04330

Glenn A. Hodgkins, Hydrologist
  Task leader for surface-water trends report

Robert W. Dudley, Hydrologist
  Surface-water trends report

USGS Michigan Water Science Center, 6520 Mercantile Way, Suite 5, Lansing, MI 48823

Lori M. Fuller, Geographer
  GIS support

Christopher J. Hoard
  Lake Michigan Basin groundwater-flow-model team

David J. Holtschlag, Hydrologist
  Surface-water-characteristics team

Carol L. Luukkonen
  Water-use and Lake Michigan Basin groundwater-flow-model teams

Brian P. Neff, Hydrologist
  Recharge team

Howard W. Reeves, Research Hydrologist
  Project Chief and Lake Michigan Basin groundwater-flow-model team

Cynthia M. Rachol, Hydrologist
  Water-use team

USGS Minnesota Water Science Center, 2280 Woodale Drive, Mounds View, MN 55112

Allan Arntson, Hydrologist
  Water-use team

USGS New York Water Science Center, 425 Jordan Road, Troy, NY 12180

William F. Coon, Hydrologist
  30 Brown Road, Ithaca, NY 14850
  Storage team

Kristin S. Linsey, Hydrologist
  Water-use team

USGS Ohio Water Science Center, 6480 Doubletree Avenue, Columbus, OH 43229

Robert A. Darner, Hydrologist
  Storage team

Greg F. Koltun, Hydrologist
  Project oversight and assistance, surface water, network analysis

Kimberly H. Shaffer, Hydrologist
  Task Leader, water use

Laura A. Simonson, Biologist
  Divides report team

USGS Pennsylvania Water Science Center, 215 Limekiln Road, New Cumberland, PA 17070

Russell A. Ludlow, Hydrologic Technician
  Water-use team

USGS Wisconsin Water Science Center, 8505 Research Way, Middleton, WI 53562

Cheryl A. Buchwald, Hydrologist
  Water-use and Lake Michigan Basin groundwater-flow-model teams

Daniel T. Feinstein, Hydrologist
  Milwaukee Project Office, Geosciences Department, University of Wisconsin Milwaukee,
  3209 North Maryland Aveneu, Milwaukee, WI 53211
  Task Leader, Lake Michigan Basin groundwater-flow-model model

Michael N. Fienen, Research Hydrologist
  Lake Michigan Basin groundwater-flow-model team, network analysis

Warren A. Gebert, Scientist Emeritus
  Recharge team

Randall J. Hunt, Research Hydrologist
  Task Leader, recharge team, and technical assistance with groundwater-flow modeling

John F. Walker, Research Hydrologist
  Recharge team

Stephen M. Westenbroek, Hydrologist
  Recharge team

USGS Eastern Region NSDI Partnership, 6520 Mercantile Way, Suite 5, Lansing, MI 48911

Stephen S. Aichele, Geographer, Great Lakes Liaison
  GIS and hydrogeography support, surface-water trends report

USGS technical steering and technical assistance:

Office of Groundwater: William M. Alley, Kevin F. Dennehy, Arlen W. Harbaugh, Thomas E. Reilly, William L. Cunningham

Office of Surface Water: Robert R. Mason

Eric J. Evenson, Eastern Region, Program Officer for the Northeast

Norman G. Grannemann, Northeastern Region, Great Lakes Focus Area Coordinator

James R. Nicholas, USGS Michigan Water Science Center, Director

Geoffrey N. Delin, Central Region Groundwater Specialist

Rodney A. Sheets, Eastern Region Groundwater Specialist, Northeast and Midwest Areas